Beloved Island

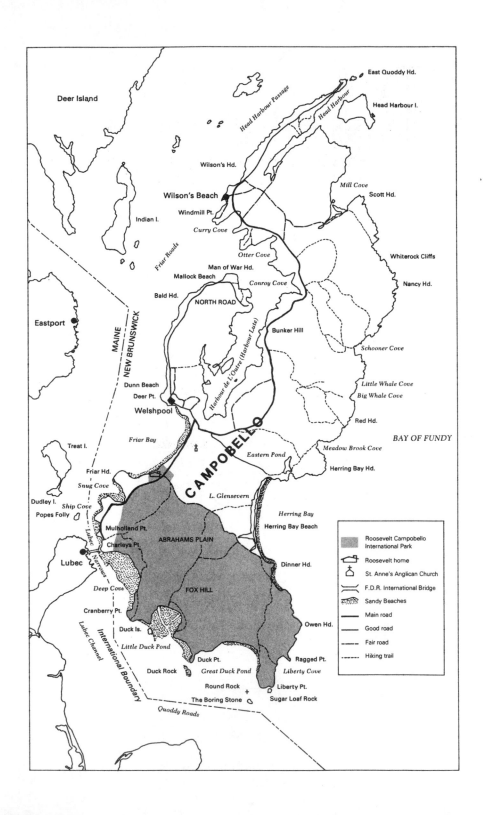

Beloved Island

*Franklin & Eleanor
and the Legacy of Campobello*

Jonas Klein

INTRODUCTION BY
SENATOR GEORGE J. MITCHELL

Paul S. Eriksson, *Publisher*
Forest Dale, Vermont

To Lois
With love and gratitude

5 4 3 2 1

Frontis piece map reprinted from *Campobello: The Outer Island*
copyright © 1993 by Alden Nowlan by permission of
Stoddard Publishing Co., Limited, Toronto, Canada

Library of Congress Cataloging-in-Publication Data

Klein, Jonas.
  Beloved island : Franklin & Eleanor and the legacy of Campobello / Jonas Klein.
     p. cm.
  Includes bibliographical references and index.
  ISBN 0-8397-1033-X (hardcover)
     1. Campobello Island (N.B.)--Biography. 2. Roosevelt, Franklin D. (Franklin
  Delano), 1882-1945--Homes and haunts--New Brunswick--Campobello Island.
  3. Roosevelt, Eleanor, 1884-1962--Homes and haunts--New Brunswick--
  Campobello Island. 4. Presidents--United States--Biography. 5. Presidents'
  spouses--United states--Biography. 6. Campobello Island (N.B.)--Social life and
  customs. I. Title.
  F1044.C2K57 2000
  971.5'33--dc21

                                                                    00-035355

Design by Eugenie S. Delaney

Acknowledgments

Throughout the writing of this book, my wife Lois's librarian skills and critical eye have been invaluable, and daughters Betsy and Leslie and their families have been constant cheerleaders.

I am very appreciative of the helpful and skilled assistance of Anne Newman of the Roosevelt Campobello International Park and Nancy Snedeker at the Franklin D. Roosevelt Library in Hyde Park. Personal reminiscences were generously contributed by a number of fellow Mainers, and I am especially grateful to Emily Herman for the use of her father's memoir. My thanks also to Patricia Fowler of Castine's Witherle Memorial Library and Marilyn Hinkley of the Yarmouth Historical Society for their anecdotal contributions.

My deep appreciation goes to Jim Fyfe, Jeanne and Jim McGowan, and Anne and Bob Perry for plowing through early drafts and providing scores of insightful comments and suggestions. I am thankful to Ed Pert, Mary McAleney, Stuart Ross, Irwin Schorr and to many others for their assistance, counsel and encouragement.

I am in the debt of many historians and biographers for their scholarship and their insights, and I am grateful for the guidance of two fine editors, Donald Ludgin and Helen Reiff. And last, but certainly not least, my heartfelt appreciation to Paul and Peggy Eriksson for their faith, expertise and warm support.

Jonas Klein
Georgetown, Maine

Contents

Introduction by Senator George J. Mitchell xi

Photographs viii

Prologue 1

1. **Childhood** 5

2. **Campobello** 16

3. **Beloved Island** 27

4. *Keeping the Name in the Family* 42

5. *Six Straight Weeks at Campo* 67

6. *I Can Forgive But Not Forget* 87

7. *I Don't Know What's the Matter With Me* 99

8. **Finding Strength** 117

9. *My Old Friends of Campobello* 135

10. *How I Wish You Could Come For Even a Few Days* 151

11. *I Have a Terrific Headache* 174

12. *The Air Has the Tang of the Sea* 195

13. **Playing the Cards They Were Dealt** 214

Epilogue 225

APPENDIX A
Chronology 234

APPENDIX B
Cottage for Sale, 1957 241

Notes 242

Bibliography 260

Index 267

*Photographs (courtesy of The Franklin D. Roosevelt Library)
follow pages 50 and 154.*

Photographs

1. Franklin D. Roosevelt, age 17, and his parents, James and Sara. Poughkeepsie, NY, 1899, p. 51.
2. Eleanor Roosevelt, age 5, and her father, Elliott. New York City, 1889, p. 51.
3. Tyn-y-Coed and Tyn-y-Maes Hotels, Campobello, 1884. James, Sara, and Franklin (18 months) first visited the island the previous summer, staying at the Tyn-y-Coed, p. 52.
4. The living room of the James Roosevelt cottage on Campobello in 1897, p. 52.
5. The James Roosevelt cottage on the shore of Friar's Bay. It was built in 1885 and first occupied the following summer, p. 52.
6. Franklin at the wheel off Campobello with a friend in 1888. Perhaps his first time in control of a sailing ship, p. 53.
7. Again at sea, this time accompanied by a family friend, Gorham Hubbard, and an unidentified helmsman, c. 1898, p. 53.
8. Franklin on the porch of the cottage with his father in 1900. James was ill and died later that year at Hyde Park, p. 53.
9. Franklin and an unidentified companion make their way along the rocks at Campobello, 1902. No matter how arduous the activity, young ladies and gentlemen were always "appropriately attired," p. 54.
10. Eleanor and her favorite aunt, Maude Hall, wading at Herring Cove, 1904, p. 54.
11. Franklin and Eleanor on the porch, Campobello, 1904. They were secretly engaged. Their engagement was announced later that fall and they were married on St. Patrick's Day, 1905, p. 54.
12. Eleanor, Anna (18 months), Franklin, and Duffy on the porch, 1907. That summer Sara was in Europe and the young Roosevelts had "Granny's" cottage all to themselves, p. 55.
13. Franklin in his favorite birchbark canoe, 1907. Canoes like this were made by members of the Passamaquoddy tribe, often from the bark of a single tree, p. 55.

14. Eleanor and Franklin at one of many Campobello beach picnics, c. 1910, p. 55.
15. & 16. Franklin and Eleanor, c. 1909, p. 56.
17. Eleanor and Franklin flanked by friends, all in casual attire, following a tennis outing, c. 1910, p. 56.
18. Sara pours tea for Anna and Eleanor aboard the *Half Moon*, 1910, p. 57.
19. The family grows. Elliot, Jimmy, Franklin, Eleanor, and Anna on the steps of Franklin and Eleanor's cottage, 1912, p. 57.
20. Eleanor, age 28, in front of her cottage, 1912, p. 57.
21. Franklin at the helm of the *Half Moon*; Eleanor and Sara seem engrossed in needlework, 1915, p. 58.
22. Franklin, in formal whites, enjoying his sail, p. 58.
23. Franklin with Eleanor supporting him on the rocky beach in front of their cottage, 1920. Only weeks earlier, he received the Democratic Party's nomination for the Vice-Presidency, p. 155.
24. Franklin and Eleanor's cottage, c. 1920, with two Roosevelt boys, p. 156.
25. A news photographer's picture of the nominee and his family on the cottage steps in 1920. From the left in the rear: FDR, Sara, and Eleanor. Next row: Elliot, Anna, and Jimmy. In front: Franklin Junior, John, and the family dog. All look into the morning sun; Eleanor averts her eyes; Sara rests her hand on her daughter-in-law's knee; Franklin, a cigarette smoker, casually cradles a pipe, p. 156.
26. Sportingly clad in knickers: from the left, Marion Dickerman, Eleanor, Nancy Cook, and Marion's sister-in-law, Peggy Levenson, in 1925. That summer, Eleanor, Nancy, and Marion and three children made a camping journey to Campobello. While on their trip, Franklin supervised the construction of Val-Kill, a stone cottage and factory for the three women in Hyde Park, p. 157.
27. Eleanor with her ubiquitous knitting on the beach at Campobello, 1925, p. 157.

28. Crew and guests on the *Amberjack II* off Southwest Harbor, Maine, 1933. FDR was en route to Campobello for his first visit after being struck down by polio. From the left in front: Eleanor, Franklin, and Jimmy. Behind his father is Franklin Junior. Next row: Nancy Cook, Mary Dreier, John Roosevelt, and, in the rear, Frances Kellor, Nancy Dickerman, and Antonia Hatvary, p. 158.

29. Franklin greets his neighbors during welcoming ceremonies at Welshpool, Campobello in 1933. Eleanor is in the white hat, p. 159.

30. Eleanor and Sara await the arrival of the *Sewanna* in front of Sara's cottage, 1936, p. 159.

31. Arriving at Campobello in 1936 on the *Sewanna* from Rockland, Maine: John, Franklin Junior, FDR, and Jimmy. The shipmate in front is unidentified, p. 159.

32. A 1930s campaign poster, p. 160.

33. Eleanor meeting with students at the International Student Service Leadership Institute held at her cottage in 1941, p. 160.

34. Franklin with Harry Hopkins (far left) and aides at Rockland, Maine, following the historic meeting with Winston Churchill at Argentia Bay off Newfoundland in August, 1941. At Rockland, Franklin first reported on the meeting and unveiled the principles of the Atlantic Charter, p. 160.

35. With her secretary, Maureen Coor, at Campobello in 1962, Eleanor relaxes under a tree. This was her last visit to Campobello. She died just months later, p. 161.

36. The rear of Franklin and Eleanor's cottage in the 1960s when it became the centerpiece of the Roosevelt Campobello International Park, p. 161.

37. The front of the cottage in the 1960s, p. 162.

38. Linnea Calder, left, daughter of longtime Roosevelt employees and family friends, in the cottage's kitchen in the 1960s. The name on the stove, "President," is pure coincidence, p. 162.

Introduction

BY SENATOR GEORGE J. MITCHELL

Americans have always answered the call to serve their country. We hold freedom and our democratic system so dear that when there has been a need, Americans have responded no matter the challenge. Some of that service has been dramatic, even epic-making like Lexington Green, Manassas, or Omaha Beach. There were the new frontiers of Lewis & Clark and Neil Armstrong; the inventions of Edison and the Wright Brothers; Salk's development of polio vaccine. America's heroes have been many and varied. They all had one thing in common, helping make a better life for all. Franklin and Eleanor Roosevelt deserve a special place on that honored roll.

Elected officials are among those who have served our nation with honor. Over our more than 200 years as a republic, men and women have acted and governed with responsibility and the courage of their convictions. They came from all walks of American life. Thomas Jefferson was born to landed colonial gentry, Abraham Lincoln began life in a frontier log cabin.

Franklin and Eleanor Roosevelt were raised in comfortable wealth and in a tradition of service. They had no need to leave the comfort and security of their birthright to test themselves in the challenges of public life. But each was committed to social change and believed that it could be best accomplished through participative government service and a political life. Neither Franklin nor Eleanor had demonstrated significant intellectual or leadership qualities in their early years, and separately they might have passed through life with little special distinction other than carrying an already famous name. But together they found the strength and resolve to become powerful advocates for democratic rights and a better life for ordinary Americans. Although they had detractors, the Roosevelts arguably were the twentieth century's most influential if not most important couple. With Franklin's political sagacity and firm leadership, and Eleanor's indomitable sense of moral imperative, they led the nation through the darkness of depression and war, and into the era of international leadership.

The Roosevelts cared deeply about how people lived and worked, how they were educated, and how they would be cared for in their senior years. This is not to suggest that Franklin Roosevelt was our greatest president, although many would claim so, or that Eleanor was the world's most admired woman, although many more would support that position. This does not suggest that they were perfect people. Their marriage was uneven, their parenting suspect, and they were often unsuccessful in personal relationships. But they shared a remarkable inner strength and an unshakable resolve to overcome physical and emotional crises and succeed to national and international leadership. Theirs is, in many ways, the quintessential story of American resilience and drive to achieve and to contribute. It is a story of perseverance and of courage.

Although we know a good deal about the Roosevelts, there is more to learn and understand. We know little about their inner thoughts, hopes and dreams. Eleanor revealed little of her feelings, Franklin even less. We know of their public accomplishments and their human fallibilities, but much less about what really made them tick, and what personally influenced their actions.

The Roosevelts had several homes during their eventful lives. Hyde Park was Franklin's birthplace and he always called it home, and Eleanor had Val-Kill on the edge of Franklin's estate. But their large summer cottage on a remote Canadian island was the only shared home that both truly loved. It was on Campobello that Franklin grew to manhood through his mastery of the challenging waters and where he learned from working islanders of lives that were not as privileged as his. Eleanor, burdened with the bleakest of childhoods, discovered real joy in the first home of her own where she found peace and refuge from an unsympathetic and demanding world. *Beloved Island* examines the Roosevelts' public triumphs and private disappointments through the view of a small New Brunswick island that played an influential role in their lives over a span of nearly eighty years.

Jonas Klein lives on a Maine island. There is an aura about northeastern islands that captivates its people. Island life and its rhythms are dictated, to a large degree, by the tides and the changing weather. Even today, many island residents make their living from the sea and the ships that sail them. Islanders, new and old, full-time and seasonal are enspirited by walking their shores and breathing the salt air. Jonas Klein recognizes that Franklin and Eleanor Roosevelt were significantly and positively affected by their island, as he is by his. Their special place was an important part of who they were, and who they came to be.

Prologue

Franklin and Eleanor Roosevelt's lives spanned an eighty-year period from late Victorianism to manned space exploration. Their period of public influence encompassed the Great Depression, World War II, the formation of the United Nations, and the Cold War. Casting giant shadows over the national and international landscape, they elicited admiration and affection or engendered derision and hatred. The Roosevelts' place in history is secure, but although they had public careers of accomplishment, they endured private lives of disappointment. Their personal courage and their perseverance, however, are legendary.

The Roosevelts achieved prominence while bearing a load of personal baggage that would have crushed most human beings. When the enormity of that baggage is understood, their accomplishments and their resolve is nothing short of remarkable. Their story is one of privilege, expectation, resolve, and loneliness. Franklin and Eleanor Roosevelt drew upon each other's virtues, the teachings of others, and their own driving need to prove their worth to themselves as well as to others.

No President and First Lady have been examined in such volume and with such passion. Although the Roosevelts' triumphs and tribulations are well known, it is far less clear how each felt about these events and how emotions governed their actions. Eleanor revealed certain guarded feelings about her marriage, family, and personal relationships, but Franklin shared little and revealed less. The search for understanding their successes and their failures is unending.

This study differs somewhat from others. While building on the rich body of existing work, it looks at the Roosevelts' lives relative to their summer homes on Campobello Island, examining the influence the island exerted on Franklin and Eleanor and the unique role it played in the development of their personal growth and their emotions. Metaphorically speaking, Campobello serves as the small end of a funnel that views their broader lives. Franklin and Eleanor searched endlessly for meaningful relationships and personal fulfillment. Campobello played an integral role in their quest.

The Roosevelts always referred to Campobello as their "beloved island." Franklin's Hyde Park home may have been first in his heart, but Campobello held a very special place. His initial visit was as an infant and his last as President of the United States. He spent part of most summers on the island until 1921, when he was stricken with polio, and although his later visits were few, brief, and symbolic, the memories of island adventures and delights were forever fixed in his mind.

Campobello held a different and broader significance for Eleanor. She first came to the island as Franklin's romantic interest, and she made her last sentimental journey just months before her death. The big red cottage that she and Franklin first occupied in 1909 was the first home she was able to call her own. She continued to visit the island after Franklin's polio and after his death, welcoming its restorative and comforting charms.

Although in distinctively different ways, for both it was truly a special place, and special places such as Campobello have unique and enchanting qualities. Situated in the Bay of Fundy, Campobello is part of the Canadian province of New Brunswick and is connected to the American mainland by the Franklin D. Roosevelt International Bridge at Lubec, Maine. With the exception of the bridge, dedicated in 1962, Campobello is in many ways little different from the remote island James and Sara Roosevelt and their infant son Franklin first visited more than a hundred years ago.

Until the latter part of the nineteenth century, Campobello had been monumentally remote and painfully short of even rudimentary conveniences or accessibility. Sometimes shrouded in dampening fog, the island is surrounded by cold ocean waters that provide unmatched sailing. Summer days are generally pleasantly mild and evenings comfortably cool. In 1881, a group of American businessmen purchased much of the island's land and quickly turned it into a rustic but refined summer community of hotels and cottage sites. Campobello lacked the abundant services and varied recreational facilities of the rapidly growing and tonier eastern summer resorts at Newport or Bar Harbor. But the offer of Campobello's unspoiled rural beauty and simple charms proved irresistible to Franklin's parents, James and Sara Roosevelt of Hyde Park, New York, and to a small number of other wealthy summer rusticators.

Campobello's heyday as a thriving community of cottagers was relatively brief, a victim of the graduated income tax and the increasing convenience of the automobile. Changing social customs and mores of North Americans in the 1920s and 1930s made obsolete, in great part, the grand scale of summer cottaging on Campobello as well as at other playgrounds of the wealthy. Campobello's zenith was brief, but the Roosevelt family enthusiastically enjoyed and drew strength from their many years on the island. They arrived at its inception as a resort community and continued to visit after its decline. Franklin and Eleanor's cottage survives as the core of the Roosevelt Campobello International Park, the world's first international park, jointly operated by the governments of Canada and the United States. The Park is a living memorial and testament to the Roosevelts, and to Campobello itself. It celebrates the memory of a love affair between American icons and a remote Canadian island.

Visiting the Park and the Roosevelt cottage is like taking a step backward in time. Red clapboard siding and green shutters give the cottage a comfortable lived-in feeling. Large windows overlook the shrubbery and green lawn that lead down to Friar's Bay. Most of the cottage furnishings are authentic and original. The light and airy rooms are painted in warm shades of yellow, green, and coral, and the wallpapers with patterns of hydrangeas and violets have been carefully restored. The spartan but functional living-room decor of wicker furniture, hooked rugs with nautical themes, and lamp shades pressed with Queen Anne's lace evokes the comfort of cool nights and crackling birchwood fires. Franklin's hat, cane, and fishing pole are laid out in his first-floor bedroom, while Eleanor's treadle sewing machine and ancient typewriter sit silently in her writing room. The megaphone she used to summon children for meals or to break up squabbles stands ready for one more call. In the sunlit kitchen, the old wood-fired cookstove, by coincidence labeled "President," stands cold, but visitors can easily imagine the warm smells of baking mixing with the scents of fresh berries and tangy sea air.

This is a cottage full of secrets and memories. It was a summer retreat for members of a family of privilege who, although unlike the vast majority of North Americans, were still touched by a full range of human events and emotions. In their reactions to these events and emotions, Franklin and Eleanor Roosevelt were both willing masters and unwilling victims.

Although they were distant cousins and shared similar birthrights, Franklin and Eleanor Roosevelt were vastly different people. Franklin intuitively perceived his destiny and understood what action was required to achieve high goals. Eleanor learned to create her destiny; her triumphs were a result of will and persistence. Their personal qualities were complementary for notable success in the public arena. These same qualities were the root of much of their disappointment in personal relationships. Through it all, their beloved island played its unique role. Campobello nurtured Franklin in his youth and sustained Eleanor in her maturity. The island was a welcoming source of both challenge and adventure, security and comfort. It was always an important part of who the Roosevelts were, and they eagerly and gratefully embraced its gifts and its legacy.

1

Childhood

James and Sara Delano Roosevelt could scarcely have imagined that their only child would one day become President of the United States and be the only President to be elected to four terms, serving through the American twentieth century's two darkest hours. Franklin Roosevelt was, arguably, one of the most important political figures in the history of the Republic and, indeed, of modern times. Although James and Sara could not have been aware of these improbabilities, they were highly instrumental in their realization. James and Sara's lineage, breeding, wealth, and social status were not only young Franklin's birthright, they were his bedrock.

The nineteenth-century Hudson River aristocracy of the Roosevelts and Delanos traced their roots to the early American colonists. Franklin, an eighth-generation Roosevelt, was a descendant of Niklaus Rozenvelt, an early Dutch trader in New Amsterdam. Phillipe De La Noye, a Huguenot, was the first Delano to arrive in the Colonies, in 1621.[1]

Both families won and lost huge fortunes in fur, lumber, shipbuilding, and the great sea trade. The Delanos acquired much of their later wealth in the enormously lucrative opium trade of the mid-nineteenth century. Warren Delano, Sara's father, amassed spectacular

(1. Notes can be found at the end of the book on page 242)

wealth while living and trading in China both before and during the Opium Wars. Financial setbacks, while not infrequent, were offset by triumphs that created substantial fortunes, providing both families with all the good things that affluent post-Civil War American life could offer.

Along with economic and financial security, this privileged class developed broad interests in travel and adventure, a cultivation of the fine arts, and a remarkable spirit of *noblesse oblige*. This spirit fostered a genuine belief in responsibility for aiding the helpless and providing service to the community. If not precisely the same ethic, this was in many ways the legacy of Jeffersonian democracy.

In nineteenth-century America, rank and privilege were accorded to wealth, whether acquired by inheritance or by commercial success. Although the Delano fortune was greater than that of the Roosevelts, both families were comfortably lodged in the first rank. James and Sara were secure in this semi-leisured class that also embraced concepts of Christian service and responsibility.

Service was demonstrated in a variety of ways, but always with a style and grace that befitted the donor's social status. This attitude was shared by the Oyster Bay branch of cousin Theodore Roosevelt and his family, who were somewhat more active socially and better financially endowed than the Hyde Park branch. Franklin Delano Roosevelt was born into this comfortable world in 1882 and was lavished with all the love and attention that his parents could bring to bear. Sara's sister Dora observed, "He was brought up in a beautiful frame."[2]

James Roosevelt, who had been widowed, was in his fifties when he married Sara Delano of Newburgh, New York. James was financially secure and reasonably healthy, and as a country squire, he had not only the tangible resources to lavish on his family, but also the time and, for a while, the energy. Sara Delano, less than half James's age, was bright, attractive, and worldly. When Franklin was born, he was loved and cherished with style and gusto. He weighed more than ten pounds at birth, and the delivery was difficult. Sara was advised not to have more children, and this admonition influenced both her conjugal relations and the intensity of the love and attention she would devote to her only child. So much attention was paid to Franklin that he never developed close childhood friendships. He had doting parents, attentive servants, personal tutors, and childhood pets to attend his every need.

For a time, Sara apparently was reluctant to recognize that young Franklin was growing up. Many early photographs showed him dressed in skirts or kilts even to the age of seven. This was not a wholly uncommon occurrence, however, for a time when society was absorbed in the sentimentality of the hugely popular book, *Little Lord Fauntleroy*.[3]

Both parents surely served Franklin well. James was an instructive companion and Sara a supportive mother. Although closely attended, Franklin was not unduly sheltered or restrained from vigorous physical activity. In fact, he was encouraged to develop "gentlemanly" sporting skills and to test himself in these activities.

Franklin acquired many of these skills and developed a variety of hobbies. In addition, he learned to withstand pain, to accommodate discomfort, and to acquire limitless patience. These were, in many ways, to become among his most prominent attributes. The ability to endure physical and emotional pain was both a strength and a weakness. In later life it served Franklin well in triumphing over disability, but it also allowed him to mask his inner self and repress his deepest emotions.

As a child, Franklin played enthusiastically, if not often, with other children who were carefully selected as playmates. At an early age, he often assumed leadership roles. Sara recalled in her autobiography that he was always the only child issuing orders, and that they were usually obeyed. When she called this to his attention, Franklin replied, "But, Mommie, if I didn't give the orders, nothing would happen."[4] This statement was surely prophetic.

Franklin was enthusiastic about his hobbies and collections. These interests remained with him throughout his life, providing him with a means to relax, a way to occupy idle hours, and a technique to escape Sara's hovering presence. When he was piloting his boat or arranging his bird or stamp collections, Franklin was in charge and determining his own order of the world.[5]

Franklin's earliest years taught him that his family were people of some importance and standing, and so was he. This early confidence served him well in achieving goals, if not in winning friends. He quickly learned how to please adults and win their respect, but at some personal sacrifice. His charm and energy delighted adults and encouraged younger children to look up to him. But these same qualities often raised walls between him and friends of the same age. As a result, he enjoyed little of the peer sharing that most adolescents crave.

European trips were constant events for the Roosevelts. Franklin's honeymoon was his eleventh trip across the Atlantic. His early experience with European languages and cultures gave him a slight British accent and continental tastes in manners and clothing. Extensive trips abroad had always been a family tradition. The Delanos and Roosevelts had long traveled worldwide. At one time, a young Sara had lived in Hong Kong.

Tutored at home until the age of fourteen, Franklin had a succession of teachers who likely impressed upon him their social and political ideas. He often recalled a French tutor's positive influence in later life. Another, a Swiss, reportedly held strong socialistic views and may have planted in Franklin some early ideas about social change.

Franklin was enrolled at Groton School two years beyond the normal entering class. Classmates had already made firm friendships, and Franklin was never fully accepted by most of them. His purposeful attitude and his enthusiasm attracted the attention of instructors but rarely his fellow students. Franklin did win prizes in punctuality and in the "high kick," a peculiar activity in which the participant would throw his feet in the air, kick at a hanging object, and then land, often on his head. Franklin succeeded in this event while others were unwilling to endure its pain. But it provided Franklin a means to excel and a way to call attention to himself. His slight build, however, was not suited to the "Muscular Christianity" of Groton's team sports.[6] Franklin competed, but he was never a successful team athlete.

Franklin was an unremarkable scholar. He may have been attentive to his lessons, but the quality of his work was mediocre, a pattern that continued at Harvard with attainment of "Gentleman's C" grades. His principal claim to distinction at Groton was his bloodline to cousin Theodore, then Vice-President of the United States. Franklin happily traded on this providential kinship. At school, as well as in later life, Franklin used whatever he had going for him.

Both parents had done what they could to ensure that Franklin would be "very nice" and that he would always be "bright and happy." Sara learned this from her father and she devoted herself to the same propositions in raising her own son. Unpleasantness was to be ignored or, better still, laughed off. When he suffered some minor disappointment at Groton, Sara told Franklin that "we must be above caring . . . keep your position and character and let no one make you feel small, go ahead your own way, and be kind to everyone if you have the chance . . . ."[7]

Sara often said that Franklin was a Delano, not a Roosevelt. Her close involvement in his life was unceasing, but Franklin eventually learned to protect his private thoughts carefully while still showing Sara both deference and love. He was the son of a mother who had been intensely devoted to her own father. Freud might have been describing Franklin when he wrote, "A man who has been the indisputable favorite of his mother keeps for life the feeling of a conqueror, that confidence of success that often induces real success."[8]

All his life, Franklin did the utmost to follow Sara's advice and to live up to her expectations. As a result, he appeared to have a peaceful and sometimes passive composure, behind which he buried all unpleasant thoughts. While he clearly charted a life of his own, he always remained the dutiful son who had perfected the art (or curse) of guarding closely his deepest emotions. Eleanor told a friend years later that his "was an innate kind of reticence. It became part of his nature not to talk to anyone of intimate things."[9] He kept his own counsel and seemed to believe strongly in his own empowerment.

Groton School meant a great deal in Franklin's development. Its founder and headmaster, the Reverend Endicott Peabody, was a towering presence in the lives of "Grotties." Peabody's goal was to turn out young men capable of bringing the highest ideals to the reform of government. He emphasized strong morals, Christian ethics, and the avoidance of sin while encouraging full mental and physical development. His influence on his students was profound. For Franklin, Peabody reinforced everything he had come to know about responsibility to his fellow man and service to the community. Franklin idolized Peabody and later attested to his belief that Peabody's influence was second only to that of his parents.[10]

Franklin's childhood was ordered, loving, and seemingly free of fear, insecurity, or desperation. Eleanor's adolescence could not have been more different. Her cousin Corinne Robinson Alsop wrote that Eleanor "knew she had a ghastly childhood, but didn't realize how ghastly it was."[11] Her early years were marked by tragedy, unrequited parental love, abject fear, and the development of a spectacular sense of insecurity.

Eleanor's father, Elliott, was Theodore Roosevelt's younger brother. Elliott showed little of the strength of character and determination of the future President. His relatively brief life was marked with disappointments, failures, and addictions. Although dashing, witty, and enormously charming, Elliott was unable to sustain any serious pursuits. He expressed admiration for brother Ted's successes but was apparently envious of them. His indulgences and idleness were closely held within the family for a time, but they persisted, and Elliott began drinking to excess.

Elliott was introduced to Anna Hall, the eldest child of Valentine G. Hall, Jr., and Mary Livingston Ludlow Hall of Beacon, New York. At eighteen, Anna Hall was a dazzling beauty, and she and Elliott fell in love almost instantly. Their engagement was announced at Algonac, the ancestral home of Sara Delano Roosevelt. Anna had been raised in wealth by her reclusive and puritanical father and a tyrannized mother. Her mother was never allowed to shop on her own or to understand family finances. When Anna's father died in 1880, Mary Hall was totally unprepared to manage a household and six children under the age of seventeen. Anna escaped from this chaotic and joyless home in marriage. She was enormously attracted to Elliott's joyful and romantic nature. He may have recognized in her a more serious mien that might give him some sense of the stability lacking in his life.

The Roosevelts welcomed Eleanor's birth in 1884, but clouds had already formed on the family's horizon. Theodore's mother and his wife Alice both died on the same day. Eleanor's birth was initially looked upon as a great relief to these tragedies. But her parents' marriage was severely troubled. Elliott's idleness and drinking continued, and Anna was unable or unwilling to handle the responsibility of caring for an infant and had little assistance from her husband.

In Anna's eyes, young Eleanor did not reflect either parent's outstanding qualities or expectations. She was considered plain-looking and joyless. Eleanor recalled in later years that as a child she was "very solemn . . . lacking in the spontaneous joy and mirth of youth."[12] Eleanor had neither her mother's beauty nor her father's gaiety.

Franklin and Eleanor first met at Springwood when he was four years old and she was two. Neither remembered this early meeting, but Franklin had dutifully and tirelessly carried an unsmiling Eleanor on his back across the nursery floor. Later, when she came down for tea, Eleanor refused to enter the parlor, standing timidly in the doorway. Anna called, "Come in, Granny," telling Sara and James that Eleanor was "such a funny child, so old-fashioned."[13] Consequently, Eleanor was convinced by what she constantly heard. She believed she was unattractive, clumsy, and a poor reflection of her glamorous parents. She held these views all her life.

Eleanor adored her father and was at her happiest when she was with him. He was affectionate and transported her into his fantasies. But his behavior had become increasingly erratic. Elliott resigned from his brother-in-law's firm and took his family on a European voyage. Aboard the *Brittanic*, they were struck by another liner, and a disorderly attempt to abandon ship followed. Eleanor was dropped into the waiting arms of her father, standing in a lifeboat. Elliott, the only male passenger to leave the *Brittanic*, was condemned for ungentlemanly and cowardly behavior, although his actions were misunderstood. The ship did not sink, but the two-year-old Eleanor felt the trauma intensely. Her great fear of the sea lasted well into adulthood.

Eleanor was constantly reminded to be brave, but the admonitions served only to increase her anxiety. Anna and Elliott were first puzzled and then irritated by her fears. Eleanor became more convinced than ever that she was a disappointment to them, and her feelings of inadequacy and despondence grew. She later wrote, "Fear has always seemed to me the worst stumbling block which anyone has to face. It is the great crippler. Looking back it strikes me that my childhood and my early youth were one long battle against fear."[14]

Elliott and Anna had two more children, Hall and Elliott, Jr. The births did nothing to strengthen the weakening marriage or encourage Elliott to stick to any of the "cures" that he undertook. By 1891, he had entered an Austrian sanitarium, and Eleanor was sent to a nearby convent school. It was a disastrous experience for her, and she felt out of place and unwanted. Elliott returned briefly to the family, but his drinking and carousing were out of control.

Elliott left the family home, fathered a child with one of the family maids, and took a New York City apartment with his mistress. Now a public scandal, Elliott was an embarrassment to the family in general and to Theodore in particular. Theodore was then rapidly rising as a public figure and he felt compelled to chastise his brother publicly, calling his spectacularly immoral behavior an "offense against order, decency, and civilization."[15]

Theodore and their sister Bamie tried to commit Elliott to an institution, but he threatened divorce and even more public embarrassment. Another "cure" and an exile to Virginia provided a brief respite for Elliott, but not for the family. Anna had taken her children to Bar Harbor, Maine, where her beauty and charm briefly made her the toast of the summer community. But Anna was crumbling emotionally and knew that she was failing her children. She made a few feeble and misguided attempts at motherly attention and companionship. Eleanor's anger grew and she blamed Anna for Elliott's long absences that deprived her of the only real love she had known. With few exceptions, there was little closeness and affection between mother and daughter.

In October, 1892, Anna underwent surgery, for an unreported cause. After the operation, she contracted diphtheria. Her mother prevented Elliott's return and Anna died in December without seeing her husband again. Then eight years old, Eleanor had lost her mother, but her beloved father soon returned, however briefly. Elliott was well over the edge, unable to grieve for his wife or care for his children. He returned to Virginia. Four months later, Elliott, Jr., died of scarlet fever. Once more Elliott returned, only to injure his head seriously while in a drunken stupor. In a state of delirium, he had a violent seizure and died. In the space of twenty months, Eleanor had lost her mother, a baby brother, and her beloved father. She later remembered that she "began living in my dream world as usual . . . . From that time on I . . . lived with him more closely, probably, than I had when he was alive."[16]

Throughout her life, Eleanor talked at length about her father, speaking of his virtues and keeping his memory alive. She published some of Elliott's collected letters so that her children would get some sense of the character that Eleanor held so dear to the end of her days.

Until the age of fifteen, Eleanor was in the care of her austere and restrictive grandmother, Mary Hall. Eleanor's only pleasure was in the companionship of her brother Hall. This close relationship with Hall continued into their adulthood, until he, too, succumbed to severe alcoholism.

Life with Grandmother Hall at Tivoli, on the Hudson, was a genuine horror for Eleanor. In addition to the grim and despotic grandmother, Eleanor and Hall shared a home with their Aunt Pussie and two severely alcoholic uncles. Pussie was incurably romantic and had a history of failed affairs. She repeatedly called Eleanor unattractive and told her that, unlike her beautiful dead mother, she would not have any beaux.

Grandmother Hall did nothing to enhance Eleanor's self-esteem or respond to her needs. Eleanor's teeth were not straightened, her clothes were not stylish, and little attention was paid to the development of her character or intellect. Eleanor's longing for love and for her lost father increased and she developed what she later called her "Griselda" moods, which haunted her for the rest of her life.[17] These periods of despair were the signs of an intensely unhappy child, if not the manifestation of clinical depression. The adults in her immediate life were chronically depressed women and alcoholic men.

By good fortune, at age fifteen Eleanor was sent to England to attend the Allenswood School under the supervision of Mademoiselle Marie Souvestre. In much the same way Franklin grew under the Reverend Mr. Peabody at Groton, Eleanor blossomed under Mlle. Souvestre. In her three years at Allenswood, Eleanor became a favorite of both faculty and students, admired for her intelligence, her character, and her heart. She took responsibility, she succeeded in her studies, and she developed both taste and skill in the humanities, especially poetry. At Allenswood Eleanor read and recited poetry aloud, a practice she continued throughout her days.

From Mlle. Souvestre she heard then radical ideas of trade unionism, the rights of nations, and the innocence of Alfred Dreyfus. Eleanor recognized that being exposed to her teacher's leftist views and atheism "did me no harm. Mlle. Souvestre shocked me into thinking, which was beneficial."[18]

Mlle. Souvestre reported to Grandmother Hall, "I have not found [her] easily influenced in anything that was not perfectly straightforward and honest, but I often found that she influenced others in the right direction. She is full of sympathy for all those who live with her. . . . As a pupil she is very satisfactory, but even that is of small account when you compare it with the perfect quality of her soul."[19] Eleanor later wrote, "Whatever I have become since had its seeds in those three years of contact with a liberal mind and strong personality."[20] After Eleanor had completed her schooling and returned to America, Mlle. Souvestre wrote to Grandmother Hall that Eleanor had "the warmest heart I ever encountered," and to Eleanor, "I miss you every day of my life."[21]

By the age of eighteen, both Franklin and Eleanor had experienced adolescences that clearly shaped their characters and personalities. Both were born to wealth and exposed to education, culture, and experience available only to the privileged. Neither was encouraged to form close relationships with peers, but both related to adults and the adult world. Both learned to keep their emotions hidden, Franklin through systematic training, Eleanor from a childhood filled with tragedy and abandonment. Both were tremendously influenced by positive preparatory school experiences and powerful mentors. One had been prepared to expect the best, one to fear the worst. Franklin looked forward to Harvard and to taking his rightful place in early twentieth-century American society. Eleanor, with more confidence and a developed intellect, looked forward with far less enthusiasm to the role that society required of young women of her station.

Franklin's loving childhood developed in him the confidence to overcome disappointment. Insecurity, in a manner, prepared Eleanor for the ordeals of her life. She said later, it "hardened me in much the same way steel is tempered." In order to protect herself from emotional crisis, she learned self-discipline. She saw what happened to those who lost self-control. Consequently, she developed "an almost exaggerated idea of the necessity of keeping all of one's desires under complete subjugation."[22] Convinced that she was neither loved nor wanted, she learned that she could win affection, or at least respect, by helping others. She believed that "the feeling that I was useful was perhaps the greatest joy I experienced."[23]

Powerful influences in their childhoods set both Franklin and Eleanor Roosevelt firmly and inexorably on their unique paths to adulthood. They were certainly influenced by later events, relationships, and the many forces that came into play in their remarkably productive lives. But it is also clear that one Roosevelt had been permanently scarred by unrelieved parental indulgence, and the other by its absolute absence.

2

Campobello

"Mist often blots out the island," Elizabeth Goodman wrote, "drifting eerily through the fir and spruce woods, accompanied by the hollow boom of a foghorn. Forests . . . where the tree limbs are draped with the grey-green lichen that flourishes in the perpetual dampness. The eastern shore has coves and beaches with multicolored pebbles and driftwood. The western shore is heavily wooded with high bluffs that make it difficult to reach the shore. Salt air mingles with the spruce scent, . . . smell of fish and cries of circling gulls . . ."[1]

Nine miles long and three miles at its widest, Campobello is the largest and outermost of a group of islands in Passamaquoddy Bay between the American state of Maine and the Canadian province of New Brunswick. In most respects, it is not unlike the many islands that dot the coasts of Maine and the Maritime Provinces. The rugged terrain features many of the geological treasures that are typical of coastal eastern North America.

Campobello's hardy residents have long relied on fishing and the boats that make it possible. The island was settled by both Native Americans and Europeans and had been occupied, at one time or another, by both the French and the English. Campobello boasts certain differences from other island retreats. One of its qualities is unique: From 1770 until 1881, Campobello was privately owned. This distinction had a great deal to do with shaping the remoteness and the independent character of the island and its residents. When, in 1881, much of the island was sold to a group of entrepreneurs who planned to develop a summer resort for the wealthy families of Boston, New York City, and Montreal, Campobello became a new "moment in time." That moment was the late Victorian age of the "rusticator" or "cottager." Resort communities grew up along the New England coast and, to a lesser extent, the Maritime Provinces of Canada, to fill a growing desire of wealthy urban families to seek relaxation and refreshment in rural seaside settings.

Newport and Bar Harbor were attracting the wealthy who sought relief from the city's oppressive heat and humidity and had both the time and resources to enjoy these new summer colonies. They were designed as exclusive havens for members of the upper classes and their social peers. Campobello met these criteria, but it was geographically more remote than the other resorts, and it was designed to be simpler and less formal. More emphasis was placed on the rural and rustic qualities of the island, and less on elaborate homes and social pomp. These features distinguished Campobello from other retreats.

Over the many years between the formation of the Campobello Company in 1881 and the present, Campobello has changed relatively little. The bridge that connected Campobello to Lubec, Maine, in 1962 caused many residents to wonder if they might cease to feel like islanders. The bridge and the dedication of the Roosevelt Campobello International Park in 1964 facilitated access to the island for automobiles and brought numbers of tourists and day-trippers. Nonetheless, Campobello had special character long before cottagers such as the James Roosevelts of Hyde Park came, and it remains distinctive long after they have passed from the scene.

Campobello Island is part of the Canadian province of New Brunswick. It might have been American, separated from Maine as it is only by a narrow and shallow channel at Lubec. Negotiators of the Webster-Ashburton Treaty of 1842 could easily have drawn the national borders differently. A story suggests that ample liquid refreshment provided to American diplomats contributed to the decision on where the line was drawn. After all, Campobello geographically relates more closely to the American mainland than to the Canadian. From the New Brunswick mainland, one must travel sixty miles through Maine to reach Campobello by land or cross more than ten miles of open water.

Most of Campobello's residents live on the eastern side near the large natural port of Harbour de L'Outre. The north is mostly ledge and low hills with thin topsoil, but the south is luxuriant with trees, fern, and flora. A forest at Liberty Point is almost perpetually in fog, and the trees are shrouded with what is known as "old man's beard."[2]

Campobello's shores are continually pounded and shaped by tides that reach heights of thirty feet. The Bay of Fundy's tides, the world's highest, have long tantalized engineers as a potential source for an immense supply of electric power. During the twentieth century, several abortive attempts were made to harness Fundy's tides. In the mid-1930s, Congress appropriated funds for engineering studies, but the task appeared too daunting, and even Franklin Roosevelt's enthusiasm for the project waned. But the tides are not the only aspects of the area that intrigue and seduce the visitor. The air, writes Stephen Muskie, is "tangy with the mixing scents of land and sea. The signs of man's presence are barely perceptible over much of her flowing fields, dense forests, tidal marshes, expansive mud flats, and jagged headlands."[3]

The residents are descended, in great part, from ten families whose ancestors date to the Proprietary Grant or fief. They live principally in three communities and fish, process fish, or build and maintain fishing boats and gear. Hand-lining, lobstering, trawling, gill-netting, seining, and weir-tending are the primary forms of fishing. Some islanders keep shop or provide service to tourists during the summer season. Sardine canning, boat building, boat repair, and carpentry provide work for others. A few are employed at the International Park and in other government positions. And in the fall many go "tipping" to gather evergreen boughs for Christmas wreaths.[4]

The weather on Campobello in summer is, at best, variable. Fog and mist often drift through the fir and spruce. On days the sun shines, the air is mild and the scents are heady, while evenings are cool, often with brilliant sunsets. The vistas are endless, both shoreward and seaward, and the sailing is unmatched. These pleasures were there for the taking, but it took a long time for them to be taken.

The first Europeans known to have settled on Campobello were the family of Jean Sarreau, Sieur de St. Aubin, in 1684. In the great struggle for control of North America that followed, the Acadian areas of the Maritimes and the valleys of the St. John and St. Croix rivers changed hands nine times during the seventeenth and eighteenth centuries. By 1693, Port Royal, on the New Brunswick mainland across the Bay of Fundy from Campobello, was the capital of Acadia. Port Royal soon fell to New England militiamen and was renamed Annapolis Royal. Little attention was paid to Campobello.

In the 1760s, following the British triumph over the French in the Seven Years War, a Welsh naval officer, Lieutenant William Owen, petitioned the Crown for some "gratuity, pension, or preferment" for his wounds and his long service. Owen was described as "a popular young hero, a man of few ideas, ingenuous but relatively honest and generous."[5]

Owen's former commander, Lord William Campbell, was appointed Governor of Nova Scotia and brought the now Captain Owen with him to Halifax. For services rendered, Lord William named him the "Principal Proprietary of the Great Outer Island of Passamaquoddy." He also arranged for Captain Owen to receive a much larger grant than his rank would have suggested.

With thirty-eight Lancashire settlers Owen landed his entourage at Halifax on May 21, 1770, and the following month at his new island fief. He promptly added thirty-seven New Englanders to the Lancashiremen. An imbalance of men to women, a lack of homesteading skills, the fierce North Atlantic winters, and Owen's inexperience in managing such a venture led to growth problems and defections. Still, the tiny colony survived.

Captain Owen named the island Campo Bello, in part a complimentary pun honoring his mentor, Lord Campbell, and in part a reference to the island's beauty. For reasons not clear, Captain Owen and a group of settlers returned to England in 1771. Perhaps they left to join the military in service against the French, or just to alleviate homesickness. Others followed but were lost at sea. Many of those who were left behind drifted away. One, Andrew Lloyd, fought for American independence and remained in the new republic. His grandson was William Lloyd Garrison, the Massachusetts journalist and fiery abolitionist. Little of the original colony remained.

Captain Owen died in British military service in India in 1778, and the second Proprietary, David Owen, a nephew, arrived in 1787 to stake his claim. Squire Owen, a tutor by profession, was even less prepared than his uncle for his new role and struggled to exercise some level of control.

After the American Revolution, many Loyalists fled to eastern Canada and a few found their way to Campobello. Among them was the American hero-turned-traitor Benedict Arnold. For some years, Arnold lived at Friar's Head, a rocky outcropping that had chiefly been known as a gunnery target for the Royal Navy.[6] It sits above Friar's Bay not far from the bluff where James and Sara Roosevelt would build their cottage a century later.

By 1835, Admiral William Fitzwilliam Owen, the English-born second son of Captain Owen, had succeeded to the Proprietorship. After naval service, he settled on Campobello, "to pursue my disposition to acquire spiritual knowledge."[7] An odd sort, Admiral Owen erected a replica of a man-o'-war quarterdeck upon which he incessantly paced in full dress uniform. While Admiral Owen and his family pursued a life of English gentility, Campobello increasingly became a community of rugged individuals and their families who fished for their survival.

In one of his few responsible contributions, Admiral Owen ordered the construction of St. Anne's Anglican Church, which today still serves the islanders. He took enormous pleasure in leading both morning and evening services. The Roosevelts later worshipped there.

The Admiral died in 1857. Captain James Robinson-Owen, a son-in-law, assumed the Owen surname and the Proprietorship. An unsympathetic landlord, he soon tried to sell the fiefdom when it continued to be unprofitable. His attempts failed in the hard financial times that followed the North American depression of 1872. Captain Robinson-Owen was still trying to sell his holdings when he died suddenly in 1874.

The hard times of the 1870s brought a new enterprise, rum-running. Fishing boats arrived from Gloucester, Massachusetts, supposedly to buy herring but in reality to purchase whiskey and gin imported from Ireland, Scotland, France, and Holland. The Prohibition Era in the United States in the 1920s again revived this illegal but lucrative practice. Campobello's fog-shrouded harbors were natural settings for the purchase and exchange of contraband. Although few of the islanders profited significantly, many participated, and their stories, embellished by time, are still told.

The Owen era and the Proprietorship ended in 1881 when Cornelia Robinson-Owen, then 61, sold her rights to the Campobello Company, a group of American businessmen. With $1,000,000 in hand, the Company quickly outlined elaborate plans to turn the island into a summer resort. The remaining members of the Owen family sailed for England, and the islanders, without participating in the decision, were about to see an enormous social change take place on Campobello. Wealth, style, and privilege were to dominate their island in a manner that was to them unknown. Overnight, Campobello became a playground for American gentility of the Gilded Age.

Miles from the Canadian mainland, Campobello became a summer community of Victorian mores and culture, Yankee style. To be sure, there were wealthy Canadians who visited from Montreal and Toronto, and a small number of English families crossed the Atlantic to rusticate, but the Campobello summer colony was essentially an American affair.

The first hotel, the Owen, was built between June and August of 1881. Rushed to completion, it exemplified the Campobello Company's zeal to get the colony established quickly. Over the next two years, the Tyn-y-Coed (Welsh for "house in the woods") and the Tyn-y-Maes ("house in the field") were built. The Owen, with four hundred rooms, was connected to the old Admiral's house by a covered walk.

The Tyn-y-Coed was described as a "fine model hotel . . . pleasantly situated near the water's edge, on a bluff 75 feet above the level of the sea." It had a large parlor, a dining room, a card room, and broad piazzas on all sides. The hotels were "provided with all the comforts of a refined home."[8] Here, "home" is the operative word, because the Campobello Company was taking the role of a gracious host.

A Company brochure described the hotels as "attractive, picturesque, and refined in all their appointments,—in fact, homelike; so that one may enjoy all the freedom of exploration or rock-climbing, come back to a home, and a good supper well cooked and well served."[9]

Every effort was made to underscore the exclusive nature of the Campobello hotels. The management emphasized a separation of the hotel guests from outsiders (islanders). "Unconsciously you feel foreign and titled when a sentinel swings open the gates for your admission and closes them quickly to the public of small boys, Indians, and loungers." In the early seasons, the Company firmly enforced a policy that "only guests of the hotel and persons arriving by steam launch . . . will be allowed on the Owen grounds. Picnic parties will not be permitted on the adjoining grounds."[10]

Islanders were referred to as industrious and thrifty, but clearly part of the background. They were thought to be "highly intelligent, ruggedly independent, and self-respectful yet at the same time deferential to their 'betters' in the English tradition."[11] The company intended to build a congenial summer colony of the "right" people.

The hotels, while quickly built to capture interest in this remote island, were but the first phase of the Campobello Company's plan. The principal challenge was to devise and establish an extensive colony of summer cottages.

F. W. Dean, a Harvard professor, surveyed the land and divided it into lots of two to six acres. The Company let the islanders know in clear terms that these holdings were to be shaped into an exclusive summer resort. They asked New Brunswick authorities to build a jail and to limit the number of dogs. At Company expense, fences were built to contain the livestock that had habitually roamed freely.[12] By the end of 1882, fifteen lots were sold and cottages quickly built. The new owners contributed to the character of the island by donating funds for a library and a church hall. The cottagers may have joined the islanders for picnics and races, but there was an unmistakable class distinction. Even so, the summer residents tried, in their fashion, to be democratic neighbors.

The St. John (New Brunswick) *Daily Sun* headlined, "Campobello, The Queen of Summer Resorts," in 1892. "American capital, American enterprise and American culture have laid hold . . . and with a quickness savouring of the days of Aladdin have transformed the old possessions of Admiral Owen into the most charming watering-place in the world." The report goes on to quote Harvard Professor N. S. Shaler's claim that "the extensive forests of balsamic firs seem to affect the atmosphere of this region, causing a quiet of the nervous system and inviting sleep." Professor Shaler asserted that despite their "hard labour and scanty diet," the Campobello fisherpeople were the "best conditioned people" he had ever seen, and "the children especially were models of vigour and health."[13]

The Campobello summer resort colony was an early success. In the late nineteenth century, the attraction of rustic natural beauty was very much in vogue. According to John Urry, this was "scenic tourism," and it was enticing to many North Americans during the years leading up to the First World War. Campobello fit Urry's mold. It was a perfect rustic Victorian landscape offering "irregularity, variation, decay and wildness in 'natural' appearance as sources of aesthetic pleasure."[14]

The Company's promotional literature extolled views of wide sweeps of ocean, the cliffs of Grand Manan island, the hilly towns of Eastport and Lubec, and the "forest-crowned" islands of Passamaquoddy Bay. Campobello was portrayed as unique and quaint. The literature refers to the islanders and their "lonely huts" who "retain an old-fashioned simplicity and courtesy." Kate Gannet Wells wrote of "the most lonesome and picturesque drive . . . the fishing boats, brilliant with the red flannel shirts of the men," and described how "you will never forget the view."[15]

The climate was appealing for those wishing to escape the swelter of city summers. This was long before the development of air-conditioning and electrical refrigeration equipment, and Campobello's summers were cool and invigorating. Crackling fires took the chill from evenings, and sunshine and gentle breezes made many summer days a delight. This is not to say that fog and rain did not have a significant presence. From time to time, planned outdoor activities were delayed until the sun's return. But for the most part, the island summers were enticing.

It was not difficult to extol Campobello's natural gifts, which were ruggedly beautiful. Vistas, particularly seaward, were often enchanting and ever-changing. Land for cottage-building was relatively inexpensive compared to some other coastal resorts. The hotels were accommodating for those who preferred not to homestead, and it was a most appealing lifestyle for those who could afford it and did not seek the flashier styles of Newport or Bar Harbor.

Opportunities for outdoor activity abounded. Campobello offered many carriage drives, paths for hiking, and superb boating and fishing. Captains and crews could be hired, and tennis courts, bowling lanes, pool tables, and eventually a golf course were available. Even Native American guides and birchbark canoes could be hired, diversion hardly to be found at Newport. And for those less athletically inclined, the leisurely pursuits of reading, lounging, gossiping, and socializing abounded.

The island boasted picturesque spots for picnics, outings, and games. Friar's Head, Herring Cove, the White Rocks, and Cranberry Point—each had its special features and its appeal. Cod, pollack, haddock, halibut, and lobsters were readily caught in the sea, and trout could be taken from island ponds. Fish was often the evening meal at a time when the pleasures of fresh seafood were not easily available in city homes. Ocean swimming was for the hardy, but mild island ponds offered pleasant freshwater bathing.

Promotional literature also emphasized the therapeutic values to be found on Campobello. *Catarrhus aestivus*, or hay fever, was first studied by Charles Harrison Blackley in the late 1800s. He believed it to be an upper-class affliction and that certain seaside locations had an ameliorating effect. These locales should have "the form and character of a small island or narrow peninsula . . . backed with high cliffs, because these act as sort of screen when a land wind is blowing."[16] Campobello, enjoying bracing air and free of hay fever, fit Blackley's bill, and offered "absolute" relief from hay fever as a major advantage in island promotion.

There was also a belief that Campobello could provide therapeutic relief from the distresses of modern civilization. This was directly linked to the antimodernism movement that grew in response to industrialization in both America and Europe. The antimodernists glorified the need to return to the tranquillity of rural life. Again, Campobello was an ideal spot to find this simple, rustic living, and, most important, it could be enjoyed in the company of others of the same social class. The industrious and respectful local residents could provide the necessary services. The rural sights, facilities, activities, and class camaraderie were an antidote to the trials of overcivilization. Campobello, therefore, promised to be a most agreeable form of therapy.

It may have been agreeable, but Campobello was hard to reach. The island was not then and is not now an easy destination. It was hardly on the way to anywhere, and there were long miles of land or sea to cross and a challenging and limited range of transport to get there. In 1882, travelers could take railroads, with several transfers, through Maine to Eastport, or through Quebec and New Brunswick to St. John. A two-mile boat ride from Eastport or longer voyage from St. John or St. Andrew's brought travelers to the small harbor of Welshpool on Campobello. Or travelers could take one of several steamships from Boston to Eastport, or a steamer from New York to Boston to Portland to Eastport. The Boston steamer took twenty-five hours; the trip from New York lasted forty-three. By 1891, the

Boston route was reduced to fifteen hours.

The steamer trips were very much like big house parties. *Cumberland, State of Maine, Harvard,* and *Yale* were crowded with Campobello friends coming together in happy reunion for the start of another summer season, a season that, in those days, might run from May to October.[17] *Yale* had an extended life long after Campobello service, serving as a troop transport in World War II and surviving the then-President Franklin Roosevelt.[18]

The Campobello summer colony thrived. Kate Gannet Wells wrote, "Each year the place became better known, but those who early made it their summer home have stamped upon it, it is hoped, that simplicity in manner of living which will prevent it from ever becoming either a [public] place for picnics or a fashionable resort. It can never lose the picturesque beauty and the exhilarating climate which make it a most beautiful summer sojourn . . . ."[19]

The tiny spruce-clad island in the Bay of Fundy, with its bracing sea breezes, clinging fogs, rugged cliffs, and unspoiled beaches, was established, promoted, and visited, by a group of rusticators, some of whom would regularly return for a half-century or more. They came for the many reasons advertised, and they made it their special place. Among those intrepid rusticators were the James Roosevelts and son of Hyde Park.

3

Beloved Island

"The 1880s were the zenith of what Mark Twain christened 'the Gilded Age,'" Alden Nowlan wrote.

The United States had been transformed from a remote agrarian republic into one of the world's industrial giants. The frontier had been all but eliminated as railways bound the continent together. Taxes were low and the work ethic was propounded and enforced as if it were a divine ordinance. It was the best of all possible times in which to be rich. The poor, according to economist and sociologist Thorstein Veblen, were quite content to derive such pleasure as they could from observing the rich consume all manner of goods on their behalf. Vicarious consumption, he called it. And among the goods that the rich consumed in vast quantities and with considerable flair was leisure. Presumably they did not feel in need of the moral discipline that work was said to provide for the poor. This was, for the few who could afford it, the age of the summer-long vacation, and of the great summer resorts . . . .[1]

Campobello Island was introduced to these few in 1881. Hotels were built in a few short months and were fully occupied the following season. James Roosevelt had heard about the island from friends, quite possibly from Alexander Porter, the Campobello Company's general manager. The sailing off the Maine and Canadian coasts was even then legendary, and the promise of a colony of genteel Victorians was extremely appealing to the very proper Roosevelts.

In 1883, James, Sara, and one-year-old Franklin visited Campobello, staying at the Tyn-y-Coed Hotel. Franklin was teething, and the Roosevelts thought the bracing sea air would be comforting to both the baby and themselves. James and Sara were so taken with Campobello that they purchased a partially built house on ten acres of land situated on a high knoll overlooking Friar's Bay. Although little else is known of what transpired during this stay, they made a commitment to Campobello and the island became an important part of each of the Roosevelt's lives. Sara christened Campobello their "beloved island."

James commissioned a fifteen-room "cottage." It was built in 1884 and first occupied the next summer. Other wealthy Americans and Canadians built cottages of similar style and size. The season was a long one, and in most cottages the women and children stayed throughout the summer. Most men spent shorter periods, traveling between the island and their business concerns. The Roosevelts often divided their summers between Campobello and travels in Europe. Business seldom interfered with the Roosevelt agenda.

The cottages were, in fact, large Victorian homes designed to accommodate significant numbers of guests in addition to the resident families and their staffs. Servants were brought from winter residences and included cooks, housekeepers, nurses, governesses, and maids. The island workforce provided groundskeepers, gardeners, and additional domestic workers. Most important, the islanders provided full ships' crews, including captains. Campobello's maritime traditions had produced some of the world's finest captains and sailors. Consequently, each occupied cottage became a center for housing, feeding, and sustaining large numbers of people to be entertained and otherwise provided for on both land and sea.

The Cow Bell, a news sheet published by the hotels, noted that "the moss-coloured roof of the Roosevelt cottage has excited universal admiration. Its owner is a most accomplished gentleman and can constantly be seen steering his pretty craft amid the islands of the bay." [2]

The James Roosevelt cottage was a pleasant shingled cottage surrounded by spruce trees and fronting on a rocky shore and pebbly beach. The balconied main hall had fireplaces at either end. In addition to providing atmosphere, a sense of coziness, and visual enjoyment, fireplaces, along with the kitchen cook stoves, supplied the heat necessary to take the chill off the cool and often damp air. For those arriving early in the season and remaining into fall, the fireplaces burned constantly in the cottages, warding off, if only temporarily, the inexorable advance of the early winter season.

Over the fifty-six years of Roosevelt occupation, the cottage's complement of rooms varied in use, depending on the need and the circumstance. The water supply was of indifferent quality and quantity, and its heating was limited. Gas lanterns and candles supplemented the illumination from the fireplaces. There was no electrical service or telephone.

Campobello cottages were typically encircled with breezy porches furnished with hammocks, wicker chairs, and tables that were generally heaped with magazines and novels. The arrival of mail by boat from Eastport was a daily highlight. The mail packet also included newspapers that brought the cottagers their only contact with the outside world.

Like other summer resorts, Campobello functioned as a meeting-place for well-to-do, socially acceptable young women and young men. Later, Franklin participated in this established custom when he, too, became an eligible suitor. The social season included dinners, a grand annual ball, poetry readings, and musical recitals. The Campobello Dramatic Club's productions were often followed by musical presentations, club and dumbbell exhibitions, or talks on subjects that ranged from flower arrangement to woman's suffrage.

There was also a Campobello Debating Society. In later years, according to legend, Franklin was barred from the debating team because of a lack of eloquence; Eleanor was thought to be the better speaker. John Calder, a local resident, was the Society's star debater, and despite his opinion of Franklin's oratorical skills, he became Franklin's closest friend on the island.

Franklin enjoyed a broad range of experiences during his youthful Campobello vacations. By the summer of 1888, James had taught him the rudiments of sailing a large yacht. A photograph shows the tense six-year-old gripping the ship's wheel while bracing himself against a stiff breeze. As Geoffrey Ward notes, he was barely as tall as the wheel but was already, if only momentarily, in command. Sailing was much more than a hobby for Franklin, it became a passion. On the water he had the means for command and control, a way to test his skills and daring, and a retreat from the rest of his world. He became a widely acknowledged expert and gained immense lifelong pleasure from sailing.

Franklin enjoyed friendship with Campobello fishermen and sailors. He liked their stories and their rugged independence. The Campobello residents, in turn, liked Franklin for who he was, not what he was.[3] He freely gave of himself and his time, and they respected him for it. He took every opportunity to ask questions, to learn and test new skills, and to demonstrate his boundless energy.

Among those who took young Franklin under their wing were Captains Franklin Calder and Eddie Lank. Lank followed James Roosevelt's lead in providing formal sailing instruction. When Franklin was about ten and had demonstrated his proficiency, Lank reportedly told him, "You'll do, now. You're a full-fledged seaman, sardine-sized."[4]

Campobello helped toughen Franklin. When he was six, he was struck in the mouth with a stick. He lost one tooth and another was broken in half, exposing the nerve. Franklin neither complained nor showed much emotion during the long crossing to the mainland to find a dentist. Sara considered his stoicism and self-control most admirable, noting that Franklin went through the entire incident "without fuss."[5]

When he was nine, Franklin protested Sara's tight regulation and precisely-timed regimen of planned activities and supervised play. He asked Sara if he could, for a day, do what he pleased. Sara agreed to a day with no restriction other than timely meals. She did not question Franklin when he returned and had no idea how he had occupied himself. The next day, he resumed his regular routine. In the usual version of this often-told story, Sara reported that Franklin returned home from his adventure "exhausted and begrimed."[6] He was gradually permitted more freedom and eagerly took advantage of it.

In 1891, James took delivery of the *Half Moon*, a fifty-one-foot yacht with an auxiliary naphtha motor. The *Half Moon* had a uniformed captain and crew of three, but Franklin often took the wheel. In 1898, James gave Franklin his own twenty-one-foot knockabout, the *New Moon*. By then, he was able to sail almost daily and learned to navigate the rocks, tides, and treacherous currents of the Bays of Fundy and Passamaquoddy. Rexford Tugwell, once a member of FDR's Brains Trust (more commonly called Brain Trust) believed that the *New Moon* may have been the most "precious possession Franklin ever acquired." It gave him the skills and awareness that were key to his character development.[7]

Learning to sail off Campobello, wrote John Kiernan, provided Franklin with "lessons in seamanship in cold waters, with dangers from fog, reefs, strong tides, and perilous currents, [that] had powerful effects on his character. The need for care and promptness, and for obedience to strict rules to avoid disaster, not only taught him the things that can and cannot be done with ships at sea, but also helped to discipline his mind . . . led to his deep interest in naval history [and convinced him of the]. . . need for a navy with strong ships and fire power and with secure lines of communications and bases."[8] At an early age Franklin read Admiral Alfred T. Mahan's seminal *Influence of Sea-Power Upon History* and was profoundly influenced by it. He often quoted Mahan's theories throughout his life.

Sailing was in Franklin's blood, and his love for the sea never diminished. He learned every cove and headland, every tide and current. He could sail "blindfolded through the difficult Down East cruising grounds" such as the Eastern and Western Ways of Mt. Desert Island or Eggemoggin Reach in Maine. He could find his way through the often-present fog to anchorages at Dark Harbor or Northeast Harbor.[9] His intimate knowledge of the Maine coast amazed and often delighted both friends and naval officers in the years to come.

A plaque at Welshpool attests that Franklin was considered as capable a sailor as any among the islanders. He had many opportunities to demonstrate his expert seamanship. When serving as Assistant Secretary of the Navy, Franklin piloted destroyers through the treacherous Lubec Narrows, the narrow channel that separates Campobello from the American mainland. One destroyer's skipper, William F. Halsey, Jr. (Admiral "Bull" Halsey of World War II), referred to Franklin as a "white-flanneled yachtsman" who "knew his business."[10]

While Assistant Secretary, Franklin took every opportunity to bring and often pilot Navy ships into Campobello's waters. The officers admired Franklin because of his love of ships and because he spoke their nautical lingo, he treated them as social equals, and his wife was kind to them when they were entertained on Campobello. They probably chuckled at the seventeen-gun salutes he insisted on having fired in his honor, and his design of a personal flag that was flown when he was aboard ship. But they respected his ability to pilot high-speed naval vessels in waters that the ships' officers were neither familiar with nor particularly eager to navigate.

The freedom to explore in the *New Moon* was exhilarating. Once, along with friends, Franklin set out to hunt for treasure that, according to local legend, had been buried by Captain Kidd on nearby Grand Manan Island. After hours of searching, they found a board carved with the initials "F.K." They triumphantly carried the find back to Campobello although it was widely believed that the board had been planted on Grand Manan as a prank by a fisherman friend.[11]

On another adventure aboard the *New Moon*, Franklin and

his comrades chanced upon a schooner moored in a secluded Passamaquoddy port. The schooner's captain told them that he was hauling potatoes from Grand Manan to Maine. Franklin thought this odd and continued questioning until he discovered that the schooner was smuggling more than a hundred Chinese laborers into the United States at $100 a head. Believing that discretion was the better part of valor, Franklin swiftly pulled anchor and departed. Smuggling was hardly unknown to the area, and the story, if not accurate in every detail, was probably true.[12]

Franklin's love of sailing and the sea was so strong that, when at Groton, he expressed a longing to attend the United States Naval Academy at Annapolis. Not surprisingly, James and Sara quickly rejected this fanciful idea. Harvard, after all, was the only proper destination for a Roosevelt. In that spring of 1898, the nation was caught up in the excitement of the "splendid little war" with Spain. Theodore Roosevelt was assembling his Rough Riders and preparing for an expedition to Cuba. Thirsting to be part of this great adventure, Franklin and two Groton classmates plotted to sneak away from school and enlist in the Navy. Mild cases of scarlet fever put an end to that romantic notion.

This incident did not mark the only time that Franklin's wish to see wartime action was blunted. During World War I, while Assistant Secretary, he asked to serve on active duty. President Woodrow Wilson refused his request, arguing that he was of greater value to the war effort remaining at his Navy Department post. The inability to claim active military service severely frustrated Franklin. He later insisted that Groton School list him on its honor roll among those who served on active duty during the Great War.

With the emphasis on physical vigor at Groton, Franklin tried mightily to succeed on the playing fields. His slight build left him behind others in team sports, but Franklin found ways to excel in other activities. Campobello, without a doubt, gave him a splendid opportunity to develop outdoor sporting skills that brought him pleasure, a sense of accomplishment and, more important, a source of leadership.

Hiking the rugged Campobello terrain was a perfectly natural activity for Franklin to undertake. After all, it was the kind of robust pastime that Theodore enjoyed. Franklin learned to negotiate the rocky cliffs, to time the tides and pools, and to turn these challenging paths into competitive events. For years, he would lead guests or children on "paper chases," often leaving them trapped by incoming tides or slowed by obstacles. Canoeing, swimming, and riding were other activities that he enjoyed and in which he excelled.

The Campobello Golf Course was completed about 1900, and Franklin played a major role in its design and plan. Although it lacked the elegance of courses being built in some other resorts at the time, it served the cottage community well. By the age of eighteen, Franklin was regularly winning tournaments while competing against older and more experienced players. When he was asked to act as both secretary and treasurer of the club, Sara thought it too much responsibility and urged him to decline. He refused her advice and rejected her offer to help with the paperwork, insisting that he would handle it himself.[13]

Once, while practicing his game, Franklin drove a golf ball through the window of a playhouse where the young Sturgis girls, among his closest friends, were painting the floor red. Hearing the crash of broken glass, he raced to the playhouse and saw the girls covered with red paint. Assuming that it was blood, he ran home, terrified, to ask the family butler for help in getting first aid to the "victims." Franklin was first relieved and then mortified to discover that the "blood" was really red paint. The story was told so often even Franklin learned to laugh at it.[14]

Gertrude Sturgis, it seemed, had eyes for the young golfer. She made formal calls on Sara on Saturday mornings to work out a strategy that would encourage Franklin to dance with her at the Saturday night balls. Years later, when she visited the White House, he asked her, "Do you remember how you used to dance with me?" "I remember," she replied, "how I used to arrange it."[15]

Stories about the cottagers' often exacting demands are still being told. Two of them are about Franklin's stern and proper father.

In one, James asked an islander to mail a letter for him in Welshpool and gave him a nickel to pay for the postage. The islander did not immediately walk the two miles back to James's cottage with the two cents change, "not wishing to embarrass Mr. Roosevelt." James reportedly went into town himself to hunt down the messenger and get his money back.[16]

The other story involved a subject often of concern to summer residents—well water. It seemed that James believed that the water from his well tasted bad. He had a crew go down into the well, bail it out, and scrub down the stone walls. The men refilled the well and passed a ladle of new water to him for tasting. He found the water still ill-tasting and ordered that the process be repeated. Again the workers descended the well, cleaned the walls, and presented James with a fresh ladle of water. Again, James was not satisfied with the water's taste. The islanders, wearied from their work, climbed down the well once more, but this time one carried a dead frog in his pocket. After the well was again cleaned and refilled, the worker climbed to the surface, waving the dead frog as the source of the problem. James, with his usual solemnity, tasted the water and triumphantly declared it fine.[17]

Stories that were told about Franklin and Sara, and later Eleanor, were generally related with warmth and often affection. The islanders always courteously catered to the needs of the summer residents, but not always with the same deference accorded the Roosevelts. One resident of an old island family said that certain cottagers "would have been surprised to know what we knew—and what we thought of them."[18]

In 1900, Sara took a photograph of father and son on the porch on Campobello. Franklin was now taller than his father, and James looked frail. The elder Roosevelt's health was failing, his business had reverses, and his beloved *Half Moon* had mysteriously blown up and sunk. Franklin offered to sell the *New Moon* to help pay for a replacement. He was saddened to see how events had taken such a toll on his father's health.

On July 16, a second *Half Moon* arrived. Franklin, his Groton chum Lathrop Brown, Sara, and James cruised up the Bay of Fundy to St. John, New Brunswick. It was the last cruise of more than a couple of hours for James, who died the following December. His death had a profound effect on both Franklin and Sara. The time she had devoted to her dear husband she could now add to that devoted to her son. The full extent of her love and attention to Franklin was now limitless. It would continue that way for the nearly forty years remaining in her life.

In 1902, Franklin and two Harvard friends set out from Boston aboard the *Half Moon* en route to Campobello. The first stop was in Beverly, Massachusetts, where Franklin pursued a romance with Alice Sohier, daughter of a prominent family, whom he had met in Cambridge. Other stops along the way would be made while they sailed down east along the New England Coast. A number of Maine venues were included in this leisurely sail, one that Franklin would virtually duplicate more than thirty years later as President of the United States.

Franklin's romance with Alice, if really that, was not progressing satisfactorily, and he was determined to put his best foot forward. Franklin was now tall, quite good-looking, and eager to please. By this time, he had begun to keep a diary occasionally dotted with coded entries designed to record his inner thoughts while protecting them from prying eyes, most probably Sara's. Following James's death, Sara had taken an apartment in Cambridge to be near Franklin during the school year. Franklin was forced to take extreme steps to protect his privacy and maintain his freedom.

By the following winter, Franklin's diary recorded that the romance was probably over and that Alice had sailed to Europe for an extended stay. She had professed to a friend her fear of giving birth to the six children Franklin had said he wanted to have. Many years later, a staunch Republican, Alice would tell a confidante that she had finally decided not to marry Franklin because "I did not wish to be a cow." [19] He did continue to see Alice that summer, taking trips, without revealing their purpose to Sara, to Northeast Harbor, Maine, where her family summered. Later in life, Franklin would alter the events to insinuate that he broke off the affair. But for the time they remained friends, and Franklin served as an usher at her coming-out party in 1904. Alice and Eleanor met only once, at a Harvard football game, but Eleanor expressed knowledge of Franklin's earlier relationship with Alice.

Then a far more ardent romance with Eleanor bloomed in late 1902, and, by 1903, Franklin entered in his diary in code, "E is an angel."[20] They had met for the first time since childhood on a train bound for their Dutchess County homes and had a warm conversation. Franklin and Eleanor continued to meet several times at parties and were most attracted to each other. He spent part of that summer in Europe and returned to Campobello in August when Eleanor made her first visit to the island. Sara apparently was unaware of the depth of any romance, but welcomed Eleanor to Campobello as she had in earlier times in Hyde Park. A member of the Oyster Bay branch of the family, Eleanor was thought by many to be a "catch," while Franklin, although a Roosevelt and pleasantly charming, had not yet given any real indication of the special talents he would later display.

Eleanor's Campobello visit was filled with picnics, walks, and some fishing. Eleanor spent as much time with "Aunt Sallie" (Sara) as she did with the smitten Franklin. They all went to church services together, and Franklin and Eleanor managed to attend only one social event without Sara, a dinner at the home of longtime friends and neighbors, the Pells. On the last day of her visit, the young couple took a carriage ride along the northern coast of the island and later read to each other from Robert Louis Stevenson. No other young women, however attractive, were then of interest to Franklin. Evelyn Carter, the daughter of the governor of Barbados, was a guest of Mrs. Hartman Kuhn at the cottage next door. Evelyn showed interest in Franklin, but he had eyes only for Eleanor. The visit was a roaring success, and Franklin and Sara took Eleanor to Eastport aboard the *Half Moon* to meet her train to Boston and New York.

By November, the romance had deepened. Eleanor went to Groton to visit her brother Hall. Franklin arrived the next day and, after obligatory social events, he and Eleanor managed to slip away. He entered in code in his diary : "After lunch I have a never to be forgotten walk to the river with my darling."[21] They had time enough for Franklin to propose marriage and for Eleanor to say yes.

Joseph Lash wrote that when Franklin proposed, he told her he was sure one day he would amount to something. Eleanor is said to have replied, "Why me? I'm plain and have little to bring you."[22]

It was typical of Eleanor to believe that she was not worthy of Franklin's love. But she must have been thrilled that he did love her, and Franklin was genuinely in love with her. Eleanor's feelings were likely the same, but she kept no diary or recorded later attestation to her love. They were both Roosevelts, and acceptable partners by all standards. But they were young: Franklin was twenty-one, Eleanor two years younger.

Perhaps Franklin's desire to marry Eleanor was motivated by more than love. He would gain instant access to the President of the United States by marrying his favorite niece. Or, perhaps, Franklin wanted to be first among peers to take the marital step. Early marriage avoided the relentless matchmaking merry-go-round that many, especially Eleanor, thought burdensome and demeaning. But he did love her, and now he faced a daunting potential obstacle: his mother.

Franklin had learned well the art of evasiveness. He cultivated what Geoffrey Ward called "the guile and easy charm, love of secrecy and skill at maneuver he brought to the White House."[23] Doris Kearns Goodwin suggests that "on occasion when his deviousness seemed to go beyond the bonds of necessity, it seemed as if he were enjoying subterfuge for its own sake."[24]

He was so good at hiding his emotions that Franklin took Sara by complete surprise when he told her of his love for Eleanor and his intention to marry her. Sara was not pleased. She was certainly fond of Eleanor and gave no indication that she thought her anything less than an appropriate mate. That is to say, she may not have believed that anyone could adequately assume such a role with her darling son. Perhaps she had not wished to believe that Franklin could love another, and, at the least, was taken aback by the depth of his ardor. She later confided, "I don't believe I remember ever hearing him talk about girls . . . ."[25]

Sara protested that they were too young to marry. She tried to distract Franklin by arranging a job for him in London at the Court of Saint James, and, when that failed, she took him and a Harvard friend on a Caribbean trip. Franklin held fast in his determination, but made a major concession to his mother. He and Eleanor would become engaged, but the engagement would be kept secret for a year.

Franklin completed his last year at Harvard, concealing his feelings and bound to secrecy. He was the fifteenth Roosevelt to enter Harvard and was finishing a college career that was marked with both triumphs and disappointments. He had been elected editor of the *Harvard Crimson*, a prestigious position, but failed in gaining other offices he desired. His kinship with the President of the United States was, however, a significant advantage for him socially. Franklin actively supported Theodore's reelection and proudly cast his first ballot for him in 1904. James, although a lifelong Democrat, voted for his distant cousin, proving that blood can be thicker than political loyalties.

While Franklin's Harvard grades were not high, he compiled a staggering list of other accomplishments. He "was captain of the Missing Links football team; was an usher and cheerleader at football games; took six courses per term; sang with the Freshman Glee Club and served as its secretary . . . [,] rowed freshman crew; belonged to the Institute of 1770, the Fly Club, the Delta Kappa Epsilon fraternity, the Memorial Society, the Signet Society, the St. Paul's Society, the Political Club, the Republican Club, and the Yacht Club; served as librarian to the Fly Club, the Hasty Pudding Club, and the Harvard Union; was managing editor, then editor of the *Harvard Crimson*." [26] Both his eagerness to belong and his energy were boundless.

Although admitted to other college societies, Franklin was rejected by Porcellian, the most elite of Harvard organizations and the one that had welcomed both his father and Theodore Roosevelt. Fifteen years later, he told a relative that his failure to make Porcellian had been "the greatest disappointment of his life." Eleanor believed that the rebuff had given Franklin an "inferiority complex," but, like other youthful defeats, it helped him "to identify with life's out-casts."[27]

By the summer of 1904, the young couple continued their usual social activities while keeping their secret. Eleanor was spending part of the summer at her Aunt Corinne Robinson's summer home at Dark Harbor on the Maine island of Isleboro. There was an active social scene in Dark Harbor, and several potential suitors paid considerable attention to Eleanor. While not beautiful in the traditional sense, Eleanor was tall and willowy and had lovely hair and complexion. Moreover, she was intelligent and interesting. She had to think of ways to deflect the young men's attentions without betraying her secret. "I really think the family must think me a dreadful flirt," Eleanor wrote to Franklin, "or an awfully poor one."[28]

Eleanor greatly enjoyed Isleboro, but she longed to go to Campobello. "I want a quiet life for a while now and above all I want you," she wrote Franklin.[29] Franklin, too, grew impatient. Why couldn't she come to Campobello sooner and take the shortest route, changing trains in Millbridge rather than going all the way through to Bangor? Eleanor didn't think it wise: If her train were late and the connection left on time, she and Franklin might find themselves stranded with only her maid for an escort. "This is one of the drawbacks, dear, to not announcing our engagement, though we did not think of it at the time," she lamented to her young fiancé.[30]

Eleanor left an unfinished letter to Franklin lying on her dressing table. While protesting their "level" of friendship, the letter opened with "My own dearest Nell." The very proper and reserved Eleanor may have left it to be seen on purpose. Despite the exposed letter, confidences were kept. "Nell" was Eleanor's pet name for Franklin. It was also the pet name her father had given her.[31]

Franklin sailed into Dark Harbor on the *Half Moon* unannounced. In his now-usual way of deceiving his mother, he wired that he had become fogbound while en route to Bar Harbor. Franklin found Eleanor and friends reading Browning sonnets. And while he appeared eager, Eleanor remained restrained and reserved. She was much the better actor in the secretive game they played.

When they finally reached Campobello, the month passed quickly. Although Evelyn Carter and Frances Pell were there, Franklin's interest in them was merely polite. He took Eleanor for walks over mossy paths and showed her his favorite picnic places. The morning fog shut out the outside world, and brilliant sunsets marked the evenings. Franklin won the President's and Challenge Cups in golf, while Eleanor and Sara took long walks. She played tennis, badly, with Eleanor Carter, went sailing with Franklin on the *Half Moon*, and portrayed a willow tree at a Club tableau that raised $80 for the island's small library. The young couple were driven to Eastern Point for a final picnic lunch under the spruce trees, then walked home together.

The next day, Sara and Franklin took Eleanor to her train in Eastport. Mrs. Kuhn, who was very much taken with Eleanor, wrote to her about Franklin's mood after she had left. "He looked so tired and I felt everybody bored him. He could not stand Evelyn's chatter." [32]

4

Keeping the Name in the Family

"I know what pain I must have caused you," Franklin wrote Sara after telling her of his plan to marry Eleanor, "and you know I wouldn't do it if I really could have helped it . . . I know my mind, have known it for a long time and know that I could never think otherwise . . . and you dear Mummy, you know that nothing can ever change what we have always been and always will be to each other—only now you have two children to love and love you—and Eleanor as you know will always be a daughter to you in every true way."[1]

After Sara and Franklin returned from their Caribbean trip, she was still unhappy. Sara wrote in her diary, "I am feeling pretty blue . . . the journey is over & I feel as if the time were not likely to come again when I shall take a trip with my dear boy . . . Oh how still the house is . . . ." Eleanor correctly sensed Sara's discomfort. "Don't let her feel that the last trip with you is over," she told Franklin. "We three must take them together in the future . . . ."[2]

Eleanor then wrote to Sara, "It is impossible for me to tell you how I feel toward Franklin. I can only say that my one great wish is always to prove worthy of him."[3] When the announcement was made in December of 1904, Franklin gave Eleanor an engagement ring from Tiffany's on her twentieth birthday. The young couple received many congratulatory notes, most of which lauded Eleanor as exemplary, and reminded Franklin what a lucky man he was. The letter that meant most was from the President of the United States. He later offered to give away his favorite niece in marriage.

March 17, 1905, St. Patrick's Day, was set as the wedding date. It was a Friday, and President Theodore Roosevelt was scheduled to be in New York City to deliver two speeches. The young couple had been guests at his inaugural on March 4 and sat just behind the President's immediate family on the steps of the Capitol. In his speech, Theodore pledged himself to a "square deal for every man." Franklin took it all in and never forgot either the process or the excitement.

The Reverend Endicott Peabody officiated at the wedding, held in the drawing room of a friend's home on New York City's East 76th Street. The drawing room was connected to the home of their cousin Susie Parish which served the overflow attendance. Lathrop Brown, Franklin's Groton and Harvard chum, was best man, serving as a late replacement for Rosy Roosevelt. Rosy, Franklin's half-brother, was James Roosevelt's son by his first marriage and was old enough to be Franklin's father. Two hundred guests were present, and the couple received three hundred and forty wedding gifts. The dazzling wedding party was bedecked in finery emblazoned with a three-feathered crest designed by Franklin. The throngs of St. Patrick's Day celebrants combined with tight security for the President prevented many of the guests from getting to the ceremony on time. They were unable to get inside the building until the reception took place.

"Well, Franklin," the President said as he kissed the bride, "there's nothing like keeping the name in the family." With that, Theodore took center stage and led most of the guests into the salon, where they were more eager to listen to him tell stories than to attend the newlyweds.[4] Theodore's daughter Alice once said of her father that he wanted to be the bride at every wedding, and the corpse at every funeral.

Following the reception, Franklin and Eleanor departed for Hyde Park to spend their first days together alone at Springwood. Having spent precious little time with each other before their marriage, they must have found this new and intimate experience daunting. They knew little of each other's frailties and insecurities. While Franklin was showing Eleanor some rare family manuscripts, she accidentally tore a page of one of the books slightly. She was terribly upset and told Franklin about it immediately. He looked at her with bewilderment and some amusement, telling her gently, "If you had not done it, I probably would [have]." "What I dreaded, I don't know," Eleanor wrote, "but I remember my vast relief. That was the beginning of my becoming more mature about my fears of displeasing people."[5]

Sara had remained in New York City. She wrote to the young couple the first evening, "My precious Franklin & Eleanor . . . It is a delight to write to you together & think of you happy at dear Hyde Park, just where my great happiness began."[6] Eleanor, although she was not aware of it at the time, never had a chance competing with Sara and the Delano-Roosevelt traditions. She had married Franklin, his ambitions, his mother, and the ghosts of Algonac and Hyde Park.

Franklin entered Columbia Law School shortly before the marriage, but, as he had demonstrated before, he was not a serious student. By delaying their honeymoon for three months, he managed to complete the first year of studies. Finally, in June, they left for a three-month European honeymoon. Almost immediately, there were tensions, as Eleanor anxiously tried to adjust to a young husband whose disposition seemed always to be sunny and whose energy was boundless. She was either unable or unwilling to keep up with his breathless pace, and Franklin often left her alone for the company of others, most usually women. Eleanor was noticeably miffed, but was unable to bring herself to tell him why she was displeased. Franklin was puzzled by her periodic gloom, and Eleanor, predictably, retreated into silence. This sequence of events repeated itself hundreds of times during the early years of their marriage.

On their return to New York City, a townhouse on East 36th Street awaited them. Sara had rented, furnished, and staffed it to her own standards and tastes. Franklin continued his studies, and they led a quiet social life. Eleanor, moved by the needs of the less fortunate, volunteered considerable time at the Rivington Street Settlement and with the Consumers League. But Sara and Cousin Susie Parish persuaded Eleanor that if she continued this kind of work, she risked bringing the diseases of the slums into her household. Then pregnant, Eleanor grudgingly conceded and confined her outside activities to serving on charitable boards.

The young couple seemed to be very much in love, but predictable routines and social responsibilities began casting long shadows over their relationship and their lifestyle. Much of this problem was attributable to Sara's unceasing control of their lives and the indisputable reality that she set the pace and the rules, made most of the important decisions, and, as she would do for the rest of her life, paid most of the bills.

Anna Eleanor Roosevelt was born on May 2, 1906. Ten pounds at birth, she was their first child and only girl. Eleanor had great concern about her ability to care for the baby, and Sara and Cousin Susie easily persuaded her that having trained nurses provide the care was better for both the mother and the child. Whatever doubts Eleanor may have had quickly disappeared, and she agreed to a nurse for Anna as well as to having servants relieve her of any responsibility for caring for the home. Not surprisingly, Sara spent a prodigious amount of time with her first grandchild, spoiling her as she would each of the others to come.

Shortly after the birth, the entire family, with nurse and servants, made the trip to Campobello. When she arrived on the island, Eleanor was determined to conquer her fear of the water since life on Campobello centered, to a high degree, on sailing. She also chose to join Franklin in as many of his Campobello activities as she could so that events that occurred during the honeymoon were not repeated. They enjoyed fishing together, and, to her surprise, Eleanor became reasonably proficient. She was, however, much less successful at golf. Knowing Franklin's love for the game, Eleanor had secretly practiced her swing. Their first and only golf outing was a disaster. She played badly, and Franklin was so impatient with her that she gave up the game then and there. Her tennis was not much better, but for a while she made the attempt.

Sara was away part of the summer but when in residence she was the supreme commander of the household and, largely, of everyone's schedule. She continued to give the orders to the captain of the *Half Moon* for many years, despite the fact that Franklin was an expert sailor. She relinquished that role only when Franklin had his own guests.

In the summer of 1907, Sara traveled to Europe, and the Campobello cottage was Eleanor and Franklin's for the season. Eleanor savored their journey by train and boat with husband, baby, and nurse. She enjoyed Anna's animated babble, Franklin's blissful sleep, and the quiet break of dawn. They looked forward to the peace and beauty of Campobello, and they must have eagerly anticipated having full control of their own lives and activities for the first extended period of their marriage. Eleanor was pregnant again and she was still trying to master the subtleties of marriage, motherhood, and an interfering mother-in-law. Neither she nor Franklin had been well prepared for these events or to understand the nuances as well as the responsibilities.

The summer of 1907 was in many ways a watershed season for the young Roosevelts, and for the entire Campobello summer colony. The weather was unusually cool, rainy, and foggy; a fertilizer plant in Eastport fouled both air and water; and rising transportation costs and the limited schedules of trains and steamships led to the closing of two of the three hotels. It marked the beginning of the slow but inexorable decline of Campobello as a favored resort destination. There was no immediate effect on the community of summer rusticators, but there were clear indications that Campobello had seen its best growth. After a mere quarter century of development, the summer community and the islanders who served it had reached a plateau. Although hardly in the same league as Bar Harbor or Newport, Campobello did share the same life cycles and rhythms. Most American Victorian summer resorts began a graceful but steady decline in popularity, victims of the march of time.

But Franklin and Eleanor had good reason to be in high spirits, and their summer vacation was highly anticipated. Their marriage was but two years old; they were the parents of an infant daughter; Franklin was soon to start a legal apprenticeship; and they had homes in New York City and at Hyde Park as well as Campobello. For Eleanor, however, they were not homes of her own. Sara rented the Manhattan brownstone for them, and there, as in Hyde Park, she was in complete control. Her omnipresence both literally and figuratively underscored the pecking order in the Roosevelt homes. In Campobello, the very same held true.

The dutiful and regular correspondence that they shared with Sara that summer provides valuable insights into the independent life Franklin and Eleanor led on Campobello and what they considered to be interesting if not important. The correspondence is in traditional diary form, typical of the time and of a Delano-Roosevelt family practice that dated back to the early nineteenth century, when the Delanos, involved in the China trade, experienced lengthy family separations.

The correspondence of 1907 is the largest single body of letters Franklin ever wrote. They are the product of a young, secure, well-born American male at his favorite playground. Like others of his class, he was insulated from the problems of the general populace and protected from need. Consequently, Franklin looked forward to a summer of boating, hiking, tennis, golf, entertaining guests, and generally enjoying the good life. Little of great importance was on his mind.

Eleanor wrote many of the 1907 letters to Sara. She paid more attention to events of some substance and indicated some personal feelings, unlike her husband. Her correspondence also reflects the protective coloration of their insulated society. But she, too, enthusiastically looked forward to her summer. Eleanor had never known this much happiness before, relatively speaking, and she was determined to make the most of what proved to be a unique opportunity for independence.

But uncontrollable forces cast their shadow on Campobello that summer. The weather proved to be, in the words of one former resident, "appalling. There were forty days of fog . . . and no one ever came back."[7] Hyperbole, no doubt, but the gloomy weather persisted and became a regular topic in the Roosevelts' correspondence. Periods of unfavorable weather were hardly unique to Campobello nor, for that matter, to all of coastal Maine and the Canadian Maritime Provinces. Cool weather is the norm and a principal reason why city dwellers wanting to escape summer heat were drawn to these areas. Fog is common to the coastal plain during the summer, and extended periods of rain are hardly unusual. As a result, beautiful summer days are celebrated, in part, for the fact that they are not predictably constant, and because they are eagerly anticipated and genuinely savored.

That summer had more than its share of poor weather, but in a continuum, a season like that was likely to occur periodically. For a resident or regular visitor, that likelihood is well understood. For the occasional visitor or guest, however, it could mean that a long-anticipated holiday and lengthy trip might have a disappointing result.

Most of the correspondence is about very pedestrian events. Franklin wrote in his news of the day that, en route from Ayer Junction, their dog Duffy had missed connections, and that two trunks had gone astray. All managed to appear shortly after arrival on Campobello. Franklin sent Sara a detailed list of clothing for her to obtain for him in London. The items ranged from dinner jackets to riding boots. Trips to Europe were always opportunities for proper gentlemen to obtain these "absolutely required" garments from English tailors and bootmakers. Eleanor, too, had a shopping list for Sara. Hers consisted of "lady-in-waiting" lingerie and clothes for the baby.

Shortly after their arrival, they enjoyed a good sail on the *Half Moon*. Franklin made good use of the family yacht until it was sold to the U.S. Navy in 1917 to be employed in patrolling coastal waters in search of German U-boats.

Eleanor reported on the physical condition of the cottage. She told Sara that the house had been "grandly painted and your ceiling looking very nice."[8] She reported on walks they had taken, the baby's antics, the guests who arrived, and the visits they made. Franklin and Eleanor had gone fishing on one occasion, and she proudly reported that they caught twelve flounder.

They had a particularly rough sail without Anna, and the baby's arrival with the nurse at the pier to greet their return created a photo opportunity. Eleanor wrote "you can't imagine a much funnier sight, particularly when F. carries her up the hill on his back with two short legs sticking straight out on either side of his head."[9]

Franklin carefully described the selection of the new crew members of the *Half Moon* with their maritime pedigrees. The boat's crew was of great importance to the Roosevelts, and replacements were carefully chosen and evaluated. He also reported the "important" arrival of his wines in Eastport. The tiny coastal towns of Eastport and Lubec were adequate sources of supply for most of the everyday needs of Campobello summer residents, but wine had to be shipped from more sophisticated locales. The arrival of such items was a major event, and Franklin enjoyed the two-mile sail across the Bay to Eastport to fetch them.

The letters describe other shopping excursions, as well as the visits of local vendors. One of them, a butcher named Babcock, was recalled by a Campobello summer resident as "quite a character. He lived in Wilson's Beach where he had a store, but he also had a butcher's cart with a canvas cover, and he came around three days a week. On Tuesday you would order what he would bring on Thursday, etc. He had meats and vegetables, but did not sell fish. As the horse seldom went at more than a walk, in order to get to the lower end of the island at a reasonable time including stops along the way, he had to leave home at five a.m. to drive the eight or nine miles or so. He had about twelve children, many of them named for the summer people, but I think Mrs. Roosevelt, Senior, prevented his naming one for her husband."[10]

A trip to St. Andrew's, New Brunswick, was a highlight. St. Andrew's remains a very English community, originally settled by Revolutionary War Tories. It was a favorite place for the Roosevelts to shop for English wares such as Wedgwood porcelain. Franklin described the sail as pleasant, although there were some rough waters in the bay. He proudly noted that "E. did not show the least paleness of cheek or tendency to edge towards the rail!"[11] Eleanor, despite her early fear of the sea, grew to enjoy sailing and secretly longed for the opportunity to take the wheel. She was resigned, however, to the fact that women were neither encouraged nor often permitted to do so.

Eleanor reported Anna's first word, "Gaga," and described her first weighing on a grocer's scale. She wrote of the things a young mother would typically tell a new grandmother. At this point in the relationship with her mother-in-law, Eleanor tried hard to please "Mama" and was always properly respectful. Sara accorded her son's wife certain, but guarded, affection.

Franklin delighted in boasting of victories at bridge or on the tennis court, or the number of fish they caught (Eleanor was usually more successful than Franklin). He proudly shared his never-ceasing ideas for improving the unsatisfactory water pumping and piping system at the cottage. Franklin's schemes for engineering projects had lofty goals, but they seldom succeeded in improving the balky systems. He was always careful, however, not to undertake any project of substance or expense while Sara was away. He did not have access to any significant sums of money, nor did Sara delegate substantial authority to him.

By the latter part of July, the foul weather was weighing heavily on the Roosevelts. Eleanor described "torrents of rain" and a "vile day, chilly and rainy."[12] On July 27, they sailed to Eastport in limited visibility to pick up Eleanor's cousins, the Parishes. The fog was so thick that Franklin was unable to find his way back to Campobello, although he was in familiar waters. A lantern hanging over the compass skewed the magnetic readings, and, after some time wandering around in the fog, they nearly ran aground near Lubec. Franklin was chagrined and mystified until he discovered that the compass readings had been compromised and he could make the necessary adjustments. He was then able to pilot them home safely. Susie Parish was not amused by the lengthy and uncomfortable voyage, and it took

1. *Franklin D. Roosevelt, age 17, and his parents, James and Sara. Poughkeepsie, NY, 1899.*

2. *Eleanor Roosevelt, age 5, and her father, Elliott. New York City, 1889.*

3. *Tyn-y-Coed and Tyn-y-Maes Hotels, Campobello, 1884. James, Sara, and Franklin (18 months) first visited the island the previous summer, staying at the Tyn-y-Coed.*

4. *The living room of the James Roosevelt cottage on Campobello in 1897.*

5. *The James Roosevelt cottage on the shore of Friar's Bay. It was built in 1885 and first occupied the following summer.*

6. *Franklin at the wheel off Campobello with a friend in 1888. Perhaps his first time in control of a sailing ship.*

7. *Again at sea, this time accompanied by a family friend, Gorham Hubbard, and an unidentified helmsman, c. 1898.*

8. *Franklin on the porch of the cottage with his father in 1900. James was ill and died later that year at Hyde Park.*

9. Franklin and an unidentified companion make their way along the rocks at Campobello, 1902. No matter how arduous the activity, young ladies and gentlemen were always "appropriately attired."

10. Eleanor and her favorite aunt, Maude Hall, wading at Herring Cove, 1904.

11. Franklin and Eleanor on the porch, Campobello, 1904. They were secretly engaged. Their engagement was announced later that fall and they were married on St. Patrick's Day, 1905.

12. Eleanor, Anna (18 months), Franklin, and Duffy on the porch, 1907. That summer Sara was in Europe and the young Roosevelts had "Granny's" cottage all to themselves.

13. Franklin in his favorite birchbark canoe, 1907. Canoes like this were made by members of the Passamaquoddy tribe, often from the bark of a single tree.

14. Eleanor and Franklin at one of many Campobello beach picnics, c. 1910.

15. & 16. Franklin and Eleanor, c. 1909.

17. Eleanor and Franklin flanked by friends, all in casual attire, following a tennis outing, c. 1910.

18. Sara pours tea for Anna and Eleanor aboard the Half Moon, 1910.

19. The family grows. Elliot, Jimmy, Franklin, Eleanor, and Anna on the steps of Franklin and Eleanor's cottage, 1912.

20. Eleanor, age 28, in front of her cottage, 1912.

21. Franklin at the helm of the Half Moon; Eleanor and Sara seem engrossed in needlework, 1915.

22. Franklin, in formal whites, enjoying his sail.

her days to regain her land legs. Most of the planned events for the next several days were thwarted by the weather. Cruises and tennis matches were rained out, picnics ended up indoors, and Susie was obliged to spend most of her time "resting."

Eleanor's brother Hall arrived and was, as always, a most welcome guest. Eleanor and Hall adored each other, and Franklin looked on him as the younger brother he never had. Hall was an eager partner for Franklin in rock climbing and foul-weather sailing. And the foul weather did persist. After a solid week of fog, Eleanor had grown quite discouraged, especially since Susie pronounced that only Campobello suffered from inclement weather, while the rest of the coast had likely remained clear.

Franklin planned an overnight canoeing and camping trip with Hall and Henry Parish. He assumed that Eleanor would not wish to come and would be content to stay at home in the parlor reading aloud with Susie. Eleanor might well have refused, but would have liked to have been asked. Susie proved to be a difficult guest, and her visit in 1907 was her last to Campobello. It is not clear whether that was her choice, or the Roosevelts'.

They welcomed a visit by Tomah Joseph, the chief of the Passamaquoddy tribe of central Maine. Chief Joseph visited Campobello each summer to build and repair canoes for the islanders. Today, the Franklin D. Roosevelt Library in Hyde Park displays a birchbark canoe he made for Franklin in its entirety from the bark of a single tree. Native Americans were regular visitors to Campobello, and their presence was usually welcomed.

Among Franklin's guests that summer were Thomas P. Beal, a Harvard classmate, and Livingston ("Livy") Davis, long one of Franklin's closest friends.[13] Franklin's guests were mostly Groton and Harvard classmates and friends. Most were invited, but some simply showed up unannounced. On those occasions, it must have been a challenge for Eleanor and the staff to accommodate them graciously. It never crossed Franklin's mind that the sudden appearance of numbers of guests might create a problem.

Franklin described in an August 5th letter to Sara "one of the vilest days here I have ever known. Fog and rain from the East 'til three o'clock when the wind ceased, and the rain came back on us with redoubled fury in a hurricane from the Northwest."[14] On this particular day, he contented himself with working on his stamp collection with a neighbor. Franklin had sent to Hyde Park for his albums. Poring over his stamp collection was a favorite lifelong pursuit, and one that continually provided Franklin with both pleasure and relaxation.

Another rainy-day activity centered around brother Hall's continuing education: both Franklin and Eleanor led impromptu classes in geography and history. Susie Parish also participated and Franklin judged her "about the foot of the class in geography and modern history, tho' . . . a little more up to date in ancient affairs."[15]

The weather cleared and they were promised a fine outlook the day Susie departed. Hosts and guests walked to Herring Cove, the first walk they had been able to take since Susie's arrival, then cruised on the *Half Moon* to Wilson's Beach prior to leaving her at Eastport for the night train home. The following day did not, however, fulfill the promise for good weather, and Eleanor wrote that "everyone is growing quite cross as a result."[16]

In the next day's letter, Eleanor reported that Franklin had omitted the "exciting fact that Anna can walk from one person to another." Eleanor said she was "to take charge of her and put her to bed to-night as Nurse is going to Eastport to say good-by to her son."[17] Anna's nurse had been experiencing problems with a grown son, and her temporary absence from Campobello required that Eleanor pay more attention to Anna's needs. Eleanor was pleasantly surprised at how easy it was to care for the baby, although the housekeeper provided additional help in the nurse's absence. It was neither usual nor pleasurably anticipated for the Roosevelts to take on the responsibility for the children's primary care. Both Eleanor and Franklin enjoyed Anna's (and subsequent children's) milestones and noted her antics. But most of the care was provided by nurses and governesses. When the Roosevelt children grew to maturity, they recalled that both parents provided less attention to them than they would have liked. They remembered Franklin's high spirits and his playfulness, but they also noted that he was often absent. The children recalled Eleanor as stern and short on motherly warmth. With an understanding of Eleanor's and Franklin's own childhoods, these perceptions and reminiscences are not surprising.

The letters describe picnics, duck shoots, and sailing errands to Eastport. Eleanor enclosed some "kodaks" (photographs) attributing their poor quality to the fact that they were processed in Eastport. She continued to take photographs of her family and guests, few of which survive today. Photography was rapidly becoming popular, and Eleanor used it as means to commemorate events and visits while remaining personally unseen. At this stage in her life, she was more eager to picture and to write of the activities of others than to be an active participant.

The weather finally turned pleasant, and Franklin and Hall set sail for Bar Harbor. Eleanor contented herself with a picnic with a friend. Feeling very pregnant, she commented in her letters about her physical condition and expanding figure. In thanking Sara for ordering lingerie, she suggested that she would enjoy having it but that she would not be a "graceful person" when Sara returned. European lingerie was as important to Eleanor as were English suits and boots to Franklin.

The *Half Moon* returned from Bar Harbor earlier than expected, carrying, along with Franklin and Hall, two unexpected guests. Franklin had sent Eleanor a wire about them, but a telegraph strike prevented its arrival. Again, this was typical of a pattern of future behavior: Franklin would invite guests and, often, neglect to inform Eleanor. Although she would be unprepared for their arrival, Eleanor would quietly make the necessary adjustments.

Eleanor reported Anna's increase in weight to twenty-five pounds (again on the butcher's scale) to Sara before turning the letter over to Franklin to describe his activities in Bar Harbor. They consisted of tennis dates, haircuts, and luncheons and dinners with old friends. Franklin relished the trips to Bar Harbor, where society's flash and sparkle thrived, quite different from the subdued rustication of

Campobello. Eleanor never enjoyed parties and the active social scene, but Franklin clearly did.

Eleanor wrote that she and Franklin had studied the interior plans of the adjoining homes that Sara was having built for herself and them on 65th Street in New York City. They were particularly concerned about lighting, bells, and telephones. Eleanor noted that electric lights would be required over dressing tables in the bedrooms rather than in the four corners of the rooms as planned by the architect, Charles A. Platt. In the early days of the century, lighting design was in its infancy; architects and interior designers were more interested in symmetry and balance than in function. Of course, no final approvals on any of the plans would be made until Sara returned.

The adjoining homes were to have connecting doorways on two floors. If Eleanor had any concerns about having a home that was connected to that of her mother-in-law, she did not express them at this time.

For once, a canoe excursion did include Eleanor, and it featured a race with two Native Americans, not an unusual event for Franklin. In this particular instance, a picnic preceded a sail back to the cottage on the *Half Moon*. Excursions could be accomplished with a different means of transportation at either end. There were plenty of servants and hired hands to provide the "transport du jour." The range of personal conveyances included canoes out, yacht back; horse carts out, dinghies back; and so on. The combinations were limited only by the numbers of participants, the destination, and the weather. An ample supply of manpower was always at the family's disposal. The fact is that there were scores of outdoor activities available to the Roosevelts precisely because of the extensive support services their staff could provide. Everything and everybody was on call.

In an embarrassing sequence of events and letters, Franklin was forced to apologize to Sara for not paying a couple of bills that were long past due. Among other things, it caused her some personal embarrassment. In a rare display of displeasure toward her son, a stern admonition arrived in a letter dated July 31: "To my sorrow I find poor Aunt Doe has been troubled by the knowledge that my dear boy's bills are not paid, though two years old. She did not say much and hesitated to tell me. I have today been to the bankers and the bills are paid. I will say nothing, as it will do no good, only it is a surprise as I am not accustomed to this way of doing business my dear Franklin and if you love me you will be more careful in the future."[18] As a matter of fact, Franklin never became adept at paying bills and performing the bookkeeping duties normally required of a head of household—in great likelihood, the result of never quite being the head of the Roosevelt household and the ultimate controller of the purse strings.

From time to time, Franklin showed interest in earning some money of his own. He considered a number of schemes that either failed in execution or expired in development. He was not driven by need since both Franklin and Eleanor had adequate trust funds and money was always available from Sara. The desire may well have been more for personal fulfillment and adventure than for generating income.

One unrealized scheme was an attempt to purchase nearby Treat Island with a Harvard classmate, Owen Winston. They had feared an impending sale of the Campobello Company and a subsequent decrease in land values. The Company was not sold at this time, but there was a flattening if not a diminishing of the value of island property. Campobello was still a viable retreat for summer rusticators, but the gradually changing vacationing habits of North Americans had tempered the continued growth.

Franklin again mentioned that he had "done stamps" with a neighbor. He asked Sara to acquire certain English, German, and French stamps for his collection. She had always encouraged and supported his stamp collecting and other hobbies from childhood. Along with stamps, Franklin continued to collect bird samples for both his own collection and that of the Museum of Natural History. Unlike Theodore, he did not stuff the birds himself but relied on a professional taxidermist. He described a trip with Owen Winston to collect cormorants. Friends were often at hand to support his hobbies, but

Franklin was content to work on his collections alone, either on Campobello or at Hyde Park.

On September 1, Eleanor confirmed that she and Franklin would meet Sara on her arrival in New York from Europe. It became traditional for Sara to be welcomed by her "children" upon her return from extended trips. Eleanor thought Sara would find her "grandaughter a sad mischief, no one has any peace now if she is round and out of her pen and her greatest joy is wheeling her baby carriage up and down the grass road to the gate so you can see that she is strong! Her big teeth seem to bother her a good deal but they are not through yet and I am sorry as I hoped they would be through before we left here. I can hardly believe that we go a week from tomorrow."[19] Eleanor's mention of teething suggests that she hoped that Anna's discomfort would not be a problem for Sara upon her return.

Eleanor reported the baby's development without expressing much joy at its wonders. It must have triggered memories of her own childhood and her mother's inadequacies. Mothering her own children was dutiful, but it failed to bring her much pleasure. Motherly joy might not have been possible for her in the light of her own cheerless childhood.

Franklin sailed to Eastport that day to collect the nurse. Eleanor reflected that the nurse "had aged (in a week) . . . but seems resigned and cheerful and like a sensible woman will try to forget about her son's behaviour I hope. Anna is happy to have her back but I am glad to say I think she missed me a little last night!"[20]

Eleanor worried about the task of securing a laundress for the homes on East 65th Street. Her letters contained many references to getting the right laundress, and that she didn't "want to discourage a new woman by having too big a wash awaiting her arrival."[21] In fairness, Sara and not Eleanor usually hired servants. In this case, Sara's absence in Europe left that responsibility in Eleanor's hands. She did not savor it.

The correspondence often refers to the state of the cottage's cistern. A Mr. Johnson had a scheme for enlarging it, and there was, undoubtedly, an increasing need to update the system. With a growing family and an ever-growing legion of guests, the Roosevelts worried that the hotel's "engine and pipes won't last much longer," and the hotel's potential demise would likely put a further burden on Sara's cistern. They believed the rumor that a New York company planned to purchase the Campobello Company, remodel the hotels, build a few cottages speculatively, "also to keep a lot of sheep and do some intelligent woodcutting."[22] A sticking point in the sale was the evil smell wafting across the bay from the fertilizer plant in Eastport.

The factory was, certainly, part of the problem in any impending transaction. An agreement was finally reached with the Seacoast Canning Company to make changes that would eliminate the odor, and a New York syndicate took title to the property. The financial panic of 1907 caused a number of members of the syndicate to miss making their subscriptions, and the Tyn-y-Coed and Tyn-y-Maes hotels were not rehabilitated but closed. The new owners operated the Owen Hotel for several more years, although with little success. They lost interest in the holdings, which eventually passed into other hands. Ultimately, an association of Campobello cottage owners acquired most of the remaining property on the island.[23]

Franklin's last letter to Sara that summer ranged from references to the legal career he was about to start as "a full-fledged office boy" to innocuous gossip about some mutual friends' couture. Franklin enjoyed commenting on personalities, fashion, and the foibles of others, and did so with a certain amount of wit. The gossip seemed to be harmless, and Sara probably enjoyed it. He mentioned that he was paying every bill he could so that Sara would be spared that chore. Franklin was highly motivated to get it right this time after being rebuked for past shortcomings in paying bills and living up to responsibilities.

The last-minute arrangements for moving his little family back to the city, and a favorable assessment of the captain and crew of the *Half Moon*, fill most of his last letter. Franklin suggested that they arrange for a new and repositioned mooring for the boat, and he assessed the state of the engine and the summer's consumption of gasoline. Although Sara had some interest in these matters, they were enormously important to him. The state of the boat's crew and equipment was always high on his list of concerns, and he was determined to demonstrate to her his thorough dedication and responsibility. In time, Sara grew to appreciate Franklin's attention to detail and his growing participation in the management of family holdings. They pleased her more than his forays into the business world and politics.

This letter was Franklin's last to any member of his family for almost a year. That task passed to Eleanor. It signaled the beginning of his professional career, and although he was no less attentive to Sara, he had less time to spend with her. The separation from his mother was uneven but inexorable. Never complete, it was the start of Franklin's independence.

In beginning the practice of law, Franklin was taking his first steps into a life and society about which he knew little. He was assigned routine tasks involving legal research and running errands. His first twenty-five years had given him little knowledge or understanding of how most people lived and thought and how things worked. New contacts and experiences helped bring him, to some extent, out from under his rock of privilege. He was embarking on a new adventure and the "three years spent with Carter, Ledyard and Milburn constituted Franklin's first immediate and real contact with a world that existed beyond Hyde Park, Campobello, Cambridge, and 65th Street. In view of the social and political philosophy he evolved in later years, this first contact cannot be regarded lightly . . . ."[24]

5

Six Straight Weeks at Campo

Franklin never completed his degree program at Columbia Law School. He was able to pass the New York State bar examination, but gave early indication that he had no intention of practicing law indefinitely. A group of young colleagues at Carter, Ledyard and Milburn heard him pronounce that he would enter politics and eventually become President of the United States. He would first get elected to the New York State Assembly, next receive an appointment as Assistant Secretary of the Navy, and then win the governorship of New York. "Anyone who is Governor of New York has a good chance to be President, with any luck," he predicted.[1]

Some years later, one of those present said that nobody had laughed at Franklin's statement. He attributed that fact to Franklin's "engaging frankness . . . the sincerity and reasonableness of what he had to say."[2] Franklin was most certainly engaging and sincere, and his statement was reasonable, considering the fact that Theodore Roosevelt had followed that particular path to the White House.

The little family continued to grow and James Roosevelt, named for Franklin's father, was born just before Christmas. Although a large baby like his sister, Jimmy suffered from more than his share of childhood illnesses. As the summer of 1908 drew near, he was still recovering from a severe bout of pneumonia, and Franklin and Eleanor determined that Campobello was too remote from specialized medical services for the baby, should they be needed. Consequently, Franklin and Eleanor rented a small cottage in Seabright, New Jersey, for the beneficial sea air and its proximity to medical services.

Located directly on the boardwalk, the Roosevelts' cottage was so close to the neighboring houses that Eleanor remembered that she "could hear [neighbors] ordering their food for the day every morning."[3] Seabright hardly presented the peace, comfort, and style of living that she had grown accustomed to on Campobello, but at the time it seemed to have been a reasonably appropriate alternative. Sara, too, was disappointed that her children and grandchildren would not be on Campobello that summer. Uncharacteristically, she changed her summer plan and remained at Hyde Park. Not surprisingly, she visited Seabright regularly.

That following winter, Sara received word of the death of Mrs. Hartman Kuhn, her Campobello neighbor. Grace Kuhn had always been fond of Franklin and especially liked Eleanor, who had often visited and read poetry to her. It is apparent that Grace had sensed Eleanor's need for a place of her own. Grace's will specified that Sara could purchase her 34-room Campobello cottage for $5,000, provided that she give it to Franklin and Eleanor. The transfer of the cottage included all the furniture, crystal, and china. Eleanor wrote, "My mother-in-law bought it and gave it to us, and the house became a great source of joy to me."[4] For the first time in her adult life, Eleanor had a home she could call her own.

In March, 1909, a third child was born, the chronically ill Franklin Jr. With Anna, Jimmy, the sickly baby, nurses, and servants in tow, Eleanor led the long journey to Campobello in much the same way Sara had for a quarter-century, and as Eleanor would continue to do in years to come. Early each summer, they boarded a train from New York for Boston, where they stayed a night in the venerable Hotel Touraine. The next afternoon, they caught a sleeper, arriving in Ayer's Junction in eastern Maine the following morning. They then switched to an ancient wooden train heated with a coal stove where their fellow passengers were woodsmen, farmers, and hired help headed for summer employment, and Native Americans who sold woven baskets and other handicrafts. Upon arrival in Eastport, the Roosevelt entourage was met by Captain Calder in a carriage that took them to the dock and a waiting motor boat that the children would dub "Chug-Chug." The wearied but excited group then made a two-mile crossing to Welshpool and changed to a rowboat that ferried them to the Roosevelt dock on Friar's Bay. As the children grew older, they would scramble on the dock and race up the hill to the cottage as mounds of luggage followed in drays from Welshpool. Eleanor coolly and efficiently managed the movement of the children, adults, and the many trunks, valises, crates, and pets that made up the caravan. It was no small accomplishment.

Throughout her life, Eleanor never tired of the red-shingled cottage. During her first weeks in residence, she rearranged the furniture countless times, using only what pleased her. Now, for the first time, she could invite her own guests, employ her own servants, and set her own routines and agenda. She had grown to love the peaceful ambiance of Campobello, and now she was free to share it with those for whom she cared. Eleanor "never apologized to her guests for the endless fogs, they comforted her," Blanche Wiesen Cook wrote. "She never tired of the howling winds; they made her feel serene. She enjoyed the long leisurely evenings reading aloud beside the fire . . . books of her own choosing."[5]

The importance of having her own home cannot be overstated. Springwood was always home to Franklin, and in a sense to the children. It never was to her. Hyde Park, Eleanor wrote, "was indeed [Sara's] home, and she made every decision concerning it. For over forty years, I was only a visitor there."[6] At Hyde Park, Sara set a relentless regimen. A gong rang thirty minutes before meals and then again five minutes before food was on the table. It was unwise to be late, and grandchildren were inspected for cleanliness before they were seated. Sara sat at the head of the table facing Franklin, who assumed his father's place. Eleanor sat wherever there was room. Sara often ordered the serving of Franklin's favorite boyhood meals, although the others did not always enjoy them. Everyone's behavior was monitored, including Franklin's.[7] Their Campobello cottage, although Sara's was just next door, provided Eleanor with an escape from her mother-in-law's domination and the opportunity to exercise some control of her own.

Eleanor wrote to Franklin from Campobello that she had "moved every room in the house around and I hope you will like the change."[8] Franklin wanted to bring with him a caribou skin, and Eleanor told him that he would find it in the closet of their New York home. It's not clear that Franklin shared Eleanor's level of excitement in having a cottage of their own. He may have had some trepidation in assuming responsibility for managing a household, since he had known only dependence on his parents.

Eleanor loved the informality and simple qualities of Campobello cottage living. "There was no telephone, no electricity, there was a little coal stove on which you did all your cooking, and the lamps sometimes smoked," she wrote, "and [you] had to learn to take care of them, and you went to bed by candlelight. But it had great charm."[9]

Franklin, Jr., did not respond to Campobello's salt air nor show any improvement when the family returned to New York in mid-September. Despite close medical attention, he continued to decline and died in November, short of his eighth month. Eleanor had difficulty dealing with his death. She suffered from bouts of depression combined with feelings of guilt and inadequacy. By summer, she was more composed and better prepared for her first full season of residence in her new cottage.

In that summer of 1910, Franklin was again unavailable to help with the move to Campobello. Earlier, he had been asked by the Poughkeepsie Democratic Committee to run for the New York Senate, and he was now stumping the district. Eleanor's anticipation of a full family vacation was tempered by Franklin's absence. He managed two brief visits, but the die had been cast. Franklin's long march to the presidency had begun and he would never again spend a full summer on his beloved island.

As happy as she was with her return to Campobello and her new cottage, Eleanor felt somewhat isolated that summer. She was again pregnant and was still mourning the loss of her baby. She missed Franklin and eagerly looked forward to his visits. But she was to be disappointed. When Franklin arrived in Campobello, he paid little attention to Eleanor. When he did, he spoke mostly of his political activities and little of things that were important to her. She was more than a little concerned by his apparent lack of caring and, as she had in the past, feared once again that she was losing love.[10]

In November, Franklin was elected by a slim margin to the New York Senate in a district that had been long held by the Republicans. He threw himself into his new position with great energy and immediately drew the attention of party leaders and the political press. Franklin's mannerisms and dress were perceived as snobbish and arrogant by the Tammany Hall Democratic Party leadership in New York City. Moreover, his open defiance of that leadership brought him insults and threats of retribution. Although an independent-minded renegade to his party, he seemed attractive and progressive to the press. Patterns of political behavior and public relations were being established that would reappear countless times throughout his political career. Franklin immensely enjoyed the combat and controversy while gaining both longtime supporters and political enemies. He took an apartment in Albany for use during the legislative session, and returned to Hyde Park as often as his responsibilities allowed.

In August, 1911, after the senate had adjourned, Franklin joined Eleanor and the three children (Elliott was born the previous autumn) on Campobello. Franklin lost little time in taking up one of his favorite activities. With Hall Roosevelt, he set sail for Bar Harbor. Delayed in Cutler by a thick fog, he wrote to Eleanor that his "hand was so stiff from handling ropes, etc. that the pen won't work quite right."[11] The boat ran aground in the fog, further delaying their visit. Freeing the boat on the next tide, Franklin managed a visit with cousin Susie Parish at Northeast Harbor and went on to pay other even more agreeable social calls. Despite a full schedule of Bar Harbor visits and events, Franklin had promised Eleanor that he would be home in three days either by rail or on the *Half Moon*. With his own captain and crew, he could choose at will either form of transport. He seldom returned to the island as quickly as Eleanor would like, and this trip was no exception.

Later, after Franklin had returned to New York, Hall and a friend were injured in a fall from Friar's Rock, not far from the Roosevelt cottage. Eleanor shepherded them to Dr. Eben Bennet, a general practitioner in Lubec who faithfully served the Roosevelts' medical needs for more than thirty-five years. Dr. Bennet maintained a small hospital in a wing of his home and did his best setting the broken bones. Hall never fully recovered from his injuries, but it hardly dampened his spirit.[12] Eleanor, somehow, assumed a certain responsibility for the mishap.

Jimmy Roosevelt once described Campobello as "a rugged place," more his father's kind of place than his mother's.[13] That may have been true at one time, but now Eleanor was the Roosevelt in residence full time, and she made Campobello her own. Franklin was in Albany for extended periods of time, and Eleanor developed comfortable routines and interests that best suited her needs. She invited family and friends who shared these interests, and their visits, often extended, helped compensate for Franklin's protracted absences.

Keeping in touch with the outside world from Campobello during his absences was not a simple task. Communications facilities were basic and often wanting. The only telephone on the island was at the post office at Wilson Beach. Electricity gradually became available but was not widely installed. The Roosevelts' cottage was not wired until it was sold well after Franklin's death. It is hard to imagine that neither electrical nor telephone service were available in the big red cottage during Franklin's visits as President during the 1930s, but it was surely so. Mail, telegraph, and newspapers were available, primarily across the bay at Eastport through the years of their residence. Campobello's own communications facilities were spartan, and its utility and availability was, understandably, geared for Canadian needs and not American. Eleanor's primary means of communication with the children from the cottage was a megaphone that hung from the ceiling of the bayside deck. With the megaphone she summoned them to meals, lessons, and appointments, or warned them of impending storms.

Many of the cottage's facilities were either rudimentary or inconsistent in operation. The light from flickering oil lamps was often wanting, and hot water was chronically in short supply. Baths were limited to a few inches of water. Even in 1941, when the cottage was used for the Campobello Leadership Conference and packed with college students, the system yielded no more hot water than in earlier years, and the restrictions continued to be applied. The second Franklin, Jr., recalled youthful times when the hot water tank in the kitchen ran out, as it often did. The holding tank emptied, and it "was a red letter day, a great occurrence . . . we didn't have to take a bath." [14]

Recreational bathing in cold ocean waters was certainly available as well as in warmer fresh-water ponds. Franklin tried to take that a step further when he had a saltwater pool built that used the tides as its source of water. The pool was heated, but Jimmy recalled that the water became stagnant and fetid, and that the concrete superstructure cracked. [15] This project was soon abandoned, like many of Franklin's other creative Campobello engineering enterprises.

Franklin did not permit the children to be careless or take risks when sailing, unlike other high-spirited activities. Of course, Franklin often took chances at sea, sometimes causing uneasiness in others on board. These risks were carefully calculated: Franklin intimately knew the waters he sailed, and he was always in knowledgeable control. With tides that rose thirty feet, treacherous rocks and narrows to avoid, and quickly moving weather patterns to watch, there were more than enough potential dangers to test Franklin's skill and daring.

Franklin especially enjoyed two trips that he took regularly. One was in a birchbark canoe he had purchased from Chief Joseph. He spent a full day circling the island with a stop to enjoy his lunch in a little inlet by Head Harbor that provided protection for fishing boats. His other favorite outing began with an announcement to his guests that they were to hike around the island, and that nobody was permitted to leave the rocks and the beaches. He knew that there were at least two places where his followers would be required to swim from one rock to another, and only he was aware of the height of the tide. Franklin took particular joy when a guest was forced to give up or retreat to higher ground.

While in Campobello planning his reelection campaign in 1912, Franklin came down with typhoid fever. Eleanor also became ill while nursing him, but quickly recovered, while her husband continued to languish. Franklin, she reported, "was still in bed and feeling miserable and looking like Robert Louis Stevenson at Valima."[16] During his convalescence, Franklin wrote to Louis Howe, an Albany newspaperman with whom he had become acquainted, and asked him to visit the island.

When Franklin had met Howe earlier in Albany, they liked each other at once. Howe agreed to manage Franklin's campaign and to act for him until the candidate had sufficiently recovered. Franklin was unable to join the fray until late in the campaign, but Howe effectively organized the reelection effort. They won by a comfortable margin, and their political partnership and friendship was sealed forever. They formed an alliance unparalleled in American political history. Franklin recognized in Howe an ally who could help him achieve high political goals. Howe believed that Franklin, under his direction, could achieve even the Presidency. In addition to their political partnership, Louis became Franklin's closest friend. In time, both Howe's friendship and his expertise were also extended to Eleanor. Louis gave himself to the Roosevelts so completely that he all but abandoned his own family.

In the summer of 1913, President Woodrow Wilson appointed Franklin Assistant Secretary of the Navy. Franklin was thrilled to have achieved this position at the tender age of thirty-one. He was now well on his way down the path that cousin Theodore had taken a generation earlier. But his new duties put even greater demands on the time and attention he could give to his wife and his children on Campobello, or at the Washington home they would occupy the next several years.

When Franklin did travel to the island, he gave Eleanor little of his time. The children clamored for his attention and his leadership in games and outings. Growing numbers of guests made additional demands on his time. Eleanor bore the brunt of organizing and scheduling events and outings, and their logistics. Franklin deftly avoided taking on most of these responsibilities, but he enjoyed and enthusiastically played the genial host. Geoffrey Ward observed that his activities as an adult were much the same as when he had been a child—he just played to larger audiences and provided enough attention to please most of them. Eleanor was not among those who were pleased.

Using his Navy Department position, Franklin ordered the battleship *USS North Dakota* to Eastport to participate in a gala Fourth of July celebration. Resplendent in white flannels, he received his first seventeen-gun salute. It fell to Eleanor to entertain the senior officers. She arranged teas, bridge games, and dinners while the active Roosevelt children loved the opportunity to play sailor on a giant warship. Eleanor dressed three-year-old Elliott in a blue sailor suit. He swaggered on board, faced the stern, and saluted the flag, just as his father had instructed him to do. The *North Dakota's* stay was extended by fog, and Eleanor played bridge with the officers until she was sure they were sick of her company.

Finally, the fog cleared, and the *North Dakota* departed with Franklin on board. A few days later, Eleanor heard alarming rumors that a flotilla would be headed their way again in August. She wrote pleadingly to Franklin, "Is it so? I could hardly bear such excitement again." Franklin reassured her, "No, no more battleships coming. I may come up in a destroyer later, but that means only three [senior] officers." Eleanor replied, "I shall welcome you on a destroyer or with a whole fleet if you will just come a little sooner on their account but of course the destroyer will be easier to entertain."[17]

En route back to Washington, *North Dakota* put in at York Harbor, Maine, so that Franklin could visit Isabella Ferguson, a close friend of Eleanor's. York Harbor was described as "a remarkably sedate vacation where liveried footmen announce the people and usher them through the blueberry patches to picnics on the stony beach." Isabella's daughter, Martha, never forgot "Uncle Franklin's arrival." When the *North Dakota* anchored offshore, they hurried down to watch a launch lowered and move slowly toward the shore. Franklin stood in the bow, looking "so handsome" in a blue naval cape. When the launch reached shallow water, two uniformed sailors climbed overboard and carried Franklin ashore so that he would not get wet on his way to dinner.[18]

Later that summer, while being watched by their nurse, the three Roosevelt children busily gathered driftwood for a bonfire on the beach below the cottage. Elliott, lumbering about in leg braces he wore to help correct a deformity, somehow tumbled into the fire. By the time he was plucked out, some of his hair and eyebrows were burned away, and hot embers had become lodged between his braces and his skin. The nurse rushed Elliott to the cottage, where he was bathed and creamed while Dr. Bennet was summoned from Lubec. To Eleanor's surprise, Elliott was unusually brave and under control, even though the burns must have been extremely painful.

Feeling guilty, Eleanor wrote promptly to Franklin about the accident. His response lacked appropriate sympathy for Elliott's pain and misfortune, and it was barely supportive of Eleanor's feelings of remorse. Eleanor was appalled by his cavalier attitude and she sharply rebuked him for his insensitivity. This proved to be an early indication of Eleanor's growing mental toughness and newfound ability to tell Franklin precisely what she expected from him in such situations.

The incident was extremely traumatic for the high-strung Elliott. He begged his mother not to make him wear the braces again, and she reluctantly agreed. Elliott claimed that he walked "with a rolling, bow-legged gait from that day . . . ."[19]

In 1914, while on Campobello, Eleanor was again pregnant. This time, the baby was due while she would still be on the island. When delivery seemed imminent, Franklin rushed to her side, piloting a destroyer for the first time through the Lubec Narrows. Franklin made a couple of frantic boat trips to Lubec to fetch Dr. Bennet, but each instance resulted in false labor. Finally, the second

Franklin, Jr., was born by lanternlight after an extremely protracted and difficult labor. The family's housekeeper actually performed the delivery as Dr. Bennet was rushing to her bedside. Bennet remarked with wonder on Eleanor's long labor and her stoicism, "Why, she is just one of us," he exclaimed. "I never [delivered babies for] summer people before." "You mean," Eleanor laughed, "that having a baby is different if you live in Maine all year around?"[20]

Late that summer, with war simmering in Europe, Franklin's half-brother Rosy and Rosy's mistress, Betty, were returning from Europe. They were aboard the Imperial German liner *Kronprinzessen Cecile,* which carried thirteen million dollars in gold and silver. They had been in England, assuming that their living arrangement would not be acceptable to the very proper Roosevelts in Hyde Park. But Betty was pleasant and agreeable, and was warmly welcomed into the family after their marriage. The *Kronprinzessen Cecile* managed to elude the eager pursuit of the British Royal Navy and slipped into Bar Harbor under cover of darkness. The United States was a neutral nation in 1914, and its ports and harbors were fair refuge for the ships of all combatants. The arrival of such a ship and cargo caused a major stir in the elegant resort. The German officers and Bar Harbor's society exchanged cordial visits. Rosy and Betty disembarked and made their way up the Maine coast to Franklin and Eleanor's cottage.

In July, 1915, Franklin made an unscheduled visit to his family on Campobello. He had unexpectedly undergone an appendectomy in Washington, and Navy Secretary Josephus Daniels gave him the time to recuperate on the island. Cousin Theodore wired his concern, and President Wilson sent his good wishes. Commander Kichisaburo Nomura, the naval attaché at the Japanese embassy and an acquaintance, expressed his "best wishes that your convalescence will be as quick as possible."[21] Their paths crossed again twenty-six years later, in 1941, when Nomura was the Japanese ambassador to the United States at the time of the surprise attack on Pearl Harbor.

In that summer of 1915, the U.S. Marines landed in Haiti to protect American interests and to assist in restoring civil order following an armed rebellion. Franklin was recuperating on Campobello and lamented that "it is a curious coincidence that as soon as I go away we seem to land marines somewhere."[22] Franklin was disappointed that he had "missed" the action there, as he had in Cuba in 1898.

Franklin did some politicking in eastern Maine in 1916, a presidential election year. He reported to Vance McCormick, chairman of the Democratic National Committee, that he found nothing for the Democrats to be alarmed about in Maine. Franklin said he saw a distinct trend toward President Wilson in general, especially among Republicans. "A large number of the men whom I talked with—factory hands, mechanics and storekeepers—were regular Republicans, who had never voted for a Democrat. These men did not wish to announce publicly that they would vote for Wilson, but told me that this was their present intention . . . ."[23] He was in error. At that time, the people of Maine voted in September, two months before the rest of the nation, and the Republicans soundly trounced all the Democrats who ran for national office.

During that summer, a polio epidemic swept the eastern part of the nation. On Campobello early in July, Franklin determinedly killed flies that had accumulated in the windows facing the bay. At that time, many believed that flies were a carrier of the disease. On his return to Washington, he wrote Eleanor, "The infantile paralysis in New York is appalling. Please kill all the flies I left. I think it really important."[24]

Franklin was right about the epidemic in New York City. Health certificates were required for all children sixteen and under, and four thousand citizens had been arrested for violating health ordinances. Useless and often bizarre home remedies were widely sold as many citizens got caught up in the panic. Six cases of polio were reported in Poughkeepsie, near Hyde Park, and Sara's coachman's three-year-old daughter, Mildred, was stricken. Although Franklin was relieved that his family was on Campobello, he felt he had to devise a safe route for them to return to Hyde Park after young Mildred had passed quarantine.

Cases were reported in Boston and Springfield, and as close to Campobello as Rockland, Maine. Many villages in New England turned away cars with out-of-state license plates. As the days passed, Franklin and Eleanor agreed that she and the children would sit tight on Campobello and remain there beyond their normal departure date in early September. She grew lonely and restless. The threat of war was looming. Unconfirmed rumors circulated of submarine sightings and landing parties of German officers on the Maine coast. "There I was entirely alone with my children," Eleanor wrote, "marooned on the island, and apparently I was going to be there for some time."[25]

Franklin was convinced that Campobello was the safest place for Eleanor and the children until the crisis had passed and he was able to arrange appropriate transport. He first planned to move them to Washington because he was so concerned about the danger of polio at Hyde Park. Eleanor, however, did not share his anxieties about the children being at Springwood. "I think the chicks will be safest at Hyde Park and even Mama does not seem to worry. They are exposed possibly anywhere and all we can do is to keep them as well as we can and I think the long season in Washington would be worse for them than the risks at Hyde Park." Having made clear how she felt, Eleanor did not press the point. "Of course if you decide it best to go to Washington or to stay later here I will do as you think best," she wrote.[26]

It seems odd that Eleanor was so eager to leave her home in Campobello for Hyde Park, where she was far from happy. It is true, however, that she liked Washington even less, and she knew the children were much happier at Hyde Park. Most important, she had once again bowed to her husband's wishes. Many found this unselfish attitude admirable in Eleanor. In later years, upon reflection, she did not find her unselfishness so admirable, and neither did others.

Franklin was in a position to requisition a ship to take his family off Campobello. But Congress had just accused Secretary Daniels of using his official yacht *Dolphin* for campaign purposes. Daniels was hesitant to allow Franklin to take the yacht until the Maine elections were over. When that date had passed and Daniels was in the Middle

West on business, Franklin saw no problem in ordering the *Dolphin* to Eastport.

The timing was right. On October 1, under the command of Captain William D. Leahy, later Franklin's military aide, the *Dolphin* arrived in Eastport. John, the fifth and last Roosevelt child, had been born in March, and Leahy had the task of shepherding the large and restless family with their servants to Washington.[27] By the time they arrived in Hyde Park, the epidemic had passed, and all bans had been lifted. Nine thousand cases of polio had been reported, and nearly twenty-five hundred people had died. Franklin had seen first-hand this terrible disease that attacked both children and adults and that medical science knew almost nothing about. There was no prevention, no cure, and only small hope for either to be developed.

Some of Eleanor's impatience at being "marooned" on the island might have been rooted in her growing suspicion that Franklin might have another romantic interest. She could not be certain of an infidelity, but her suspicions grew that summer. His long absences from Campobello and his lack of attentiveness when he was there fueled her unrest.

In Washington that winter, Eleanor once more endured the tedious official and social life that she had grown to abhor. As the wife of a government official, she was expected to spend most of her days making and receiving meaningless social visits with other officials' wives. Eleanor found this routine stultifying and unrewarding. Nonetheless, she persevered and the family continued to function much as it had in the previous years of their residence in the capital. But when the summer of 1917 arrived, Eleanor delayed her departure from the oppressive heat of Washington for the cool shores of Campobello. She had little trust in Franklin's faithfulness while she was away.

Franklin sensed Eleanor's concern about leaving him alone in Washington and tried to calm any suspicion she might have. The day after her departure, he wrote, "I really can't stand that house all alone without you, and you were a goosy girl to think or even pretend to think I don't want you here all summer, because you know I do! But honestly you ought to have six straight weeks at Campo, just as I ought to, only you can and I can't! I know what a whole summer here does to people's nerves and at the end of this summer I will be like a bear with a sore head until I get a change or some cold weather—in fact you know I am unreasonable and touchy now—but I shall try to improve." [28]

Franklin had bundled Eleanor off to Campobello so that he could pursue his romance with Lucy Mercer. Lucy was an attractive young socialite with limited financial resources who had taken a position as Eleanor's social secretary. Eleanor and the children liked Lucy, who easily fit into the Roosevelt household. When the United States entered the war in April, Lucy enlisted in the Navy and, to little surprise, was assigned to Franklin's section. Franklin casually wrote to Eleanor on Campobello of outings he had taken that included Lucy, although he was quick to point out that she was "escorted" by Nigel Law, a minor official at the British Embassy. Law, a favorite companion of Franklin's, apparently functioned as a "cover."

Franklin and Lucy had been seen together by Alice Roosevelt Longworth, Theodore's daughter. Alice, a legendary sharp-tongued gossip, thought little of Franklin and even less of Eleanor. But Alice went out of her way to encourage the romance. While Eleanor was away, Franklin and Lucy were dinner guests at Alice's. The romantic affair was good for Franklin, Alice observed. "He deserved a good time: he was married to Eleanor." [29]

In late July, Franklin came down with one of his many throat infections. Eleanor rushed from Campobello to Washington to be at his side. It is apparent that her return was prompted as much by her suspicions as by Franklin's not-too-serious illness. She wrote to him when she returned to Campobello in mid-August, "I hated to leave yesterday. Please go to the doctor twice a week, eat well and sleep well and remember I *count* on seeing you the 26th. My threat was no idle one." [30]

But this time Franklin did go to Campobello as he had promised. Again, he used his office to requisition Navy transportation. Ensign William M. Rand, a young Boston businessman who had received a provisional Navy commission, was assigned to special duty as Franklin's aide. Rand recalled fifty years later in a memoir:

I hadn't been on the Aztec more than eight weeks when I was ordered for "additional duties" to report to Bar Harbor Section Commander for special duty as Aide to the Assistant Secretary of the Navy during his trip from Bar Harbor, Maine, to Campobello Island, where I was to deliver Franklin Delano Roosevelt.

We had chosen one of the better steam yachts in the reserve fleet for the trip, the *Cherokee*, being William Douglas's yacht transferred to the Navy and armed. Her civilian skipper was enrolled in the Navy and continued to be *Cherokee's* captain. He had little knowledge of or interest in naval etiquette, and her crew was made up of reserves. When I went aboard, I arranged for a tender to be cleaned up, a blue border towel to cover her stern sheets, and found a good oarsman in the crew. In 1917, an outboard motor was unknown in Navy ships. Then I got the crew to line up and stand at attention, practicing for the moment when F.D.R. should come onto the quarter deck.

Then came the situation about the flag for the Assistant Secretary. The *Cherokee* had no flag. The nearest regular Navy ship had a flag, but it was too big for the *Cherokee*. It was Saturday afternoon, and the Assistant Secretary was to arrive the next morning. We must make a flag! The stores were closed, but Bar Harbor hadn't seen such a high-ranking government official, so the owner of a dry goods store came down, opened up, and I bought some blue and white bunting and took it to an elderly seamstress who had been recommended. I drew out on a piece of brown paper the fouled anchor and star, asking the lady to sew a fouled anchor and four blue stars on each side of the duly hemmed and reinforced white bunting. The seamstress had the job done by midnight.

The next morning, we went through a 'dry run' of the proceedings before our guest arrived. All went well—the lined-up crew and officers, and the man at the flag halyards to break out the Assistant Secretary's flag as he stepped aboard the quarter deck.

I met Mr. Roosevelt at the dock, and the bluejacket did a seamanlike job of rowing him to the *Cherokee*. The boatswain's whistle blew, and I glanced up from the tender as the [Assistant] Secretary stepped aboard, and the boy at the halyards had pulled the [Assistant] Secretary's flag out of the stops but had forgotten to lower the force commander's flag, which was flying from the mast. I doubt if Mr. Roosevelt noticed that a very much lesser personality's flag was flying alongside his for a time. At four o'clock in the afternoon we were off the coast.

Our first stop was at Jonesport in Moosabeck Reach. That was before politicians and the Army engineers put in the ridiculous bridge between Jonesport and Great Wass Island, which closes Moosabeck Reach to all but small craft—a bridge which probably has the least usage for its size of any bridge in the world. We anchored in the reach in a swift tide, and the fog so thick that visibility was only a few feet. Mr. Roosevelt wanted to go ashore, so I ordered the tender put overboard. The blue bordered towel was in place over the stern sheets, and the oarsman in clean blues, shoes shined, was standing ready at the starboard ladder. I then went into the cabin, saluted, and said 'Your boat is standing by, Mr. Secretary.' He replied, 'Can you row, Rand?' 'Yes, sir,' I answered. 'Well, let's you and I go ashore.' So I relieved the bluejacket and took the bearing to a spot where I thought the town landing was and, allowing for a swift tide, rowed as fast as I could for the shore. It seemed a long time before the loom of some buildings showed up ahead. I had been in Jonesport before, and I recognized the William Underwood sardine factory which was a good half mile from the center of town, so I turned and rowed along the shore.

Mr. Roosevelt was charming. He visited the Post Office, the drug store, and ended up in the grocery store sitting on a cracker barrel and chatting with a storeful of men who seemed to come from nowhere.

Soon he decided to return to the *Cherokee*. When we got to the dock, the fog was just as thick, if not thicker, than it was when we came in. I was not sure which way nor how strong the tide was running, nor was I sure just where the *Cherokee* was anchored or how far out she was. I rowed hard in a direction which I thought would take us to the ship, and when I got to a point which I hoped was near the vessel, I stood up, cupped my hands and shouted four times in each direction, 'Ahoy, *Cherokee*.' No answer. The Secretary looked at me with a twinkle in his eye and said, "You're a hell of a navigator, you are, Rand!" I turned the tender around and rowed back, judging the strength of the tide by lobster buoys which we passed, came back to shore and tried again—the second time successfully.

When we got into the Bay of Fundy, passing inside the Grand Manan Island, the fog cleared, and as we came to West Quoddy Head Mr. Roosevelt went onto the bridge and said to Captain Sparks, 'I'll take her, Captain, through Lubec Narrows.' The expression on Captain Sparks's face spoke volumes! He had never had his authority of command on his beloved vessel challenged, and he couldn't imagine this man who had never steered the *Cherokee* taking her through the dangerous channel between Quoddy Head and Campobello Island. However, he reluctantly stepped back, and Roosevelt took the vessel through the Narrows, turned her to starboard, and we dropped anchor in the semi-circular bay before the Roosevelt estate.

Again I ordered the tender and the oarsman, and the [Assistant] Secretary and I were rowed ashore. As we neared the dock, a sight I long remember took place. From the house there came a number of children running down the broad, daisy-speckled field followed by Mrs. Roosevelt in a long white dress. I said good-bye to Mr. Roosevelt just before he was smothered by the enthusiastic greeting of his children.[31]

The children hungered for Franklin's attention, and they competed with each other and with the charms of Campobello for his time and energies. It was a summer vacation that seems to have been thoroughly enjoyed as well as eagerly anticipated by all the Roosevelts. When he left the island on September 2, Eleanor wrote to him, "It is horrid to be without you, and the chicks and I bemoaned our sad fate all through breakfast."[32]

Of course, Franklin had to return to his duties at the Navy Department. The war seemed to get a bit closer to Campobello when there had again been rumors of German submarines in the North Atlantic, close to the American and Canadian shore. That possibility was on Franklin's mind when he had written to Eleanor earlier that summer "that if by any perfectly wild chance a German submarine should come into the bay and start to shell Eastport or the Pool, I want you to grab the children and beat it into the woods. Don't stay to see what is going on, I am not joking about this, for while it is 500 to 1 against the possibility, still there is just that one chance that the Bosch will do the fool and unexpected thing . . . ."[33]

The Germans did not shell Campobello, but Eleanor must have felt that her marriage was under attack. On her return to Washington that fall, she threw herself into the war effort while remaining wary and vigilant about Franklin's social activities. His lack of attention to her, his lengthy summer absences from Campobello, and her highly tuned sensitivities suggested to Eleanor that something was amiss in their marriage.

None of the Roosevelts made the journey to Campobello in 1918. Their attention was on the war, and Eleanor was doing her best to help in the civilian support effort. In addition to organizing women knitting sweaters for servicemen, she tirelessly greeted soldiers and sailors as they passed through Washington and helped arrange for their care and feeding.

Navy Secretary Josephus Daniels, a courtly, conservative North Carolinian, relieved Lucy of her duties at the Navy Department. He had quite likely seen or been informed of her close relationship with Franklin. Daniels deeply believed in the sanctity of marriage. He probably wanted to protect his assistant's reputation and felt that Lucy's discharge was for the good of the service.

Meanwhile, Franklin requested a naval commission so he could have the opportunity to see action. President Wilson directed him to remain in his civilian post, but Franklin managed to arrange permission to sail to Europe on an official Navy Department mission. He was able to get close to the action and it gave him some satisfaction to see and hear the firing of big guns. He tried using this proximity to battle for recognition of his wartime service.

Again, illness struck while Franklin was in France. He came down with a serious case of pneumonia and was shipped home in early September. Eleanor met the ship and watched as he was carried off on a stretcher. While unpacking his things, she found a packet of love letters written to Franklin by Lucy Mercer. Eleanor was devastated; her worst fears had been confirmed. A quarter century later she confided to Joseph Lash, "The bottom dropped out of my particular world, and I faced myself, my surroundings, my world, honestly for the first time."[34]

6

I Can Forgive But Not Forget

The affair between Franklin Roosevelt and Lucy Mercer created the great personal crisis of the Roosevelt's marriage. It changed their relationship forever. Franklin's monumental indiscretion, while romantically exhilarating for him, was a crushing betrayal to Eleanor. The intra-family debate that followed was highly charged and the intensity of the deliberations was worthy of the highest judicial courts.

It is clear what happened, or, more precisely, what did not happen. Eleanor offered Franklin his freedom to marry Lucy Mercer, but he concluded that the price was too dear. Divorce would have meant giving up his five young children and an uncommonly loyal and decent wife. It seems abundantly clear that Sara had a great deal to say about any consideration of divorce. Had her beloved son made the choice to leave his family and marry another, Sara could not possibly have accepted his decision. She could abide his clumsy business schemes, and she was gradually becoming accustomed to his pursuit of a public career. But a divorce and the abandonment of his wife and children—and to marry a Roman Catholic—that was absolutely out of the question. Sara was intransigent, and her threat was crystal clear. Should Franklin choose divorce, he would be cut off without a cent, and he would relinquish forever his right of succession to the Hyde Park estate.

If Franklin still needed help in bringing this drama to its final resolution, Louis Howe delivered a loud and clear message. Never one to mince words with Franklin, Howe announced in no uncertain terms that a divorce would mean the absolute and unequivocal end to any and all political aspirations. Period.

Eleanor never doubted Franklin's love for the children or, in many ways, that he cared for her. But she believed that Howe's declaration of political finality was the critical factor that led to Franklin's decision. Eleanor's terms included Franklin's promise not to see Lucy Mercer again.

Although Eleanor offered Franklin his freedom, it is not at all certain that Lucy would have married a divorced man. It is also far from certain what Franklin really wanted. What terms did he believe were acceptable? Did he apologize? Was he mortified or contrite? What did they say to each other when they struck their final agreement? Eleanor referred to the entire affair only obliquely in later writings. Sara's diaries for the years 1917–1919 are missing and were probably destroyed. And Franklin, not surprisingly, wrote nothing of Lucy or the aftermath of the affair, and probably never discussed it with anyone.

The obstacles to any thought of divorce were clear and many. Franklin and Lucy parted, but not forever. She married Winthrop Rutherfurd, a wealthy businessman. He was more than twice her age and died not many years later. In secret, in 1933, Lucy attended Franklin's first inauguration at his invitation. At least once during his presidency, his special train car pulled off to a siding near her New Jersey mansion.

Lucy Mercer Rutherfurd visited Franklin a number of times at the White House and at Hyde Park in the late years of his presidency. These visits were arranged with the help of his daughter, then acting as his social secretary. Bernard Baruch, the Wall Street financier and Democratic Party benefactor, had Lucy and Franklin as guests at his South Carolina retreat. And, in a classic twist of irony, Lucy was at Warm Springs, Georgia, in 1945 when Franklin suffered a fatal cerebral hemorrhage. Eleanor did not know of any of these meetings until after Franklin's death, and she learned of Lucy's presence at Warm Springs while making the funeral arrangements.

According to one story, Eleanor was kind and tolerant during the family deliberations in 1918 that decided what was to be done about the marriage. Reports of her tolerance and understanding are probably exaggerated. In later years, she confided to intimates, "I have the memory of an elephant. I can forgive, but I cannot forget."[1] Many believe that she could not forgive, either.

Many years later, the three older Roosevelt children had a great deal to say about the relationship between their parents at that time of family crisis. Anna, the oldest, was only twelve years old at the time, and their assessments are probably something less than reliable. Yet they believed that they knew much about their parents' intimacy or lack of it. Anna wrote that Eleanor had told her that "sex was an ordeal to be borne."[2] Elliott concluded that Lucy provided his father with "a woman's warm, enspiriting companionship, which my mother by her very nature could not provide."[3] Elliott married five times in search of his own enspiriting companionship.

In 1918 and 1919, Franklin and Eleanor tried to resurrect marital and family harmony, but it was not an easy task. Franklin spent more time with the children, and showed Eleanor more attention. For a while, he cut down on the number of his outside activities. Eleanor tried to enjoy social events with Franklin, always taking pains to ensure that they would both arrive and depart together, not often the case in previous years.

However, Eleanor became more introspective and withdrawn. She lost weight and lapsed into periods of melancholy. She often sought solitude to reevaluate her life and recent events. A frequent destination was a quiet spot in Washington's Rock Creek Park where she sat for hours at a Saint-Gaudens statue. Placed there by the historian Henry Adams, the female figure was believed to be a likeness of his wife Clover, who had committed suicide. The few photographs taken of Eleanor at this time reveal a grim, pale, dejected woman, whose face is averted from the camera. Even the heartening news of the Armistice and war's end in November could not lift Eleanor from her gloom.

On New Year's Day 1919, Franklin and Eleanor sailed for Europe. Franklin was on a mission to organize the dismantling of American naval installations. He had pleaded with Secretary Daniels to allow Eleanor to accompany him. Daniels was sensitive to the Roosevelts' domestic upheaval and must have been relieved that his assistant had chosen his family over divorce. It was Eleanor's first trip to Europe since their honeymoon.

President Wilson faced growing opposition to his Fourteen Points and the League of Nations in his own party as well as among the Republicans. Franklin incurred Wilson's wrath by publicly agreeing with Britain's former Foreign Secretary Sir Edward Grey, who opposed the League, and supporting amendments proposed by Republican Senator Henry Cabot Lodge. Wilson had lost all confidence in Franklin and he exploded with anger when Franklin and Eleanor openly and regularly entertained Grey. Wilson confided to Secretary Daniels that he now "hated" Franklin, whose days in the administration were clearly numbered.[4]

En route to Europe, Franklin and Eleanor learned of the death of Theodore Roosevelt. Eleanor, although saddened by the loss of her uncle, wrote in her diary with little emotion, "Another great figure off the stage."[5] By now, there had been a significant cooling of relationships between the Hyde Park and Oyster Bay branches of the family. Theodore's sons believed that Franklin was trading on their father's good name, and Alice Roosevelt missed no opportunity to demean Eleanor and, on occasion, Franklin. Some time later, someone asked Sara what had caused the rift between the Roosevelt branches. She replied, without hesitation, "I can't imagine, unless it's because we're better looking."[6]

Eleanor took the opportunity to visit former Allenswood classmates in London. She also found time to spend with Franklin's Aunt Dora, who had remained in Paris all through the war. Eleanor toured U.S. military hospitals and was shocked by the shattered bodies of the wounded veterans. Still very much the Victorian, Eleanor deplored the immorality then rampant in Paris, but she did love revisiting the shops and bookstores that she had first seen with Mlle.

Souvestre. All in all, the trip was a welcome and needed diversion.

Eleanor and the children spent the early part of the summer of 1919 in Washington, hoping to have more time with Franklin. But the sweltering heat was discomforting, and Campobello seemed too distant and, perhaps, too lonely. They went to Springwood, but their stay in Hyde Park was not a success. Eleanor and Sara disagreed often, and Eleanor, uncharacteristically, freely expressed her mind. Later in July, she took the children to the Delano estate in Fairhaven, Massachusetts, for the rest of the summer. When they returned to Hyde Park in September, the disagreements with Sara continued.

Sara expected Eleanor to suppress all personal emotion and maintain a cheerful demeanor for the sake of all the family. That would be, of course, in the best Delano-Roosevelt tradition. They quarreled often and grew even more distant. Eleanor, however, felt remorseful and in October she wrote Sara a letter of apology. "I know, Mummy dear, I made you feel most unhappy the other day and I am so sorry I lost my temper and said such fool things for of course you know I love Franklin and the children very dearly and I am deeply devoted to you. I have, however, allowed myself to be annoyed by little things which of course one should never do and I had no right to hurt you as I know I did and am truly sorry and hope you will forgive me."[7] No more mention was made of their differences, and peace and harmony were restored, but the problems were hardly resolved

In August, Eleanor's Grandmother Hall died on the twenty-fifth anniversary of Elliott's death. Memories of her unhappy childhood must have been suppressed as Eleanor mourned her death. She considered her grandmother's life a sad one. She later wrote, "I wondered then and I wonder now whether, if her life had been less centered in her family group, that family group might not have been a great deal better off. If she had some kind of life of her own, what would have been the result?"[8] This event encouraged Eleanor to consider the course of her own life carefully. "I determined that I would never be dependent on my children by allowing all my interests to center in them," she wrote. Unlike Grandmother Hall, Eleanor would no longer allow anyone "to feel assured" of "love and unquestioned loyalty unless it was justified by specific behavior." [9]

Eleanor grew increasingly uncomfortable with the Delano women whom she had always thought to be models of generosity and familial love. They now seemed to be overbearing and out of touch. Was she thinking of just the other Delano women, or was she thinking also of Sara, when she wrote to Franklin, "They all in their serene assurance and absolute judgments on people and affairs going on in the world, make me want to squirm and turn bolshevik." [10]

As to her own aunts, Tissie lived in England, Maude and her new husband were in Portland, Maine, and Pussie had tragically died in a fire with her two young daughters. Eleanor could count only Isabella Ferguson as a close friend, and the Fergusons lived in New Mexico. Clearly, some changes had to be made in her life, and Eleanor resolved to make them.

That October, Eleanor made her first contact with a number of women's working movements. She attended the International Congress of Working Women and met several women who became lifelong friends and colleagues. Eleanor was impressed with both the women and the ideas they expressed.

In that fall of 1919, Franklin left Washington for a hunting trip in New Brunswick. He prepared to spend a week "in the heart of the woods," and wrote to Eleanor, "Got here, Fredericton, in time for lunch . . . Yesterday I had a nice day at Portland. [Aunt] Maude met me at the station . . . after lunch golf with Dr. George Derby, then tea at Maude's . . . Mrs. Sills, wife of the President of Bowdoin College, came . . . it is very cold but a wonderful day . . . ." [11] Franklin's first extended holiday was a treat, and his return to Maine and New Brunswick, although not to Campobello, refreshed his spirits.

In 1920, Franklin and Eleanor were diligently trying to please each other. There was at least an outward appearance of harmony and tranquillity. Both pursued individual interests, and although their marriage was no longer one of romantic intimacy, they were supportive of each other's activities and concerns.

Later that year, prior to the Democratic National Convention, Franklin's name had been circulated as a potential vice-presidential candidate. Louis Howe was determined that Franklin be made available for nomination to higher office. Eleanor saw no particular role for herself, and Franklin did not encourage her to attend the convention. With no compelling responsibilities of importance at that time, she packed up the children and servants and headed for Campobello for their first stay since 1917. She had hopes that Franklin would join them once the convention was over.

Eleanor was particularly looking forward to her return to Campobello, in part because 1920 had been a year of unrest in the streets of Washington. Strong anti-Communist feelings had erupted, and government agents were aggressively Red-hunting. In addition, there had been deadly race riots and several incidents involving anarchist-engineered bombings.

One night, just as Franklin and Eleanor were returning home, an explosion took place on the steps of the house directly across the street, the home of the fiercely anti-Communist Attorney General Mitchell Palmer. Franklin and Eleanor ran inside their house to make sure that the children were unhurt. The anarchist who placed the bomb was blown apart by his own charge. He was the only casualty.

The Roosevelts' housekeeper was hysterical, and Franklin and Eleanor found twelve-year-old Jimmy standing in the upstairs bedroom window, intently watching the arrival of the police and the gathering crowd. Jimmy remembers how his unnerved father embraced him with relief and how his mother coolly chastised him for being out of bed at so late an hour. Without further word to her excited son, she then turned to calm the housekeeper.

President Wilson had suffered a debilitating stroke, and the Democratic Convention was seeking a successor to the ailing President. Franklin was prepared to support Al Smith, the Irish-Catholic governor of New York, with whom he had an uneasy relationship. As a result of Franklin's maverick terms in the state senate, he was estranged from the Tammany Hall organization that ran the

Democratic Party in New York, but believed it in his best interests to support Smith.

Smith withdrew when it was clear that he could not win the nomination, and the New York Democrats switched their support to Governor James Cox of Ohio. Cox finally prevailed on the forty-sixth ballot. In the interest of peace and party harmony, Tammany leaders agreed to support Franklin's nomination for vice-president. Franklin's youth, his sparkling personality, his Eastern support base, and the Roosevelt name appealed to Cox, Smith, and other party leaders. And it appealed to the convention as a whole as Franklin won the nomination by acclamation. It was, assuredly, good news for Franklin, but the bad news was just as clear: Wilson and the Democrats had fallen into wide disfavor during the deliberations over the League of Nations and the international turmoil that accompanied them. The Republicans were overwhelming favorites to recapture the White House.

Franklin reveled in returning to Hyde Park and a tumultuous welcome. Eleanor hurried from Campobello to be there, but she arrived too late for the reception. Her initial public response to his nomination was predictably guarded. "I was glad for my husband but it never occurred to me to be much excited." Until she became active in the campaign, she "felt detached and objective, as though I were looking at someone else's life." [12]

Eleanor returned to Campobello and followed the campaign with great interest. Franklin wrote to her that he planned to get to the island. "I can hardly wait. I miss you so much. It is very strange not to have you with me in all these doings." "I like all your interviews," she answered, " . . . Oh! how I wish I could be in two places at once." [13] She may have felt detached at first, but now she felt just plain left out.

Franklin arrived at Campobello aboard the destroyer *Hatfield*. Lashed to the deck was the *Vireo*, a boat he was bringing to the island to replace the *Half Moon*, which had been given to the Navy during the war. Franklin again triumphantly piloted the destroyer through the Lubec Narrows and returned to his beloved island as the

Democratic nominee for the vice-presidency of the United States. He told the press that he planned to do some shooting, take cliff walks, teach Jimmy to handle the *Vireo*, and begin work on a toy sailboat for the children.

When he safely anchored at Welshpool, Franklin savored the excitement he brought to his Campobello neighbors and those at nearby Eastport. His trip, however, also caused a stir in the press and gave Franklin his first public relations problem. The *New York Journal*, a newspaper owned by William Randolph Hearst, charged that Franklin "had no right to use a fighting ship belonging to the American Navy and the American people . . . for commuting purposes." It went on to criticize Franklin, asking, "What right has a man to burn up coal enough to heat the homes of fifty families all winter to carry his 165 pounds . . . to a summer resting place? Is a first-class ticket . . . not good enough?"[14]

Now Franklin, and all the Roosevelts, had become newsworthy. Shortly after his arrival, a newsreel camera crew set up its equipment on the grounds of the cottage. Eleanor's on-screen persona was decidedly self-conscious and joyless. She picked flowers, led the children down the cottage stairs, and generally tried to do the cameraman's bidding. The boys scowled, and the younger ones clutched their mother's side. Only the nominee and Anna, now fourteen and with long blonde hair, were photogenic subjects. It was not a happy experience for Eleanor, but she learned from it. In coming years she would become better able to accommodate the press, if not master it.

There was time, that summer, for the Roosevelts to enjoy most of their favorite Campobello activities together. Franklin probably did lead one last cliff walk. John Gunther believed that Franklin made a special point of taking this rugged trek once every summer. Gunther speculated that if it were Theodore Roosevelt, he would have done it every day, and before breakfast at that![15]

With or without the cliff walk, Franklin was at the top of his game. He was but thirty-eight years old, a candidate for national office, and proceeding on his self-predicted journey to the White House well ahead of schedule. Franklin was ready, willing, and able to hit the campaign trail and sell himself to the American people. If he harbored any doubts, they were certainly far beneath the surface.

Franklin's summer neighbors on Campobello were mostly Republicans who gave little support to his candidacy. But the fellow islanders who had embraced him from childhood felt some pride and admiration. Local citizens were interviewed by the press about the Roosevelts, and their reflections served as high praise, "down east" style. "They were not ones to sit around the kitchen" or "they weren't ones to stand in front of the fire"[16] attested to the Roosevelts' vigor if not their egalitarianism. The Roosevelts were well respected on the island and Campobello residents demonstrated this admiration and acceptance toward them for the rest of their lives.

Franklin spent a few days campaigning in Maine, where the governor's race would be settled on September 19. The Democrats hoped to keep the expected Republican margin of victory below 20,000 votes. It didn't happen. The GOP won by more than 60,000 votes and captured all three Congressional seats. This was neither the first nor the last time that Franklin would campaign in Maine with little success. The state that welcomed him as a young man, and that he visited countless times, never supported him politically. His 1920 experience was not only typical, it was surely a harbinger of what was to come in November and in future years.

Theodore Roosevelt, Jr., followed Franklin into Maine to campaign. Young Ted, who had always disliked Franklin, stumped the state, disparaging his cousin's claims and insisting that it was the Republican Party that had won the war. Ted shadowed Franklin throughout the campaign, doing what he could to undermine the Democratic effort. There were many citizens, particularly in the west, who were confused about who was who in the Roosevelt family. Some supported Franklin because they believed he was Theodore, Sr.'s, son. Some swore to oppose him for the very same reason. Theodore, Jr., thought that everything had come to Franklin too easily and that he, not Franklin, should be the Roosevelt to lead the next generation politically.

As Franklin embarked on a national campaign, Eleanor and the children followed the events as best they could from Campobello. Jimmy wrote his father that he won a prize at the annual Campobello Field Day, while Eleanor's letters indicated envy that she was missing all the excitement. She was angry when Franklin agreed at the last moment to speak at a Labor Day rally in Brooklyn instead of coming to Campobello for five days of rest as he had promised. "Of course it is hard to refuse," she told Sara, "but I think he should have cut Monday out and come here directly, however, there is no use in saying anything."[18]

Eleanor joined the campaign when Franklin's entourage headed west in September, but not until she had enrolled Jimmy at Groton. Jimmy's adjustment to prep school was slow and painful, not unlike that of his father. But Eleanor stayed with the campaign, dispatching Sara to Groton to look after a stomach ailment that turned out to be nervous indigestion and a portent of the ulcers that would plague Jimmy all his adult life.

As Franklin thrived in the limelight, Eleanor slowly learned to adjust to political campaigning. More important, she began to form a close personal relationship with Louis Howe, after years of cordial but distant feelings. Spending many hours together on the campaign train, they discussed many subjects, including politics. They enjoyed reading poetry to each other, and they generally supported each other's unique role in the Roosevelt contingent. She had referred to him as "Mr. Howe" when the trip began, but wrote of "Louis" when it ended at Buffalo. Eleanor wrote ahead to Sara asking that Louis's daughter Mary, a student at Vassar College in Poughkeepsie, be invited to tea at Springwood. Sara was hardly an admirer of Louis, but she decided that members of his family were acceptable guests in her home.

When the election results were in, the Republicans had won 61 percent of the vote, taking 404 of the 531 electoral votes. To Franklin's embarrassment, the Democratic ticket failed to carry his home state, New York. Al Smith lost the governorship, and the national and state Democratic Party was in disarray.

"Franklin rather relieved not to be elected Vice-President," Sara noted in her journal on election day.[19] Franklin was outwardly upbeat. The defeat, although lightly brushed off, must have disappointed him, but Franklin was determined to persevere. He had an active family and believed that he should go to work to support them. Franklin had been a public official since 1910, and, while he and Louis continued to look to a political future, his first concern was to find a stable business situation.

7

I Don't Know
What's the Matter With Me

In 1921, Franklin was faced with a need for decision and rededication. His vice-presidential campaign had provided national political exposure, and he had compiled a solid record of public service. To a great extent, Franklin had paralleled cousin Theodore's public career. It was clearly time to establish a route to the next political objective. But first, there were problems to solve.

Franklin's turn-of-the-century progressivism was out of vogue. What's more, he had to deal with the Tammany organization that held a stranglehold on the New York Democratic Party. Tammany leaders remembered Franklin's opposition to many of the party's programs and candidates during his tenure in the state Senate. In addition, the "city gang" disliked and distrusted his airs and perceived an arrogance in Franklin's Hudson River aristocracy. His *pince-nez* glasses, his formal dress, and his habit of throwing back his head and looking down his nose exaggerated the differences in social backgrounds. He was held in esteem by many political leaders outside of New York, but Franklin had yet to demonstrate that he could be a consistent winner or that he was able to develop more than a limited base of influence. To exercise significant political leadership, he needed the support of a broad state and national constituency.

Franklin joined a law firm that became Emmett, Marvin and

Roosevelt. He continued to find the practice of law unappealing and grew more interested in establishing the means for an independent income. Despite his and Eleanor's trust funds and Sara's willingness to help, he found it increasingly difficult to support his family and their lifestyle. Franklin may also have wished for a little less dependence on his mother's largesse.

His friend, Van Lear Black, headed the Maryland-based Fidelity and Deposit Company, a large surety bonding house. Black offered Franklin a vice-presidency as head of the New York office. The annual salary of $25,000, a significant amount for the times and for Franklin's limited business experience, was five times his Navy Department earnings. Franklin was also offered and had accepted the leadership of the Navy Club and the New York Boy Scout Council. He made the leap from public service and a political life to a full plate of business and personal commitments. Eleanor at first thought he had taken on a heavy load. However, noting Franklin's prodigious energy, she hoped that these meaningful activities would occupy most of the time that he had recently been devoting to shallow social organizations and parties.

Eleanor began the new year in full force. She enrolled in a business school to learn typing, and she found a housewife to teach her to cook. She joined the League of Women Voters and continued to explore participation in other women's organizations. Sara, ever the arbiter of appropriate Roosevelt social custom, didn't approve of these new activities. Sara would have preferred to have Eleanor "pour tea" and support charities as was the established custom of other members of the leisure class. Eleanor, strengthened by her ordeal and resolved to live her own life, would now have none of it. She wanted to be involved in important public issues and to work with others on ideas and causes in which she believed.

Eleanor met a number of women with education and purpose. She was taken with Esther Lape and Elizabeth Read, among others, who introduced her to contemporary ideas and, most important, to the notion of personal empowerment. Lape and Read were leaders of a growing group of nontraditional women who met regularly to discuss public issues, read poetry, and generally enjoy the company of women of similar mind. Eleanor was warmly welcomed into this circle. She first had to overcome feelings of inadequacy and inferiority when she was among others with more advanced education and experience. In a short time, however, she began to understand that she had something of value to contribute and, to her surprise and delight, that others were interested in her views.

Although hardly a militant feminist, Eleanor was especially concerned about women's rights and issues of child welfare. She quickly grew to understand the power of political activism in advancing these concerns. She attended conventions, Democratic Party meetings, political lectures, and organization meetings. And, when it suited her, Eleanor elicited Franklin's views. They began to share ideas and opinions on issues of mutual interest. For the first time in their marriage, Eleanor's point of view was heard and, mostly, respected.

Franklin took considerable pleasure in coaching Eleanor in political tactics. Prior to one important League of Women Voters meeting, he was specific on what she was to do after a particular report was to be read. Eleanor followed his suggestions precisely. She placed herself at the front of the room, got on her feet, and moved that the report be tabled. She gleefully reported to Franklin that "it worked, you should have seen their jaws drop."[1] Eleanor now took enormous pleasure in doing exactly what Franklin had told her to do in similar circumstances. She wrote to him from Cleveland after a particularly tedious League convention, "much love, dear, and I prefer doing my politics with you."[2]

Meanwhile, despite his new professional and business duties, Franklin continued to enjoy an exuberant social life. Eleanor was indignant when one afternoon she found him at home in bed badly hung over. On another occasion, at an Oyster Bay Roosevelt family wedding, Franklin's uproarious behavior attracted considerable attention. It was the "Roosevelt spirit," his detractors noted. The snide comments embarrassed Eleanor and irritated Sara, who was by now more certain than ever that her son surely must be less a Roosevelt and much more a Delano.

Franklin was mostly bored by both the surety bonding business and the tiresome practice of law. His attention was now necessarily focused on an infamous event that had taken place at the Newport Naval Base a year earlier. He found himself in the uncomfortable position of facing the possibility of defending himself from charges brought by a Congressional subcommittee about any official role he might have had in the Newport "homosexual ring" scandal. The charges involved a systematic entrapment of sailors by a specially appointed squad of informants. Franklin's participation, active or passive, as well as that of Secretary Daniels, was in question. It was alleged that he either had significant responsibility for directing the operation or was derelict in his duty to discover what was actually taking place. By springtime, it was not clear just how far the Congressional investigation would go.

The far-away charms of Campobello began to occupy Franklin's thoughts as he tried to push Newport from his mind. He busily prepared himself for what he had hoped would be a long, relaxing summer with his family at their cottage. As was his custom, Franklin wrote to Captain Franklin Calder to alert him to the family's needs for boating services.

The letter asked for the usual arrangements, gently suggesting that usual fees might be less since the price of gasoline and the "general wage schedule" had come down. He asked that the *Vireo* be ready by the end of June and indicated that the family would probably stay on Campobello until mid-September. The letter also lamented the news that some cottages had been broken into. Franklin suggested that, rather than hire a watchman, it might "be better to offer a reward confidentially to three or four people for the arrest and conviction of any thieves."[3] He demonstrated an insensitivity to his neighbors by insinuating that some islanders knew the identity of those doing the break-ins and that such knowledge could be purchased.

While Franklin finished his duties in New York, Eleanor, the children, and their support staff journeyed to Campobello. Louis and Grace Howe and their son Hartley joined them for the summer.

Franklin and Louis hoped to formulate political plans for the following year. Eleanor now looked forward to Louis's company and to that of other guests. Franklin wrote to her to "tell Louis I expect those [model] boats to be all rigged and ready when I get up there and I am greatly put out not to be there now. Kiss all the chicks and many many for you."[4]

On July 10, Franklin joined them on the island, but his visit proved painfully brief. Three days after his arrival, a bicycle messenger from Welshpool brought a telegram: "Committee ready to report Monday [July 18] on Newport. Libelous report of majority. Can you go to Washington at once. Answer. [signed] Josephus Daniels."[5]

Franklin's worst fears had been realized. He had been promised an opportunity to testify, but now a "libelous" committee report was to be released to the press before he had any chance to defend himself. Franklin wired the chairman and demanded the opportunity to testify. The chairman wired back that if Franklin insisted, he could appear before the committee on Monday morning, July 18. With anger and even more trepidation, Franklin was forced to leave his cool island for the hot seat in Washington.

On his arrival, he was faced with the impossible task of reviewing six thousand pages of testimony in less than twenty-four hours. He had no alternative but to appear as he had requested. All he was able to accomplish in his presentation was to charge the Republican majority with falsifying facts and violating the standards of fair play. The committee's majority reported that, if he could not be held directly responsible for despicable actions, he was certainly extraordinarily derelict in not knowing what was happening on his watch. Daniels was similarly excoriated.

The always proper New York Times reported on its first page:

Lay Navy Scandal to F. D. Roosevelt. Senate Naval
Sub-Committee Accuses him and Daniels in
Newport Inquiry. Details Are Unprintable.[6]

Franklin's testimony and rebuttal were buried on inside pages. Fortunately for Franklin and Daniels, there was nothing more about the hearing in the afternoon papers. At that time, every sizable city had both morning and afternoon newspapers, and several of them at that. Franklin could only hope that the inconclusiveness of the subcommittee's findings would bring an end to the press coverage and conjecture. Indeed, the newspapers now seemed to take more interest in what was taking place in the new Harding administration than what had happened in the recent past. One can only conjecture about how today's media would have covered such a scandal, and how the "unprintable" nowadays would crowd out all else.

Although he was relieved that the subcommittee took no further action, the innuendo caused Franklin to fear that the inquiry and the publicity could, at some time, negatively affect his political aspirations. He continued to worry about Newport for all the years leading to 1932 and his first presidential campaign. He even arranged for a friendly biographer to include a lengthy press release of his detailed refutation of the subcommittee charges. Only then was Franklin able to exorcise the Newport ghost.

Tired and angry, Franklin had piles of unanswered mail and plenty of unfinished business at his two offices to occupy him for a week and a half. Eleanor, who tried to be as supportive as she could, wrote, "It must be dreadfully disagreeable for you . . . but it has always seemed to me that the chance of just such attacks as this was a risk one had to take with our form of government & if one felt clean oneself, the rest did not really matter."[7] But, for Franklin, it did matter.

On Thursday, July 28, a weary Franklin and about fifty other prominent men associated with the New York Boy Scout Council boarded a steam yacht for a trip up the Hudson River to Bear Mountain. Their mission was to inspect eighteen camps that served 2,100 city boys who participated each summer. It was a congenial trip and the sort of function Franklin enjoyed. The day's events included speeches, parades, demonstrations of knot-tying, bonfires, and a fried chicken dinner. Franklin enthusiastically played toastmaster at the bonfire and posed for photographers. One photograph shows his lithe, athletic body in full parade—the last photo ever of Franklin walking under his own power.

Geoffrey Ward concludes that when Franklin sailed back to New York City that evening, a mysterious virus "inhaled or ingested at some point during the hot, hectic day . . . [was] already moving through his bloodstream . . . ."[8] Franklin's thoughts were of boarding a boat for another trip, to Campobello.

Despite Franklin's absence, Eleanor and the children, along with her guests, were having a most agreeable summer. They had not enjoyed such a long stretch of time on Campobello for years without the concerns of war or the tensions of a strained marriage. They had plenty of visitors to help keep them occupied, Among them were members of Franklin's Harvard Fly Club who arrived unannounced by yacht.

Louis built model boats for the children, and endlessly hit baseballs to Elliott and Hartley. The older children found many other activities to amuse themselves now that they had more freedom to explore. Although Eleanor disapproved, Anna, James, and Elliott roamed around the now long-closed hotels, searching the dark halls for treasures. The buildings had fallen into disrepair, and Eleanor feared for the children's safety. The boys tried their hands at roping the sheep that ranged freely to clip the grass on the island golf course, while Chief, Anna's German shepherd, enjoyed chasing the poor animals into the sea. The sheep's owners, not surprisingly, were not amused.

Regular domestic routines served the Roosevelt cottages' needs. A butcher from Wilson's Beach brought meat twice a week, and a dairyman delivered vast supplies of milk, cream, butter, and eggs. Eleanor and the children often scrambled into Captain Calder's "Chug-Chug" for the frequently choppy trip to Eastport for fruit, vegetables, and the mail and newspapers they eagerly anticipated. Eastport, although not a large town, provided the summer residents with many of the items not readily available on the island. The Roosevelts grew to be comfortably familiar with Eastport as their link to home and the outside world.

At Franklin and Eleanor's cottage, the resident staff and island services handled housekeeping chores. A laundry wagon collected towels and bedding weekly, and the caretaker, Anna McGowan, did the rest of the personal wash. She hung the laundry on clotheslines inside a latticed fence that concealed it from outside eyes. Linnea Calder, a longtime employee and commentator on the Roosevelt scene, reported that, for modesty's sake, Eleanor's undergarments were dried inside a pillow case.[9] Propriety and discretion were constantly and vigorously pursued.

Eleanor organized all the events at the crowded, busy cottage. She arranged for the almost daily picnics, sending servants ahead to spread the blankets and distribute the wicker baskets of hot and cold food. Eleanor firmly but kindly supervised the staff of both live-in and day servants, making sure that the Irish Catholic serving girls could chug across the bay to attend Sunday Mass in Eastport.

When there were no formal activities in the evenings, Eleanor customarily read aloud in the living room. The strenuous daily outings, the usually large dinner, and the lazy ambiance provided by a birch log fire and the flickering kerosene lamps would often put several of those assembled to sleep. This apparently did not bother Eleanor at all, and may indeed have amused her. She believed it to be part of her responsibility as hostess to relax her guests after the day's more vigorous pursuits.

But the varied activities did not satisfy the children's longing for Franklin. Jimmy recalled that "Campobello was [Franklin's] second home and he inundated us with fun . . . . Sometimes we felt we didn't have him at all, but when we did . . . life was as lively and exciting as any kid could want it to be."[10] Franklin was the acknowledged leader of all the robust, adventurous activities on Campobello, and the children loved him for it. They especially liked his "hare and hound chases" on the slippery trails. Eleanor, who was never captivated by these hikes, was less than certain that every guest enjoyed these particular adventures. But she, as well as the children and the guests, looked forward to the return of the energetic, enthusiastic Franklin.

Franklin, too, was eager to return to Campobello, although he did not look forward to the long overland journey to Eastport, with an overnight stay in Boston and three changes of trains. But it would take him back to his beloved island, his family, and his friends. Exhausted by the frustrations of Washington and the tedium of New York, Franklin gratefully accepted an offer from Van Lear Black to join him aboard his 140-foot steam yacht *Sabalo* to cruise the Maine coast and be delivered to Campobello.

The entourage left on Friday, August 5, for what Franklin hoped would be a restful and uneventful trip. But the seas would not cooperate, and rough weather and darkened skies persisted. The *Sabalo's* captain was based in Maryland and was unfamiliar with New England waters and tides. He gladly turned the wheel over to Franklin, who piloted the boat for many hours, spinning yarns and calming his shipmates' concerns. He had, after all, safely steered warships through these waters.

Late on Sunday, August 7, Eleanor and the children enthusiastically greeted the *Sabalo* as it arrived in Welshpool. Franklin embraced each one in turn and promised them fishing and camping trips in the days ahead. After a tour of the lavishly appointed ship, the children were dispatched back to the cottage while Franklin and Eleanor remained on board for an elegant dinner served by uniformed, white-gloved stewards.

After dinner, as if by design, a horn signaled the start of an event unique to local custom. Franklin, who had observed such occurrences in the years of his youth, eagerly led the party out to watch the islanders seine their herring catch by torchlight. In a dramatic panorama, they watched the red-shirted island fishermen haul giant nets filled to overflowing with silvery herring glistening in the light of flares. Eleanor recalled the scene as one that was "almost biblical." She conjured a view of the apostles drawing their nets and filling their boats.

The next morning, Franklin and his guests arose early to go fishing aboard the *Sabalo's* tender. Ever the good host, he baited their hooks, crossing frequently fore and aft along a three-inch-wide varnished plank. Perspiring freely from the frantic activity and the heat of the engine, Franklin slipped and fell overboard into the icy waters of the Bay of Fundy. "I'd never felt anything as cold as that water," he remembered. "I hardly went under, hardly wet my head, because I still had hold of the motor-tender, but the water was so cold it seemed paralyzing. This must have been the icy shock in comparison to the heat of the August sun and the tender's engine."[11]

That evening, Franklin felt tired and aching, but he thought it only a touch of lumbago. Black and his entourage were also wearied by their host's energetic and hectic pace. Pleading the press of urgent business in New York, they said their good-byes and the *Sabalo* steamed south. With Black's departure, Franklin was finally at his family's disposal.

The next morning, he took Eleanor, Jimmy, and Elliott for a sail on the *Vireo*. As they cruised among the islands at the entrance to Cobscook Bay, they spotted a forest fire on one of the smaller islands. Franklin brought the boat in as close as he could to the beach, and they splashed ashore. Armed with boughs stripped from evergreen trees, the four Roosevelts spent a frantic hour beating out the flames and embers until they were satisfied that the fire was extinguished. Weary and covered with ash and soot, they reboarded the *Vireo* to sail back to the wooden slip at the foot of the sloping path that led to the big red cottage.

Oddly enough, Franklin still felt the need for more exercise. He challenged Jimmy and Elliott to run with him two miles to Lake Severn, a favorite freshwater pond. A horse-driven wagon and servant were dispatched to ferry them home. After a customarily raucous swim filled with horseplay, the trio scurried across a narrow spit of land to plunge into the bracing waters of the Bay of Fundy, one of Franklin's regular and eagerly anticipated routines.

"I didn't feel the usual reaction," he remembered, "the glow I'd expected." The boys wanted to race back to the cottage, and Franklin joined them. "Walking and running couldn't overcome the chill. When I reached the house, the mail was in, with several newspapers I hadn't seen. I sat reading for a while, too tired to even dress. I'd never felt quite that way before."[12]

Eleanor was only mildly concerned with Franklin's condition. She suggested that he go upstairs to bed and have his dinner served on a tray. Whatever malady he had, she didn't want to risk the chance that the children might get it. But Franklin was not hungry, and he had difficulty sleeping. He continued to shiver all night under the weight of several warm blankets.

When he arose the next morning, Franklin's left leg seemed to buckle under his weight. He managed to drag himself to the bathroom and shave, but he had pains in his back and a throbbing headache. Obviously, something was seriously wrong. Eleanor took his temperature and recorded a 102-degree fever. The planned camping trip was dispatched without its leader. The children would be gone for three days, and Eleanor hoped that Franklin would be recovered by the time they returned.

Franklin was by now very concerned. He later wrote, "I tried to persuade myself that the trouble with my leg was muscular, that it would disappear as I used it. But presently it refused to work, and then the other."[13]

Eleanor became worried and sent to Lubec for Dr. Bennet. The country doctor was baffled by Franklin's condition. He had tended to the basic medical needs of the wealthy summer people for years, but was often intimidated by them. With little experience in diagnosing illnesses that he was less than familiar with, Dr. Bennet determined that Franklin had, most probably, a very bad cold.

By the following morning, Franklin was unable to stand if Eleanor and Louis did not hold him upright. Something needed to be done, and done quickly. Louis accompanied Dr. Bennet back to Lubec and used the doctor's telephone to call summer resorts up and down the Maine coast in search of knowledgeable physicians. He located Dr. W. W. Keen, a well-known Philadelphia surgeon who had once removed President Grover Cleveland's cancerous tumor. The eighty-four-year-old Keen agreed to the drive up the coast from Bar Harbor only when he heard the identity of the patient.

Howe sat rubbing Franklin's feet while waiting for Dr. Keen to arrive. By this time, Franklin's usually positive spirits were flagging.

He kept repeating to his friend over and over, "I don't know what's the matter with me, Louis, I just don't know."[14]

Dr. Keen arrived early Sunday morning. After a thorough examination, he pronounced that Franklin's condition was caused by a blood clot from a sudden congestion that had settled in his lower spinal cord. The clot, Dr. Keen said, had temporarily interfered with his power to move, though it had not affected his power to feel. Dr. Keen recommended vigorous massage, and Eleanor immediately wired to New York for a professional masseuse. Dr. Keen thought that it would be an extended process, but he believed that some absorption of the clot had already begun.

When the children returned from their camping trip, they were instructed not to enter Franklin's room. Hartley Howe remembers that his father totally ignored him. All of Louis's and Eleanor's attention was on Franklin. Taking turns, they rubbed his inert body for hours on end, despite the constant pain it caused. Franklin's condition continued to worsen. He now had no movement below the waist, and Dr. Bennet had to show Eleanor how to administer an enema and insert a catheter. For Eleanor, after years of no intimacy with her husband, the task was most formidable. Despite the pervasive fear of infection, she performed the procedures remarkably successfully over a period of three weeks. A friend later called this a "service of love." Eleanor, uncharacteristically, took considerable pride in her often complimented nursing skills.[15]

Eleanor slept on the window seat each night and ministered to Franklin's every need. His fever soared, and he had periodic episodes of delirium. Eleanor feared that he might be losing his mind. Years later, Franklin told Frances Perkins, his long-time aide and Secretary of Labor, that he had been "in utter despair, fearing that God had abandoned me."[16]

On Thursday, a letter arrived from Dr. Keen. He had reconsidered his blood clot theory and now believed it was more likely a lesion of the spinal cord. This condition was, he thought, more serious than the clot and promised a slower rate of recovery. He also enclosed a bill for $600 for his services, a rather steep rate for the time.

Eleanor wrote to Franklin's half-brother Rosy to alert the Roosevelt family to her husband's condition. Louis sent a detailed letter to Franklin's uncle, Frederick Delano, asking him to use his influence and wide circle of contacts to relay the symptoms to medical specialists. Uncle Fred suggested that Dr. Keen, although a fine surgeon, might not necessarily be the most able of diagnosticians. He quickly made contact with Dr. Samuel Levine, a young member of the Harvard Infantile Paralysis Commission and an attending physician at Boston's Beth Israel Hospital. From Uncle Fred's description of the symptoms, Dr. Levine believed that Franklin had poliomyelitis, then popularly called infantile paralysis. He urgently recommended that the family locate a physician in Bangor, the only city of any size close to Campobello, to perform a lumbar puncture at once to relieve pressure on Franklin's spine. The fairly straightforward procedure was not done, for reasons unknown, and Dr. Levine always maintained that not performing it had tragic results. Richard Thayer Goldberg, in agreement with Dr. Levine's conclusion, wrote that if the lumbar puncture had been performed in a timely manner, "the course of the disease might have been altered and the final outcome might have been less disabling." [17]

Uncle Fred was now convinced that Dr. Robert W. Lovett, who chaired the Harvard Infantile Paralysis Commission and was the leading American authority on infantile paralysis, was urgently needed to make the final diagnosis. Uncle Fred was so persuaded by Dr. Levine's preliminary findings that he prevailed upon a somewhat reluctant Dr. Keen to track down the vacationing Dr. Lovett. His search was successful, and Dr. Lovett agreed to cut short his holiday in Newport and proceed at once to Campobello to examine Franklin.

On August 25, two weeks after Franklin had dragged himself to the bathroom, Drs. Lovett, Keen, and Bennet arrived for their examination. Franklin now had some paralysis in his face, his hands were not functioning properly, and his leg and hip muscles, although not destroyed, were extremely weak.

After their examination, the physicians retired to Anna's bedroom, and there Dr. Lovett confirmed his diagnosis to his colleagues:

Franklin definitely had infantile paralysis. Anna, who was hiding in her closet, was the first family member to learn the awful news. When Dr. Lovett told Eleanor, she was crushed. Like most, both she and Franklin had for some years been terrified by the threat of polio, and she remembered the scare of 1916. She now had to be satisfied that the children were in no danger. In almost numbing irony, Eleanor was instructed to stop all massage treatments immediately. The massages had not only prolonged the pain, but also might have damaged the muscles. That great labor of love Eleanor and Louis had performed on Franklin may have slowed any recovery, and had needlessly caused Franklin intolerable pain. Eleanor and Louis were both stunned and disheartened, but there was little they could do but watch and wait.

Dr. Lovett said that Franklin might recover, perhaps completely, but there was no way to be sure. Franklin took the news with an outward calm. But Eleanor later recalled that the expression on his face at that moment was one that she would see only once again, on the fateful Sunday in 1941 when the Japanese attacked Pearl Harbor. Franklin's outward reaction to momentous events, personal or otherwise, was always one of apparent calm. No real inner emotion was ever allowed to show.

The watchful waiting period was almost unbearable for Franklin. He became more anxious as he lay virtually motionless in his bed. For a man of such prodigious energy and vigor to be so confined was unthinkable. Eleanor and Louis became even more concerned with Franklin's continually deteriorating muscular function and his increasing anxiety.

Dr. Bennet sent a night letter to Dr. Lovett asking for direction. Franklin, although he understood that massage was of no useful value, yearned to have somebody do something. At least with massage, however painful, there was some "hands on" treatment. He wanted some kind of action.

Another problem was yet to be faced, a huge one. Sara was due to arrive in New York City from Europe. Franklin and Eleanor had always met her on her return from such trips, and Eleanor needed a reliable family member to meet her and gently break the news of Franklin's illness. She wrote to Rosy, "Do you think you can meet Mama when she lands? She has asked us to cable just before she sails and I have decided to say nothing. No letter can reach her now & it would simply mean worry all the way home & she will have enough once she gets here but at least then she can do things. I will write her a letter to quarantine, saying he is ill but leave explaining to you or if you can't meet her, to Uncle Fred or whoever does meet her . . . ."[18]

Rosy and Uncle Fred met Sara at the dock and handed her Eleanor's carefully worded letter:

> Dear Mama,
>
> Franklin has been quite ill and so can't get down to meet you . . . to his great regret, but Uncle Fred and Aunt Kassie [Sara's brother and sister] both write they will so it will not be a lonely homecoming. We are all so happy to have you home again, dear, you don't know what it means to feel you near again.
>
> The children are all very well and I wish you could have seen John's face shine when he heard us say you would be home soon.
>
> . . . we are having such lovely weather, the island is really at its loveliest.
>
> Franklin sends all his love and we are both so sorry we cannot meet you.
>
> Ever devotedly,
> Eleanor[19]

"It was a shock to hear the bad news, . . . but I am thankful I did not hear before I sailed," Sara wrote to her sister Dora. Sara reached Campobello late on September 1 after the two-day, three-train journey from New York to Eastport. Franklin dutifully put on his serene face in "a major act of cheery nonchalance for her benefit."[20] Sara seemed determined to be hopeful. Eleanor marveled at her mother-in-law's composure but assumed that she shed many tears in private. The Delano calm, both Sara's and Franklin's, was so powerful that there was never any display of emotion.

Franklin sent messages to the state Democratic Party and to his two business offices in New York. He allowed that he was "under the weather." Both he and Louis were determined to keep the extent of his illness under wraps, at least for the present. Louis signed all letters, because Franklin's thumbs were now paralyzed. Ever the master of public relations, Louis fended off inquiries from the press about the cause of Franklin's "indisposition." Nothing contained a hint that it was polio.

Louis traveled to New York to meet his daughter, Mary, who was arriving from a trip to Europe. Warmly welcoming her, he gave no hint of Franklin's condition. While in New York, he shopped for a watch that Eleanor wished to give to Captain Calder for his special service to the Roosevelts during Franklin's illness.

Louis wrote to Franklin, "I love the way Eleanor telegraphed to go into Tiffany's to buy a watch for Calder without mentioning whether it was to be a $1,200 Jorgenson or a Waterbury Radiolite; also to have it inscribed without mentioning what to inscribe on it. Lord knows, I have acted as your alter ego in many weird commissions, but I most positively and firmly refuse to risk my judgement on neckties, watches or pajamas."[21] Louis scouted out watches at Tiffany & Co. and arranged to have Eleanor make her choice by telegram.

The progressive atrophy in his legs alarmed both Franklin and Dr. Bennet. Dr. Lovett assured them that a warm bath a day was the only permitted activity for the patient. At all other times, he was to remain, as best he was able, without motion. Franklin was sadly tired of his bed-ridden isolation, and he longed to get back to New York City, where he could, at the least, resume his business affairs if not his political career.

Louis returned to the island to stage-manage Franklin's departure from Campobello and journey to New York. It was no simple undertaking. Dr. Lovett had provided a certificate that attested that Franklin's condition was of no harm to the public. This calmed Dr.

Bennet's concerns about any actions by public health authorities on the U.S. mainland. Then, on September 13, Captain Calder supervised Franklin's departure from his bedroom to a waiting boat.

Five sturdy islanders, all probably well known to Franklin, gingerly carried him down the long winding cottage stairs and out the door on a homemade stretcher of canvas and native pine. As he was transported down over the broad verandah past his cherished views of Friar's Bay, Franklin smiled at his frightened children. They had never before seen their robust father as a helpless invalid being taken by stretcher to some unimaginable other place. With a broad Rooseveltian grin, Franklin assured the younger boys, "Don't worry, chicks, I will be all right."[22] And then they tearfully watched their father and his island bearers carefully descend the long sloping path that led to the family dock.

Franklin was placed on board Calder's dory. Accompanied by Eleanor, Louis, and Edna Rockey, a nurse from New York, they motored across rough seas to Eastport. Although the boat's rocking motion must have been painful, Franklin never complained. Perhaps he took some pleasure in being once more, however briefly, at sea.

They arrived at Eastport as the tide was going out and made the delicate move of lifting Franklin from the dory and carrying him up the wet and slippery steps. A wrong step could have resulted in drowning. Louis had deliberately directed waiting reporters to another landing place, and Calder's men now hurried to place Franklin on a flatbed baggage truck. Franklin endured a short and bumpy ride over cobblestone streets to the depot where the train awaited with a private car that Uncle Fred had dispatched to Eastport.

The flatbed reached the depot, and Louis noticed that the entrance to the railway car was too steep and too narrow for the stretcher. By knocking out the window frame of the sleeping compartment, Calder's men were able to lift Franklin through the window and onto his berth.

The train started just as the reporters and spectators arrived. Franklin, with a cigarette in his mouth and his dog on his lap, was able to smile, wave, and shout greetings to the gathering as the train pulled out of the depot. Louis's masterful plan had worked to perfection. Franklin was on his way, and the press had not gained any real knowledge of his true condition.

By September 16, Franklin was ready to have his condition announced to the press. Louis released a carefully worded message, and the front page of the *New York Times* carried the news of Franklin's polio. Now everyone knew what had happened, but had no idea of what lay ahead.

Eleanor gave the inscribed watch to Captain Calder as the train prepared to leave Eastport. The thoughtfulness of the Roosevelts was much appreciated. Calder wrote to Eleanor thanking her for the watch "which I can accept from you and Mr. Roosevelt, as the spirit in which it is given is so different, also for the real good friendly note which accompanied the same. Who could dare be disloyal to a friend like you? I only hope that Anna can be just like you as she grows older."[23]

This ordeal by fire forged a new and more lasting bond between Eleanor and Franklin. They would come to realize a deepened level of dependence upon one another. Franklin now needed her as he had never needed anyone. Polio cemented their bond just as it underscored their need for strength and determination. They would learn how to navigate the turbulent waters ahead and reset their personal and professional goals. Eleanor's devoted nursing and judgment were everlasting proof to them of both her skills and her resolve. Franklin refused to abandon his hopes of a meaningful recovery. They were about to embark on the reinforced partnership that was to serve them and the country extraordinarily well for the next quarter-century.

As for Louis Howe, the faithful friend, colleague, and companion, a momentous and even more challenging line had been drawn in the sand. Louis never lost his belief that Franklin could achieve the Presidency. He now "married himself irrevocably to his crippled friend's fortunes . . . could not desert his only close friend[s] after they plumbed the depths of tragedy together at Campobello."[24]

8

Finding Strength

Following his return to New York from Campobello, Franklin spent the first six weeks at Presbyterian Hospital. Dr. George Draper, an associate of Dr. Lovett, took charge. He was no stranger to Franklin: they had been at Harvard at the same time. There was little improvement during the period of Franklin's hospitalization. He continued to lose function below the waist, but the pain had diminished. His spirits continued to be high, for the most part, and all the Roosevelts maintained a general attitude of hopefulness.

After six weeks of hospitalization, Franklin returned to his New York City home but shortly suffered an unexplained relapse. He ran a high fever, briefly experienced eye pain and vision problems, and suffered extreme contraction in the knee muscles of one leg. Plaster casts halted the contractions, the eye concerns passed, and his fever broke as mysteriously as it had appeared.

In November, Dr. Draper wrote to Dr. Bennet in Lubec:

> Let me ask your forgiveness for having delayed so long in sending you any word about Franklin Roosevelt. He has done . . . well ever since his arrival, although his progress has been slow. There is still . . . tenderness in the muscles and, of course, practically no return to power in

any of the affected ones, but his general condition is very much better and he has come out of that state of nervous collapse in which all of these cases find themselves for some little time after the acute attack. He is now at home and able to get about in a wheel chair into which he is partially lifted and partially swings himself by means of a strap and ring hung from the ceiling. He is cheerful and hopeful and his general morale is high.

As soon as we can, we propose to get him on crutches with braces to make his legs rigid.

I am ordering sent to you one of the little books on poliomyelitis that I spoke to you about and likewise enclosing two dollars which you so kindly provided for tipping the ambulance men . . . .[1]

Initially, there had been extreme concern that Franklin's back muscles might be affected. This worry was soon put to rest. He maintained strength in his upper torso and enhanced his partial control of movement by learning to raise and even lift himself with rings and bars. Although bed- or chair-borne, he enthusiastically arm wrestled, threw playful punches, and generally demonstrated his strength and upper body control. As time passed and his limbs remained lifeless, Franklin took immense pride in the strong upper body muscular functions he still retained.

Soon Franklin was able to raise himself from the bed and lower himself into a chair. He later learned to crawl, bump himself up and down stairs, and, eventually, take some toddling, wheeling steps while on the arm of a strong aide. Only in water was Franklin able to move freely without any help. The following summer, he tried swimming in the small pond at Hyde Park and in neighbor Vincent Astor's pool. He recalled the icy waters of the Bay of Fundy: "Water got me into this fix, water will get me out again!"[2]

Franklin and Eleanor were facing, perhaps, a lifetime of his disability and the attendant personal adjustments. Added to their burden was the immense apathy and ignorance of the general public toward similar illnesses and disabilities. In the 1920s, public attitudes toward paralytic patients and their treatment were remarkably archaic and unsympathetic. Many sufferers died from infection or other complications, while others developed side effects such as pneumonia or kidney problems. Therapy was largely unknown or ineffective, there were no known drugs or medicines to relieve suffering, and mortality rates were high. Moreover, institutions housing the afflicted were needlessly grim and depressing. Names of facilities were indicative of the public's general feelings about the disabled: the House of St. Giles for the Crippled and the New York Society for the Relief of the Ruptured and Crippled, for example.

Treatment was not only non-rehabilitative, it was often debilitating. Few orthopedic devices existed, wheelchairs were bulky and heavy, and no buildings or vehicles had handicapped entrances or ramps. Clearly, any person who survived a severe case of paralytic polio in the 1920s faced a depressing and uncertain future. This was true for those who wished for a rewarding and useful life in general, to say nothing of a career in politics. No severely paralyzed person had ever been successful in American national political life. Prevailing attitudes discouraged even the attempt.[3]

The first winter after the polio attack was, in Eleanor's words, "the most trying . . . of my entire life."[4] Of course, hopes for Franklin's eventual recovery and rehabilitation were paramount in everyone's minds, but the means to those ends and the realities of living through these trials were difficult, if not chaotic. There was a desperate struggle for Franklin's body, mind, and soul, and it was all being played out in the name of love and respect.

Eleanor's low tolerance of illness was severely tested. She wanted to do all she could to encourage Franklin and help him maintain his intense struggle to regain function and to thrive. Instinctively, Eleanor knew that without goals that were ostensibly achievable, Franklin would barely survive, if at all. In addition, she now desperately wanted a life of her own and had taken steps to break out of the fixed pattern of subordinated wife and mother. Nonetheless, she never lost her tenacious drive to help Franklin realize his dreams.

Eleanor had unqualified help from Louis Howe. Eleanor had asked him, "Do you really believe that Franklin still has a political future?" Howe replied: "I believe that someday Franklin will be President."[5] She had only Louis's unquestioned determination as a basis to accept this goal as realistic. To reinforce their effort and commitment, Louis moved into the Roosevelt home, leaving his family in Poughkeepsie and joining them only on weekends. Jimmy Roosevelt later called this decision tantamount to family desertion, but for Louis there was no other choice. Franklin must be President, and Louis's unswerving mission was to help get him there.

The Roosevelt children were not pleased with their new housemate. They were accustomed to having Louis around and had always been courteous, but living with him on a full-time basis was another matter. Louis was rumpled and gnome-like, chain-smoked Sweet Caporal cigarettes, and had a persistent, hacking cough. Eleanor decided to give him Anna's room and the unhappy fifteen-year-old was forced to move to a smaller room and share a bath with her younger brothers. Predictably, Anna turned to her grandmother for support.

Sara had always sided with, fussed over, and spoiled her grandchildren. They, in turn, happily turned to her for the kind of comfort and attention that Eleanor found difficult to give. What's more, Sara had never been fond of Louis and his habits. She was never able to warm to this little man who gave himself so completely to her beloved son. Although she eventually came to recognize Louis's remarkable contributions to Franklin's success, Sara never graciously accepted him into the households in New York City or Hyde Park.

Sara was never enthusiastic about Franklin's legal or business careers and, at this point in time, didn't consider that he would be able to continue a political life. She had accepted his professional activities with reservations while he was able to pursue them actively. But now, Franklin was severely afflicted with a debilitating illness that, both by accepted standards and by her reckoning, was more than enough to inhibit an active, self-supporting life. Her solution was obvious. He would gracefully retire to Hyde Park, where he would enjoy the quiet life of a country squire. His father had done just that, and Sara thought this solution both appropriate and eminently appealing. If he would allow her, Sara wanted to bring her boy home.

Franklin continued his rehabilitation in New York City. During the first several months of 1922, the leg casts were removed. He was fitted with heavy braces that enabled him to stand erect when they were locked at the knee and he was lifted to a standing position. Using crutches, he began learning to ambulate (it could hardly be called walking) by a series of pivoting actions. Although his knees were locked and he had no feeling or flexing ability in his toes or feet, Franklin was able to move, although he had neither sense that his lower body was in motion nor any precise idea of his distance from the floor. However, the toddling gave him a sense of accomplishment and a feeling that he was finally regaining some semblance of forward motion.

During these months, tensions and emotions ran high in the Roosevelt household. Franklin concluded that his rehabilitation expenses were too great and that he wished Eleanor to assume a more active nursing role. Eleanor would have none of it, and the professional nurse-therapist was retained.

Eleanor's emotions were constantly on a short tether as she was caught between Franklin's needs and her own. One afternoon, while reading to the younger boys, she suddenly burst into tears and fled from the room. The long-suppressed torrent of feelings came pouring forth as she sobbed uncontrollably. Louis tried without success to soothe her, and it took several hours before Eleanor was able to compose herself. She later wrote about this unusual loss of self-control, acknowledging that "it was the one and only time I ever remember in my entire life going to pieces in this particular manner."[6]

Louis's recognition of Eleanor's frustration and pain was a clear indication of their growing friendship. He was the only adult to offer comfort. They had learned to lean on each other for support and to reinforce the resolve that was necessary to endure the trying days and months that lay ahead.

The children learned to cope in their own way. Jimmy went off to Groton, while Anna and the other boys lived at home and attended private schools. They visited with Franklin daily and were exposed to his shrunken legs and his infirmity. The boys continued to have physical contact with their father, who enthusiastically wrestled with the older boys on the floor, and welcomed the younger ones into his bed.

Living with their crippled father in a tension-filled home was not easy for any of the Roosevelt children, but for Anna it was particularly challenging. Anna had not easily made the adjustment to a new school in New York. She had trouble making friends, and she had lost her room and private sanctum to Louis Howe. Moreover, Anna was unable to find much warmth and understanding from a crippled father and a distracted and distant mother. Anna's growing defiance of Eleanor and resistance to the socially-required customs of the time added to the turmoil.

Anna particularly recoiled at being forced to attend dances and the traditional "coming-out" events that were taking place that spring at Newport. She hated these formal and constricted relics of the Victorian Age but she dutifully participated, however reluctantly. Adding to Anna's unhappiness, Susie Parish told her of her father's affair with Lucy Mercer. The stunning news hardly enhanced the teenager's enthusiasm for the events at Newport, but it did change her feelings toward Eleanor. This marked the start of a new closeness between mother and daughter.

In May, Franklin went "home" to Springwood. Eleanor and the children remained in New York City until the end of the school year before joining him in Hyde Park. A summer in Campobello may have seemed appealing, but Eleanor dismissed any notion of taking her family that far away for several months, leaving Franklin alone during this critical period of his rehabilitation. Sara took Anna and Jimmy to Europe, and Franklin and Eleanor and the younger boys made Springwood their own for the remainder of the summer.

In the autumn, Eleanor continued to participate in political meetings and discussion groups. She met Molly Dewson, Nancy Cook, and Marion Dickerman, friends with whom she quickly developed lasting relationships. Dewson was a lifelong friend and political ally to Franklin as well as Eleanor, and Cook and Dickerman became close friends and, eventually, Eleanor's associates and housemates.

Like Esther Lape and Elizabeth Read, Nancy Cook and Marion Dickerman were highly motivated women active in support of women's and children's rights and deeply involved in the political process. And like Lape and Read, Cook and Dickerman were emotionally committed to each other. They were first uncharitably referred to by Franklin as Eleanor's "she-male" friends, but they were central to Eleanor's personal growth and political development. Cook and Dickerman grew to be close to Franklin when he realized that they had much to offer him as well as Eleanor.

Franklin exhaustively searched for polio "cures" and relief in every corner. Some of these so-called remedies bordered on the bizarre and required a complete suspension of reality. All were uniformly useless. His thirst for solutions other than the widely accepted therapies and exercises of Drs. Lovett and Draper frustrated both Eleanor and Louis, no less the physicians themselves. Consequently, Lovett resigned Franklin's care in 1924 and told him that he would be much better off if he listened to Eleanor and Louis rather than the "quacks." Franklin's reaction was to declare himself his own doctor.

Missing the satisfaction of useful activity, Franklin made an abortive attempt to return to his law practice. His limited ability to get out of an automobile, climb steps, and cross marble floors without drawing attention proved too frustrating and extraordinarily embarrassing. Franklin seemed resigned to a semi-indolent existence as he searched for a cure and for some meaning to his life.

He had no lack of company for the more idle of his pursuits. Franklin purchased an aged houseboat he renamed *Sirocco* and spent a great deal of time sailing in southern waters with a coterie of amiable companions that included Missy LeHand, his personal secretary, and his old chum Livy Davis. Eleanor had little patience with this sort of idleness and self-indulgence. She was far more interested in pursuing her new life and, in her fashion, tending to her family. But the aimlessness afloat, for a while, helped bolster Franklin's spirits and it served as some kind of prelude to a more lasting reaffirmation of his personal commitment.

Politics proved to be the elixir for both Roosevelts. Political involvement could not cure Franklin's polio nor replace Eleanor's forty years of unfulfillment. But it could—and did—help provide a new meaning and direction to their lives.

In 1924, Governor Al Smith asked Franklin to head a committee supporting Smith's nomination as President of the United States. Smith was Roman Catholic, a product of the city, and an anti-Prohibition "Wet." As head of a committee for Smith, Franklin supplied his good name to the campaign as well as his Protestantism and the upstate rural support that Smith desperately needed. The two former political adversaries formed a loose alliance that lasted for six years and transformed the political face of New York State. Eleanor took an active role in the Women's Division of the Democratic Party. She endorsed Smith's candidacy but was even more interested in supporting progressive programs of reform of child labor laws, a livable minimum wage, and an eight-hour work day.

Smith asked Franklin to place his name in nomination for the Presidency at the Democratic National Convention. Franklin laboriously "walked" across the stage to the rostrum on Jimmy's strong arm as the crowd cheered. His speech clearly made him the star of the convention as he dubbed Smith the "Happy Warrior." The speech did not win Smith the nomination, but it did earn Franklin the respect and admiration of both the attendees and those who listened to the first political convention to be broadcast on national radio.

People liked what he said, they were thrilled by his courage, and they reveled in his obvious charm. The *New York Herald Tribune* said he "has easily been the foremost figure on floor or platform." Tom Prendergast, later Harry S Truman's champion and long-time Kansas City political boss, told a friend, "Had Mr. Roosevelt . . . been physically able to withstand the campaign, he would have been named by acclamation . . . he has the most magnetic personality of any individual I have ever met . . . ."[7] For Franklin, it was truly a defining moment. A lost national political career had been reborn.

Eleanor still had to be convinced that Franklin was fully back in the quest, especially for the Presidency. She wanted him to have his political day and told Frances Perkins, later Franklin's and the country's first woman cabinet member, "I do hope that he'll keep in political life. I want him to keep himself interested in politics. This is what he cares for more than anything else. I don't want him forgotten. I want him to have a voice . . . it's good for him."[8]

With this regained impetus, Louis began an active campaign to keep Franklin's name in the political spotlight. For the next several years, Eleanor became his "point person," appearing at various political gatherings and events, keeping the Roosevelt name active, and reporting back to the candidate-to-be and his lieutenant. Louis organized letter-writing campaigns and produced news-releases that steadily increased in tempo and volume through the middle years of the 1920s.

Eleanor planned strategy for the state Democratic Party and was appointed finance chair of the Women's Division of the national party. She vigorously stumped the state for Smith in his successful reelection campaign for governor as he defeated her cousin Theodore Roosevelt, Jr. She so maligned young Ted that the breach between the two branches of the family became unbridgeable.

Along with her political activities, Eleanor's personal life had prospered. With Nancy Cook and Marion Dickerman, she undertook the kind of adventure seldom attempted by "unescorted" women in 1925. They took an extensive automobile trip through the Adirondacks into Quebec, down through New Hampshire's White Mountains, across to the Maine coast, and then on to Campobello. It would be Eleanor's first trip to her island home since 1921 and Franklin's polio. The entourage consisted of the three women and Franklin, Jr., John, and George Draper, the son of Franklin's physician. Significantly, there were no adult men on the trip.

They set out in a seven-passenger Buick, planning to camp outdoors each night. When they could find no available public camping sites, Eleanor, the most persuasive in the group, asked farmers for permission to pitch tents in their fields. In one instance, a farmer asked where their husbands were. Eleanor replied, "Mine is not with me and the others don't have husbands." The farmer replied, "I don't want women of that kind."[9] This was a discouraging but not an unusual point of view for the 1920s.

The trip proved to be an adventure. They visited Montreal and then turned south into New Hampshire, where they traveled up Mount Washington on the cog railway. After crossing another mountain on burros, Eleanor reported it all to be "great fun."[10] The little group then traveled across Maine to the pretty coastal town of Castine, a village whose eighteenth-century history had been marked by capture and recapture by French, British, and American forces. Here they stayed with Molly Dewson and Polly Porter—the first of many visits with her friends in Castine. Eleanor and the boys stayed in a guest cottage "down by the water."[11]

Their arrival in Campobello was described second-hand in a letter that Franklin sent to his half-brother Rosy: "All goes well. Eleanor and the rest of the caravan reached Campobello in safety, the only accidents being first, Franklin Jr. cutting his foot with the axe, instead of the tree; second, skidding off the road into the ditch and having to be pulled out; and third, upsetting a dray just as they approached Lubec and dumping the load of lumber and the small boy who was driving it—total cost of damages $10."[12]

The boys were on their own as they revisited Campobello's joys, this time without Franklin's leadership. Eleanor happily showed her friends the island that she had missed so much. They comfortably combined business with pleasure as they welcomed several visitors, including Molly Dewson; Rose Simkhovitch, a forceful settlement-house leader from New York's Greenwich Village; and Maud Swartz and Rose Schneiderman of the Women's Trade Union League. These women shared with Eleanor their considerable knowledge of trade unionism in general and the concerns of America's working women in particular. All were active and important participants in Franklin's successful campaigns for Governor of New York and President of the United States.

Eleanor shared Campobello and its memories with her friends.

She led them to her favorite picnic grounds, overlooks, and paths. The boys, unaccustomed to this much freedom, roamed all over the island, getting in and out of scrapes.

In the evening, when the boys had gone to bed, Eleanor read aloud by lantern light. She chose books by Henry Adams and Ray Stannard Baker. Baker's *The Countryman's Year* was especially compelling as she read, over and over, "Back of tranquillity lies always conquered unhappiness."[14] Eleanor thought that this particularly resonant phrase had been written with her in mind. She reported all of this in regular correspondence to Franklin, who replied that her letters made him homesick for Campobello.

While the women and boys made their camping trip and visit to Campobello, Franklin was in Hyde Park busily directing the construction of Val-Kill, a home and craft furniture factory for Eleanor, Nancy, and Marion. The three women had become so attached to the countryside and their picnics and outings that they were disappointed when Sara closed Springwood in the winters.

Two miles from the big house, Val-Kill was constructed of native fieldstone. Franklin provided his support, architectural and construction assistance, and, most important, the land on which to build. Val-Kill was built on a plot that Franklin personally owned abutting his mother's estate. He was delighted that he could provide assistance and that Eleanor and her friends would have a Hyde Park place of their own where they could come and go as they pleased. The cottage had a swimming pool, and Franklin was always a welcome guest. The Campobello cottage was Eleanor's, but it was distant and not easily accessible. Val-Kill became, in a sense, a second home of her own.

The stone cottage was occupied in 1926 and Eleanor began teaching two days a week at the private Todhunter School in New York City. Marion Dickerman, the school's headmistress, persuaded Eleanor that she would make a fine teacher. Eleanor learned to alternate her time between Val-Kill and New York City and to compartmentalize her life as well.

Franklin had by then become interested in a run-down rehabilitation facility in Warm Springs, Georgia. He believed that the mineral waters would be of therapeutic value to polio sufferers. Franklin gave the aging and mostly abandoned resort his attention, his energy, and a considerable amount of his own money, restoring and upgrading it in order to bring it to respectability. Although it is questionable whether the water therapy actually improved the physical condition of the guests, it did provide emotional support. Franklin delighted in directing the programs and activities and interacting personally with patients of varying ages and degrees of disability. He had learned the magic of giving to the less fortunate the invaluable gift of hope.

In the summer of 1928, while in Warm Springs, Franklin accepted an offer of his party's nomination for the governorship by telephone from Al Smith at the New York State Democratic Convention in Syracuse. Eleanor placed the call to Franklin and then handed the phone to Smith. She immediately left the convention in order to distance herself from Franklin's decision.

Louis Howe was clearly upset when Franklin accepted. Louis believed it still too early in his rehabilitation and political comeback. Eleanor wired Franklin, "Regret you had to accept but knew you felt it obligatory." Louis was less understanding. He wired, "Mess is no name for it. I have no advice to give." [15]

Franklin actively participated in the Democratic National Convention and campaigned vigorously for the governorship. With the confidence in Tammany in New York City and his natural constituency in the Hudson Valley, Franklin was able to turn most of his attention to the small towns and rural areas of upstate New York. He won the race by a narrow margin in the face of a national Republican sweep. Al Smith lost his run for the presidency largely on the backlash to his big-city persona and his Catholicism.

Eleanor did not campaign for Franklin, apparently by mutual decision, but worked hard for Smith. She was depressed by Smith's loss and was less than excited and gracious about Franklin's triumph. She undoubtedly feared that she would be forced to withdraw from her active and deeply satisfying public life. Eleanor made an offhand, ill-advised comment to a reporter inquiring about her pleasure in Franklin's election. Her candid but uncharitable reply was, "No, I am not excited by my husband's election. I don't care. What difference can it make to me?"[16]

Eleanor's activities to that date had spanned the spectrum of progressive causes, most of which had been cornerstones of Al Smith's administration. They included public playgrounds, school lunches, medical care in schools, visiting nurses for homes, improved sanitation, and, preeminently, setting enlightened minimum wages and maximum working hours for women and children. She worked to outlaw war and to further trade unionism and equal rights. Eleanor was now one of the best-known woman Democrats in the United States. She had written a boldly feminist article in *Redbook* entitled, "Women Must Learn to Play the Game as Men Do," and she had been editor of the *Women's Democratic News*. It was easy to see that being the First Lady of the State of New York held little appeal for the now-ardent activist.

Al Smith planned to influence, if not control, Franklin's administration by offering the governor-elect his two most trusted and influential aides, Belle Moskowitz and Robert Moses. But Franklin rejected Smith's offer and cast Moskowitz and Moses from his staff. He had already refused a pre-written inaugural speech and was fast perceived by the Smith-controlled state party organization as disloyal and intransigent. The result was Franklin's bitter and permanent break with Smith and the legacy of a life-long enmity with the power-seeking Moses.

Franklin's administration, however, was in most ways a continuation of Smith's progressive reforms. His agenda included plans for low-cost electricity, a humane minimum wage, and child-labor reform. These issues were much the same as those being promoted by Eleanor and her friends. Although Franklin was not fully successful in securing legislation for all of his proposed reforms, he managed to advance the concept of better living standards for large groups of the population, especially those living in rural and less industrialized areas.

Eleanor cared little for living in Albany and spent little time in the governor's mansion. When in residence, she occupied a small third-floor bedroom, and the obligatory hostess functions fell largely to Missy LeHand. The constant companionship of Louis Howe gave Franklin enough of the personal support he needed.

In 1930, with the Great Depression deepening, Franklin's progressive leadership earned him reelection by a landslide. The second administration was hardly distinguishable from the first, continuing a strong push for social reform. He now had the full support of leading women progressives who had been shepherded to his cause by Eleanor as she increasingly expanded her circle of influence.

Eleanor continued her Val-Kill/Manhattan/Albany commute. Anna married and started a family; Jimmy finished Harvard and began a business life; Elliott refused to attend college and struck out on his own; and Franklin, Jr., and John were at Groton. Eleanor could concentrate her time, efforts, and interests where she pleased.

Polio had disabled Franklin, but it had helped him find inner strength and resolve. Louis Howe later reflected, "There are times when I think that Franklin might never have been president if he had not been stricken. You see, he had a thousand interests. You couldn't pin him down. He rode, he swam, he played golf, tennis, he sailed, he collected stamps, he politicked, he did every damn thing under the sun a man could think of doing. Then suddenly he was flat on his back with nothing to do but think. He began to read, he began to think, he talked, he gathered people around him—his thoughts expanded, his horizons widened. He began to see the other fellow's point of view. He thought of others who were ill and afflicted and in want. He dwelt on many things that had not bothered him much before. Lying there, he grew bigger, day by day." [17]

Richard Thayer Goldberg thought that Franklin's struggle with polio gave him greater emotional strength and understanding. He believed that Franklin's compassion for the less fortunate was not so much the result of heritage and *noblesse oblige* as it was something he acquired by sharing the plight of fellow sufferers from all walks of life.

Eleanor also thought that "polio was a turning point." It was, she believed, almost a blessing in disguise. Polio "gave him strength and courage he had not had before. He had to think out the fundamentals of living and learn the greatest of all lessons—infinite patience and never-ending persistence."[18]

Rexford Tugwell thought these "fallow" years allowed Franklin to mature. He developed a new ease with public affairs and began to read meaningfully and study history.[19] Frances Perkins believed that he "underwent a spiritual transformation during the years of his illness."[20] Unquestionably polio's physical and emotional influence on Franklin was defining. He developed a new resolve, a doubling of effort, an intensifying of purpose. He learned the techniques necessary to help him achieve his lofty goals. To that point, it seemed to be working, and he was well along his reenergized path to the White House.

One technique was especially well-learned. The more Franklin appeared in public, the more staging was required to minimize the effects of his polio and to make it either unnoticed or acceptable. Staging required great physical effort and meant that Franklin and his supporters had to control settings, create illusions, and carefully orchestrate mutually respectful relationships with the working press. Franklin appeared to be a man of action and one of great energy. Yet he could not walk on his own and had to be lifted, carried, or wheeled into place before appearing in public. Photographs and newsreels never showed Franklin carried or wheeled. Although there are many photographs showing him standing or seated, there are only two extant of him in a wheelchair, and only four seconds of film of him "walking." Such control of the press could never have been achieved under the scrutiny of today's media, but, in the 1930s, the Roosevelt/Howe plan worked in spectacular fashion.

Was there an active and comprehensive plan to shield the public from the fact that Franklin suffered from polio and had severely limited mobility? Christopher Clausen writes that the "notion that the press concealed the facts of FDR's paralysis from the public is without foundation. *Time* on February 1, 1932, six months before [FDR's] nomination, ['reported'] swimming at Warm Springs several times for months each year and special exercises at Albany have made it possible for the Governor to walk 100 feet or so with braces or canes. When standing at public functions, he still clings precariously to a friend's arm.'"[21] *Time,* the most widely read national news medium at that time, reported in a later article that FDR had sent a nine-year-old girl to Warm Springs for treatment at his own expense. The magazine referred to the child as "also a cripple from infantile paralysis."[22]

News photos clearly show his leg braces, and a few show him using crutches. Clausen wonders whether the same public acceptance of a presidential candidate's infirmity would apply today. He thinks it not likely because of America's current obsessions with health and youthfulness. He suggests that "ashamed of this fact, we claim that our parents and grandparents must have been deceived. The thought that in some respects they have been more tolerant than we are is insufferable."[23]

———

Through the rest of the 1920s and early 1930s, the Roosevelts did not visit Campobello. Although they expressed disappointment, Campobello was not then a viable destination. In the later twenties, Franklin summered in Warm Springs, while Eleanor and the maturing children did everything but vacation as a family. The Campobello house was available for lease and was, in fact, rented for part of at least two summers. There was a real question in the minds of the family as to whether Campobello might have any place at all in their future.

Mostly on their minds was the quest for the Presidency. Franklin had expressed no interest in the Presidency during his second gubernatorial term. In early 1932, however, he and Louis decided that he would enter the North Dakota primary. He quickly put a large support organization in place under the leadership of Howe and James A. Farley, the chairman of the New York State Democratic party. While Louis organized publicity programs and ran the headquarters, Farley traveled through much of the country, lining up support. A personable and extremely able front man, Jim Farley ingratiated himself with local Democratic leaders and returned to New York with a pocketful of political markers. By convention time, Franklin was a leading candidate for the nomination.

Franklin assembled a team of speechwriters and policy consultants and a solid base of financial support. In gathering experts and specialists, Franklin made it abundantly clear that he was always in control. He listened, questioned, and sifted through the information the experts provided, but he alone made all final decisions. This pattern continued throughout his public career, and it was the source of Franklin's genius. He was not an innovator but a collector and disseminator of the carefully selected available wisdom of others. After appropriate consideration, he would act. Never afraid to make mistakes, he could recognize that he had made them and try something else. Unlike the incumbent President, Herbert Hoover, whose sphynx-like inaction in the first years of the Depression fanned the flames of despair, Franklin could provide hope—action, experimentation, and always hope.

The 1932 Democratic National Convention became deadlocked early in the proceedings. Al Smith again tried to win the presidential nomination, and William McAdoo, Woodrow Wilson's son-in-law, had strong support. Meanwhile, Howe lay wheezing with asthma on the floor of a sweltering Roosevelt headquarters room, masterminding moves and promoting deals. Farley worked the convention floor and negotiated with state delegations and influential leaders.

With the aid of the financier Joseph P. Kennedy, a deal was struck with the powerful newspaper publisher William Randolph Hearst. McAdoo, who headed the California delegation, delivered its large block of votes to the Roosevelt camp with the blessing of Hearst and the support of the Texas delegation, and it was over. Franklin had been nominated as the Democratic Party's candidate for the Presidency of the United States.

At that time, tradition held that candidates did not appear before the convention to accept their nominations. But Franklin was not a traditionalist. Along with Eleanor and members of the family, he made a tedious succession of flights from New York to Chicago. Franklin's acceptance speech featured the introduction of both the phrase and the concept of a "New Deal." A roaring convention greeted the physically challenged candidate with resounding support.

Franklin and Eleanor campaigned vigorously, much of the time on an extended national train tour while the enigmatic President Hoover barely ever appeared in public. The summer of 1932 saw the Veteran's Bonus March and the packing-crate encampments called "Hoovervilles" that appeared in large cities. The needless, ugly, forced eviction of the Bonus Marchers from their Washington encampment by U.S. Army troops under the command of General Douglas MacArthur and the widespread news photos of this highly-charged event crippled Hoover's campaign before it even began.

Taking advantage of the ineptitude of the barely visible Republican campaign, Franklin cranked up the Roosevelt charm and hinted at programs for relief. Mostly he just radiated a spirit of hope. That was more than enough. His victory over Hoover in November was overwhelming: he carried forty-two of the then forty-eight states.

Franklin publicly saluted Howe and Farley as the two people most responsible for his successful election. He may have privately thanked Eleanor for her substantial contributions, but members of the Brain(s) Trust, Franklin's policy advisors whose contributions were not publicly acknowledged, were quick to trivialize any importance attached to Eleanor's efforts. No matter to Eleanor; Howe and Farley spoke highly of her assistance.

Eleanor was characteristically calm on election eve. She described her pleasure in her husband's achievement, but without emotion or joy. Eleanor did not look forward to living again in Washington, residing in the White House and being the nation's First Lady.

In fact, Joseph Lash wrote that Eleanor was an admirer of Socialist Party candidate Norman Thomas. Some years afterwards, Eleanor's radio and television agent reluctantly confessed to her that he had voted for Thomas in 1932. To his amazement, Eleanor replied, "So would I, if I had not been married to Franklin." [24]

President Hoover conceded the election at 12:30 a.m., and Franklin and a reserved Eleanor left their hotel headquarters shortly afterward for their 65th Street home. Sara met them at their door and embraced an ebullient Franklin with, "This is the happiest day of my life!" [25]

9

My Old Friends of Campobello

When Franklin was inaugurated as the thirty-second President of the United States in March, 1933, he was fifty years old. The years had been marked by public service, personal loss, marital crisis, and the crushing effects of polio. Franklin devoted his first half-century to the search and the adventure. That goal now realized, he would be president the rest of his life.

In the first months of 1933, while the Roosevelts were adjusting to the almost staggering pressures of Franklin's public responsibilities, they were still learning to reshape their own personal relationship. Although they hardly had an intimate marriage, they clearly were partners in social progressivism. Franklin and Eleanor were dedicated to improving the desperate lot of the millions of Americans who had been physically and emotionally devastated in the Great Depression.

They continued to be mutually supportive and fiercely protective of each other, but they had little of the old emotional attachment. They increasingly spent less private time together and experienced little of the sharing endemic to successful marriages.

It was not surprising, then, that both Franklin and Eleanor sought others for the personal attention and companionship they were unable or unwilling to provide to each other. In Franklin's case, casual and uncomplicated friendships came naturally and easily. He selected with care from those who were attracted to him, and cultivated those friends and companions who suited his comfort and his schedules.

Louis Howe was the closest and perhaps the only real friend Franklin ever had. Louis gave Franklin far more than political guidance and tactical advice. He was ever the devoted friend and companion. He had the soul of a poet, an imaginative and inventive mind, and a marvelous sense of humor. A Renaissance man, Louis was an expert conversationalist, choral singer, watercolorist, amateur poet and playwright, and master of practical jokes and tricks. He could always be relied upon for whatever form or style of support, advice, or amusement the often mercurial Franklin required, especially during the long years of confinement and therapy.

Other than Eleanor, Louis was the only person who could speak his mind to Franklin. Louis was the only member of the extended Roosevelt family who maintained a lasting, unshakable relationship with Franklin that was solidly built on mutual trust and admiration. The enormous amount of time they spent working and relaxing over the many years they were together proved to be remarkably successful, highly gratifying, and certainly enduring.

Harry Hopkins served as Franklin's closest aide and confidant in the years of international turmoil and war that followed Howe's death in 1936. But Hopkins had neither the emotional nor the artistic spirit, the long personal history with Franklin, nor the dogged fraternal love of the devoted Louis.

Other longtime associates filled vital roles politically and administratively, but not many did so on a highly personal level and few could be called close friends. Franklin had always been flirtatious in spirit. He enjoyed the company of women, tried mightily to charm them, and encouraged their attention, particularly during the presidential years. But, with the Lucy Mercer affair excepted, his relationships with women during the earlier years of his marriage seemed to be innocent and proper. He was a playful, attractive, socially active young man in the years he served in the Navy Department in Washington, and a fair amount of partying was typical of his position and social set. Even after polio, Franklin was still attractive to women. He liked laughter, he enjoyed a good martini, and he loved to gossip. He sought these simple pleasures with both men and women, but there were few men, save Louis, whose company he really seemed to enjoy.

Marguerite "Missy" LeHand was a prominent participant in most aspects of Franklin's life from 1920 on. She became his personal secretary during his unsuccessful vice-presidential campaign and served in that role through the fallow years, during the governorship in Albany, and in the White House until she suffered a debilitating stroke in 1941. Missy's devotion to Franklin rivaled that of Louis Howe. She accompanied Franklin on trips, she attended him and acted as hostess during his long stays at Warm Springs, and she served him unfailingly in Albany and in the White House. Missy was a superb executive secretary who could handle a staggering range of assignments and responsibilities. Beyond that, she was a skilled hostess, mixed a good drink, and fitted in easily with the family on social occasions. Missy lived at the White House, as did Louis, other Roosevelt friends, and colleagues. Everyone in the family liked Missy, including Eleanor, and they admired and depended on her untiring service and devotion.

Missy filled many of the roles that a wife and First Lady would normally perform. There was always a marked spirit of informality in the White House private quarters. It was commonplace for Missy, often in her bedclothes, to move in and out of Franklin's bedroom in the evening, delivering papers, his stamp collection, or a refreshment. One of the Roosevelt children speculated that Franklin and Missy might have had a physical relationship, but, in the absence of credible evidence, it's hardly worthy of speculation. It is clear that Missy worshipped Franklin, and he cared for her, in his fashion.

The companionship of other women brightened many of Franklin's non-official hours. Cousins Laura Delano and Margaret "Daisy" Suckley were long-time favorites. When Daisy died in 1991, a battered suitcase was found filled with her diaries, and with a trove of letters to and from Franklin. These newly-discovered papers revealed how much she thought Franklin enjoyed their easygoing, unqualified friendship, and suggest that she and Franklin had an even deeper relationship during the late 1930s and early 1940s.[1] Franklin had acknowledged that Daisy and Laura were the only companions with whom he could completely relax. There is no other evidence that he felt that there was any more to the relationships than that. They were adoring, solicitous, and available on demand, and they asked little in return. The ubiquitous cousins were with Franklin, as was Lucy Mercer Rutherfurd, in Warm Springs when he suffered his fatal cerebral hemorrhage in April, 1945.

There were other women who competed for Franklin's attention. The flirtatious Princess Martha of Norway was a regular wartime visitor to the White House, as were other war-exiled royals. How much Franklin really gave of himself to these devoted friends and companions is conjecture, but they filled a welcome role in the private side of his enormously public life.

In Eleanor's case, lasting personal relationships and friendships were much more complicated. She shared Val-Kill, and much of her professional and private life, with Nancy Cook and Marion Dickerman for a dozen years. Esther Lape and Elizabeth Read, Molly Dewson, and Polly Porter were close friends and colleagues and Eleanor was comfortable with them and energized by their intelligence, energy, and purpose. She was closest with Nan and Marion, and she enjoyed including them intimately in most aspects of her life. Despite Franklin's uncharitable "she-male" comment, there is no indication that Eleanor's personal relationship with them was anything other than collegial companionship and sisterly affection.

During the Albany years, state police sergeant Earl Miller was assigned to protect Eleanor. Miller was an outgoing, athletic, handsome man fourteen years her junior. In his role, he was a constant companion who served "his lady" with loyalty and friendship. Miller taught Eleanor to ride, helped her learn to swim and dive, and introduced her to many of the outdoor pursuits Franklin had long since dismissed as activities for her to enjoy. Their friendship was relaxed and informal. Photographs showed them in seemingly innocent physical contact.

Eleanor and Miller spent a great deal of time together, and he fit in easily at Val-Kill and with her friends. Jimmy Roosevelt suggested that there may have been more to the relationship between his mother and Miller than just that of an aide and friend. Unquestionably, they had a warm companionship and Eleanor treated Miller as a close and dear friend all their lives. Both Eleanor and Franklin had encouraged a romance between Earl and Missy LeHand. It did not develop, and shortly after leaving the Roosevelts' service, Miller married a younger woman. It is just possible that the Roosevelt children who suggested that their parents may have had physical relations with others might just have been jealous of Franklin's closeness with Missy and Eleanor's with Earl.

Despite warm friendships with others, there was relatively little of that kind of warmth with and among the members of the immediate family. The Roosevelt children, perceiving that their parents had something less than a fully successful marriage, proceeded to repeat history. They compiled a dismal record of failed marriages. Each married more than once, and Elliott tied the knot five times. Two of the Roosevelt children's spouses from these many unions eventually took their own lives.

━━━━━

With the completion of the administration's first hundred days in the spring of 1933, Eleanor's thoughts turned northeast as she prepared for the first of two trips to Campobello. None of the Roosevelts had been on the island since the mid-1920s, but now the joys of Campobello were at hand, and they would prove to be memorable.

Vacation time approached as Congress prepared to adjourn. While Marion Dickerman tended to closing the Todhunter School for the academic year, Nancy Cook stayed at the White House to help Eleanor transform the dreary second-floor rooms into comfortable living quarters for the Roosevelts. Although she had little idea that it would be their home for the next twelve years, Eleanor enjoyed the luxury of nesting when permitted the opportunity. The brass bed in Franklin's room was too short, so the skilled Nan crafted a fine four-poster for the President in their factory at Val-Kill. Franklin used it for the rest of his life.

Franklin, too, looked forward to a well-earned and long-awaited vacation. He was understandably exhausted from the whirlwind administrative pace. In that time, Franklin had closed and reopened national banks; abandoned the gold standard; established a Civilian Conservation Corps (CCC); designed the Federal Emergency Relief Act; and established the Tennessee Valley Authority (TVA), the Agricultural Adjustment Administration (AAA), and the National Recovery Administration (NRA). The necessary legislation was pushed through Congress at a breathtaking pace and in record time. The Depression was far from over, but the dynamic new president had proven that he was, as he had promised he would be, a man of action and a restorer of hope.

Franklin had decided on a cruise along the New England coast, making his first visit to Campobello since the onset of polio. In the intervening years, he had often expressed his homesickness for the red cottage. He asked Jimmy to sail with him, while Franklin, Jr., and John would join them off the coast of Maine at the conclusion of their semesters at Harvard and Groton. The Navy provided escort, and he would return to Washington aboard the *USS Indianapolis* after two days on the island. The yacht that would take him to Campobello was the *Amberjack II*, a schooner-rigged ship almost forty-six feet long. Aboard were her owner, Paul Rust, Jr., and a friend, Amyas Ames. The captain was George Briggs of Marblehead, Massachusetts. The trip began on June 15 in Marion, Massachusetts.

After *Amberjack II* had set sail, Eleanor, Nancy, and Marion left Hyde Park to drive to Maine. They rested the first night at Der Danske Denby, a recreated Danish village in the Maine town of Scarborough, and stopped at L. L. Bean in Freeport, then a small purveyor of hunting boots and camping supplies. They next traveled up the coastal route to Southwest Harbor on Mount Desert Island, arriving at the home of Mary Dreier, a leading social reformer and friend. Mt. Desert Island had long been home to the summer resorts of Bar Harbor and Northeast and Southwest Harbors. Franklin knew these summer enclaves well, visiting them often by sail from Campobello. Eleanor, Nan, and Marion planned to proceed to Lubec and then on to Campobello to prepare the cottage for Franklin's well-publicized arrival.

Festivities were the watchword as Campobello, Lubec, and Eastport awaited the triumphant homecoming of "one of their own," now the President of the United States. The *Lubec Herald* on June 22 headlined: "Welcome to President Roosevelt. The President will arrive in Quoddy [Passamaquoddy Bay] June 29th, and Mrs. Roosevelt will arrive this week."[2]

In its extensive coverage, the *Herald* described the President's sailing plans and shipmates, how and when he was due to arrive, and some of the history of his many years on Campobello doing "what the other fellers did."[3] Franklin's return to his beloved island marked the first time an American president spent a holiday in Canada.

Describing the preparations, the *Herald* noted that "In anticipation of the coming of the President and the 'First Lady of the Land,' Lubec and Eastport have had a professional decorator come and trim the business places with flags and bunting, with plenty of 'Welcome' banners so that the two towns present a gala appearance. Lubec has not planned for any special celebration on the arrival of Mrs. Roosevelt, but at Eastport a big Field Day is to be held on the 29th, with parades, ball games, short address by the President, a number of warships in the harbor, bands and Bugle & Drum Corps galore, and everything that goes with a day of this kind."[4]

The *Eastport Sentinel* on Wednesday, June 28, published a day-by-day report of *Amberjack II*'s progress, complete with weather conditions. It chronicled the local excitement in the ports of call and the small adventures caused by the presence of a presidential cruise. The *Sentinel* noted that Raymond Moley, former member of the Brain Trust and then an administration aide, had briefly boarded on official business. The World Monetary and Economic Conference on currency stabilization and the gold standard was then taking place in London. It was Franklin's first major participation in international politics and economics, and he was able to stay in touch with his envoys and the official proceedings throughout his journey by aides and by dispatch. Mail pouches and dispatch cases arrived by courier at many selected ports along the way.

Franklin, Jr. and Johnnie joined their father at Chebeague Island, in Casco Bay, off Portland. They were delivered by the destroyer *Ellis*, which joined the growing fleet anchored in Casco Bay. Jimmy's wife Betsey and their new baby, christened Sara Delano Roosevelt, also visited the *Amberjack II*. The inestimable Missy LeHand was also a caller.

Franklin took the ship's wheel several times during the trip. In the midst of the sail in foul weather, his intimate knowledge of the Maine coast and its dangerous waters came as a great relief to Captain Gibbs. Franklin was also at the wheel other times when his spirit urged. One of these times was just inside Seguin Island, a rocky outcropping with a towering lighthouse near the mouth of the Kennebec River.

Mary Elizabeth Crockett was vacationing with her family on Squirrel Island, just off Boothbay Harbor. Her father, a "dyed-in-the-wool" Republican, set out with the whole family on their fifty-foot ketch, hoping to spot the President. They met the *Amberjack II* in the narrow passage between Seguin and the mainland, unescorted, because the Navy ships were unable to run in so close to land. "FDR was at the helm," Mary Crockett remembered, "the familiar cigarette holder set at a jaunty angle from his mouth and a wide grin on his face." Her father challenged him to a race, and Franklin enthusiastically shouted, "You bet." Just as the ketch was closing in, so was the naval escort, and a bullhorn warned the ketch to stay a mile from the Presidential vessel. Crockett recalled that Franklin threw his hat down in disgust when the naval escort spoiled his fun. But one of his sons sportingly dipped *Amberjack II*'s presidential flag, conceding victory.[5] Franklin grudgingly now understood that security considerations would often restrict much of his accustomed free movement.

When Eleanor and her friends awoke at Mary Dreier's home in Southwest Harbor on the morning of June 25, they were pleasantly surprised by a visit from Jimmy, Franklin, Jr., and John, who had come ashore from the moored *Amberjack II* to join them for breakfast. The women were thrilled and surprised that their paths crossed that of Franklin's boat. They motored out to the mooring to greet Franklin, and then separated to complete their individual journeys to Campobello. Eleanor looked forward to having a few carefree days on the island with her friends prior to the *Amberjack II*'s arrival.

The previous day an eighty-seven-year-old fisherman had presented lobsters to Franklin, and at Jonesport he was greeted by a group of town dignitaries and supporters. He enjoyed the attention and continually asked the naval escort to ease the tight ring around him so that the people of Maine could catch a glimpse of their president.

Eleanor and her friends arrived in Lubec on Monday, June 26. The *Herald* reported the event on page one. The same edition carried a piece entitled "Lubec Filled With Strangers for Roosevelt Celebration." This article details the amazing sight of a twelve-cylinder Pierce Arrow car that followed Eleanor on a trip to Machias and Jonesport to meet Louis Howe. The *Herald* excitedly reported that the town was filled "with strangers, secret service men and dozens of out-of-state cars."[6]

Back on the front page, the *Herald* went on to describe the Eastport field day:

> Delegations of Veterans Posts from all over Maine and New Brunswick, together with the famous York Regiment of New Brunswick in line. At 3:30 Governor Brann (Maine) and staff will be present and the Governor will deliver an address. The United States Cruiser Indianapolis and the destroyers Ellis and Beranardou will be in the harbor with 1,200 men on board. After the address there will be ball games, band concerts, a grand ball at the armory, and a display of fireworks at 9 o'clock.
>
> At Campobello the program starts at 11 a.m., with water sports, motor boat races, etc. At 1 p.m. the Connors Bros. big fleet of sixteen boats will parade all gaily decorated. At 2 o'clock President Roosevelt will be officially welcomed to the island by J. F. Calder, President of the

Campobello Board of Trade, on behalf of the island residents, and by Premier L. P. D. Tilley, on behalf of the Province of New Brunswick, to which Mr. Roosevelt will probably respond.

At 3:30 there will be a ball game between the Kiwanis Champs and the USS Indianapolis team. Meals will be served in the village of Welshpool and the Lubec Car Ferry will be on the island to take charge of traffic.[7]

While on the island, Eleanor wrote daily to Lorena Hickock, a national wire service journalist, who had been assigned to cover her throughout the presidential campaign and the early days of the new administration. Lorena, or "Hick," had become a close friend of Eleanor. "Lunch and a trip to Eastport to buy essentials with the engine breaking down as usual, and the rain in our faces for a time." Later Nan and Marion came in to tea by the fire. "No telephone. Absolute peace. It is a joy."[8]

Eleanor really wanted to enjoy the few days that she, Nan, and Marion would have on Campobello before Franklin's arrival and before all the formal festivities would begin. "I hope we have good weather so I can give Nan and Marion some nice trips, and especially do I want good weather when Franklin and his fleet are there. I love the place and like people I like to see it at its best. Fog is nice if you know a place and are here with someone you like. It is like a winter storm. It shuts you in and gives you a close and intimate feeling and adds to the joy of your fire. But you don't want to meet a new place in a fog any more than you want to be intimate with a new acquaintance."[9]

Eleanor, Nan, and Marion were able to enjoy a cruise in the motor launch up the St. Croix River to St. Andrew's. Eleanor wrote to Lorena, "The sun is out, and the fog is rolling out to sea, and I'm sitting in the bottom of the boat, sniffing salt air and every now and then looking over the water to my green islands and grey rocky shores. I do think it is lovely, and I wonder if you will."[10] Lorena had not yet been to Campobello, and Eleanor hoped that she, too, would enjoy its many pleasures.

Marion Dickerman recorded in her journal: "We opened the house. The island at that time was rather a primitive place (no electricity or telephone); and getting ready for the big picnic we were to have when the President arrived took all of Nancy's expertise, along with a lot of neighborliness on the part of the island women. We had some of them bake rolls, others cook a huge ham, and others prepare bowls of potato salad and so on—because there was to be at this picnic a large number of people, including the Governor of Maine, Norman H. Davis, Henry Morgenthau, Canadian officials, dozens of Navy officers, and many local Roosevelt friends. Louis Howe was there, of course."[11]

Thursday, June 29, dawned with a thick fog blotting out views of the *Indianapolis* and the other naval craft that had preceded Franklin to Eastport. The local herring fleet, Marion wrote, was "properly dressed for the occasion," and lay at anchor off Welshpool. Then, as if by magic, the fog lifted, and the sun shone through a cloudless sky. "The schooner [*Amberjack II*] sailed quite majestically through the Narrows and tacked across Passamaquoddy Bay, and Franklin landed at Welshpool for the first time in a dozen years."[12]

On Friday morning, June 30, the assembled dignitaries and islanders pressed forward to listen to the President of the United States. He stood bare-headed, propped up in the rear of a touring car, and addressed the friendly crowd:

> I think that I can only address you as my old friends of Campobello—old and new. I was figuring this morning on the passage of time and I remembered that I was brought here because I was teething forty-nine years ago. I have been coming for many months almost every year until about twelve years ago when there has been a gap.
>
> It seems to me that memory is a very wonderful thing because this morning, when we came out of the fog at West Quoddy Head, the boys who were aboard said 'There is Land All Ahead,' and I started full speed because I knew it was the Lubec Narrows. That was one of the things I

learned up here, one of the things I learned, for instance, from Ed Lank, one of the things I learned from John Calder, and old Captain Mitchell who, by the way, gave me a few minutes ago a very delightful photograph of my Father's first old boat away back in the early nineties. I am mighty glad to have it.

I was thinking also, as I came through the Narrows and saw the line of fishing boats and the people on the wharves, both here at Welch Pool [sic] and also at Eastport, that this reception here is probably the finest example of friendship between nations—permanent friendship between nations—that we can possibly have.

I was glad that I had with me the American Delegate to the Disarmament Conference in Geneva, Mr. Norman Davis, because he will go back to Geneva and will be able to tell them that he has seen with his own eyes what a border-line without fortifications means between two great nations.

I am very happy to have had this very wonderful reception, all of this kindness from the Governor of the Province of New Brunswick and also from the Dominion Governor, and especially a very delightful telegram of welcome from the Governor General of Canada, the representative of His Majesty, the King.

I have had a very wonderful couple of hours and I am going to have a very wonderful two days before I have to leave.

I hope and am very confident that if peace continues in this world and that if the other nations of the world follow the very good example of the United States and Canada, I will be able to come back here for a holiday during the next three years.[13]

The neighbors, friends, and guests loved Franklin's speech and pressed around the touring car to greet him personally. The remainder of that day and much of the following he had some time to reflect on what must have been a highly emotional experience. There has been speculation that he might never have returned had he not been able to come back in triumph. A quiet, private homecoming for a fading, career-less semi-invalid might well have been too painful for him, and the memories too bittersweet. But Franklin's enormous success permitted him a gracious return to the scene of many of the happiest days of his life.

It was evident that he needed some time for quiet contemplation. A Washington correspondent later told of walking in the woods with a young lady on a foggy morning at Campobello:

> All at once, not five yards off in the fog, there was the President's Ford with big Gus Gennerich, the President's bodyguard, asleep against the wheel. And there beside the car was the President. He was sitting on the trunk of a tree, his legs folded out in front of him, his hands over his face. And suddenly, before they could move, the hands came down and there were his eyes looking straight into their eyes just a few steps off and not seeing them at all, the way a man's face will look at you not seeing you from a flash in the movies; there was a kind of drawn grimace over his mouth and over his forehead like a man trying to see something in his mind and suffering. And then all at once they could see his eyes focusing and it was like a shutter clicking down on a camera the way the smile came back over the look in his eyes and he called out: 'Hello, there, Billy. Picking flowers?' They turned and got out of there. They could hear his big laugh back of them in the spruce . . . .[14]

Was the story apocryphal? Was Franklin experiencing a powerful emotional reverie? Was he overwhelmed by the conflicting feelings engendered by his return? Was he contemplating the full scale of his responsibilities? Franklin was seldom, if ever, caught off guard like this. There in the fogbound evergreen forest of his youth, he may well have been wishing to turn back the clock and the ravages of time. Or, perhaps, he had concluded with wistful resignation that for him there was truly no "going home" again.

Eastport held its planned celebration on Thursday, and Campobello on Friday. And then Franklin's long-interrupted return to Campobello was over. He never recorded his feelings or emotions about his return. But his warm reception and departure brought a life's chapter to an end with a certain finality. For Franklin, Campobello marked the end of immaturity and self-indulgence. Returning to Campobello may not have fully banished his demons, but it may have brought some satisfactory closure.

Franklin and his party said their good-byes and were taken by launch to the *Indianapolis*, lying at anchor off Eastport, for the return trip to Washington. *Amberjack II* was lifted aboard and the holiday was over. Eastport had first seen Franklin in official pomp aboard a battleship in 1913 when he brought the *North Dakota* to Maine for the Fourth of July celebration. Another ship named for a landlocked midwestern city ceremoniously took him away just twenty years later.

The grand return to Campobello seemed to please everyone. Franklin reveled in all the attention, and the islanders, townspeople, and dignitaries successfully did everything they could to make the event memorable. Eleanor was able to perform her "First Lady" function graciously and play hostess to the Roosevelt guests. Campobello, Lubec, and Eastport briefly had their day in national spotlights, and the local residents had accumulated many stories and anecdotes they could store away for retelling to children and grandchildren in the years ahead.

Eleanor, Nan, and Marion returned to New York City shortly after the President's departure. Eleanor couldn't wait to return to the island to show Campobello to Lorena Hickock. Several weeks later, Eleanor and Hick set out on an extended drive from New York through Quebec and Maine. Their trip first took them around the Gaspé Peninsula, with its rugged headlands, crashing seascapes, and tiny French villages. They stopped often to meet with local residents and experience the unique Quebecois culture. Eleanor, in her usual modest way, did not advertise the fact that she was America's First

Lady, allowing only that she was the niece of Theodore Roosevelt. Remote French-speaking villagers in Quebec knew and cared little of the politics of their giant neighbor to the south and did not recognize that she was the wife of the incumbent president.

Eleanor and Hick enjoyed the majesty of Percé Rock at the northern reach of the Gaspé and the lonely, rugged coast. Turning south, they took the long drive through western New Brunswick and finally reached the Maine frontier and the broad potato fields of Aroostook County. Eleanor wrote:

> We stayed at a farmhouse that night. I was interested in finding out what conditions were, so I bought a paper which told me a good deal about the potato situation. I found an opportunity to start the farmer talking about how long he and his family had been on the land and what he grew, and so on. I aired the small local knowledge I had just acquired. He seemed much surprised that I should know the price of potatoes or any of the problems of that region, and when I told him that my husband was interested in farming, he finally asked who I was. I had a feeling that no Maine farmer would look with favor on the wife of a Democratic president, but he was kind enough to say that he was keeping an open mind. He added, however, that I had better not mention who I was to some of the neighbors; if I did, they might not want to show me their farms, and he was arranging to take me around so I could see them the next morning.
>
> The news spread, nevertheless, since I think he could not help telephoning to some distant friends and relatives to come over early in the morning. In spite of my politics, the farmers in the neighborhood were kind enough to let me see their farms, so we spent a most interesting morning learning about farming in the area.[15]

From the fields of Aroostook County, Eleanor and Hick drove

to Lubec, where, after garaging the Buick, they met Calder's boat for the short trip to Campobello. Climbing down the ladder from Lubec's wharf to the launch, Hick had her first "encounter with the long and slippery steps which at low tide make the descent to any boat a matter for some consideration."[16]

The trip had additional significance: It was the first of many that Eleanor would discuss at great length with Franklin. Her mobility and her energy permitted her to get to the more remote, more rural, and less accessible parts of the country. Franklin learned to trust her eyes, her ears, and her perceptions. After this trip, as with others like it, they would have a long uninterrupted meal, and he would question Eleanor about all she saw. He wanted to know what kinds of homes the people lived in, what their farms looked like, how their villages were arranged, what they ate, what kind of education was available, what work was offered—and, after this particular trip, how did the Native Americans seem to be getting along. In Aroostook County, they belonged to the same Passamaquoddy tribe as did old Tomah Joseph, the chief who often visited Franklin in Campobello.

Similar trips and their subsequent "debriefing" conversations were repeated many times in the next dozen years. Eleanor traveled extensively and always with great purpose. Franklin realized and often acknowledged the value of these fact-finding trips, and Eleanor was enthusiastic about performing a useful advisory function.

In her book *This I Remember*, Eleanor failed to report on the first of her two trips to Campobello in the summer of 1933, Franklin's homecoming. The residents of the island and those of Lubec and Eastport would long remember the event, and it had tremendous significance to Franklin. But, perhaps, Franklin's home-coming was less personally memorable to her than that of her island holiday and her deepening relationship with Lorena Hickock.

In a letter, Eleanor wrote of Franklin's return to Campobello: "After speeches he came home and I think [he was] happy." And now it was her turn to be happy on the island with Hick. She was "settling down again into this quietest of places and loving it."[17]

10

How I Wish You Could Come For Even a Few Days

Eleanor's visits to Campobello in 1933 were welcome respites from the challenges and frustrations of her complex life in Washington. Although she now had a powerful national voice and had dutifully assumed an important role in Franklin's administration, these roles were challenging and still in flux. Franklin had frozen her from any influence in his handling of international affairs, and she found it necessary to dispute his leadership, or lack of it, at the recent World Monetary and Economic Conference. Eleanor feared that America's isolationists were influencing his judgement. She had yet to determine and define the full scope of her public activities now that she was the wife of the president. At the same time, she continued to wrestle with the personal forces tugging at her, particularly her relationship with Lorena Hickock.

Within her quasi-official context, Eleanor struggled for a balance between her growing political agenda and her continuing quest for a more satisfying personal life. She had never liked living in Washington during Franklin's Navy Department days, and she disliked the official duties that history and tradition had assigned to First Ladies. Pouring tea, welcoming women's groups, and performing mundane ceremonial functions dredged up the painful memories of the social burdens of her late Victorian young womanhood. She believed these activities of little intrinsic value or utility, and she performed as few of the official hostess duties as she could. Eleanor remained in Washington only when required or when she found it convenient. Most of her interests were elsewhere; her children were grown, and her husband filled few of her personal needs. Missy LeHand happily attended to some of Eleanor's official duties, and Franklin was comfortable with that arrangement.

Val-Kill was still Eleanor's home, as it was Nancy Cook's and Marion Dickerman's. But these relationships were beginning to change. The women remained friends and business partners for a time, but Eleanor's time was taken with the demands of Franklin's presidency, her expanding public activism, and her intensifying relationship with Hick. It had become something of a pattern for Eleanor to form close friendships and then, after a time, move on to others. Earl Miller, her former bodyguard and companion, had married, and the relationship with Nan and Marion was losing some of its intimacy. They continued their friendship and shared Val-Kill and Campobello holidays, but Eleanor had less time to spend with her old friends.

Although Franklin did not plan any Campobello holidays, the big red cottage continued to play a role, albeit a lesser one. He accepted a position on the board of directors of the Campobello Island Club. The directors looked out for the interests of the summer community, concentrating on protective concerns such as fire prevention. Occasionally they ventured into subjects of governmental taxation and administration.

For years, Franklin had been concerned about the duties and taxes levied on American rusticators and their guests when they reentered the United States from vacations in Canada. In the 1920s, he had protested to the Treasury Department about charges from which he believed American summer residents and visitors should be exempted. Franklin cited the proximity of Campobello to the American mainland and the fact that United States citizens spent considerable sums of money in Eastport and Lubec during their Canadian residences, contributing significantly to the local economies.[1] There is no indication that the Customs Service paid any heed to Franklin, who at that time was merely a private citizen with a prominent name.

Now, in the 1930s, the Campobello summer community, like others, felt the pinch of the Depression. Directors of the Campobello Island Club took their case for lower tax assessments to the New Brunswick local government, the Queens County Council. Franklin wrote to William M. Patterson, chairman of the board, that he "long thought non-resident property is over-assessed . . . I agree with you that the only way out is to have all the non-resident owners join in an appeal to the County Council. I am sure that my Mother would be willing to join as well as myself."[2] At this time, Franklin's home and property was assessed at $6,500, Sara's at $4,500. He may have been the President of the United States, but the state of his personal finances was always of some concern. The Club's Campobello agent reported to Patterson that the County Council had refused their request.

Meetings of the Board were held regularly, including one at the White House on March 21, 1935. Correspondence indicates that the Campobello Company was often behind in receivables from the islanders. Among these were the stumpage fees residents paid for the wood they cut for building fishing weirs, constructing their homes, or firewood to heat them. The Company's agent often had to pursue woodcutters for their payments, because money on the island was a commodity that was constantly in short supply. Agent Mac Gillivary sent individual letters to tardy islanders, at times threatening lawsuits or cancellation of permits.

Patterson wrote to Franklin on December 13, 1933, telling him of Mac Gillivary's concerns and his actions. He enclosed a letter written to Patterson from an islander, Price Batson: "In reply to yours of 6th instant—again I say I do not owe for the five cord of wood you refer to. No matter what you have looked up, I do owe stumpage and when I am able to pay, I will do so. I am not trying to beat the Company out of anything. When you talk of collecting by law, perhaps I have as many friends in the Campobello Camp as you that I can state my case to."[3]

The principal relationship between the islanders and the cottagers continued to be one of personal service. When Franklin called the islanders his "neighbors" on his return in 1933, he may have exaggerated their closeness. Geoffrey Ward suggests, "There was always a considerable gulf between the fishermen and their families who occupied the island through the bitter winters, and the wealthy American visitors whom they found it profitable to serve in the summer, a gulf best symbolized perhaps by the seating in St. Anne's, the board-and-batten Episcopal church at Welshpool to which all the Roosevelts walked every Sunday morning; the pews in the center were reserved for the summer people; islanders sat along the walls."[4]

Franklin certainly had made some lasting friendships with the Calders, the Lanks, and some others on Campobello; and Eleanor was both liked and well-respected. Franklin Calder had been a guest at the White House, but most of the personal relationships went just so far. The Roosevelts, however, had more cordial relations with islanders than did most of the cottagers.

The members of the Club continued a perceptible coolness toward Campobello's residents and, at this time, toward Franklin. He was a valued member of the organization, but not special, even though he was the president. Most, if not all, Club members were Republicans, which accounts for the merely polite and businesslike tone of all communications between them.

During his presidential years, Franklin received many offers and requests from former Campobello neighbors and visitors. He politely declined all invitations to participate in Campobello events such as the library's fiftieth anniversary. So, too, did he decline the offers of gifts. One letter writer offered to sell Franklin a sword that had belonged to old Admiral Owen. Others offered memorabilia from the former Hotel Tyn-y-Coed or requested his assistance in selling Campobello property. He also received a number of "remember me?" notes from former playmates and neighbors. Franklin always acknowledged and graciously declined requests expressing his appreciation and often cordial remembrance.

Later, in 1935, Aubrey Calder wrote directly to the President.

23. Franklin with Eleanor supporting him on the rocky beach in front of their cottage, 1920. Only weeks earlier, he received the Democratic Party's nomination for the Vice-Presidency.

24. Franklin and Eleanor's cottage, c. 1920, with two Roosevelt boys.

25. A news photographer's picture of the nominee and his family on the cottage steps in 1920. From the left in the rear: FDR, Sara, and Eleanor. Next row: Elliot, Anna, and Jimmy. In front: Franklin Junior, John, and the family dog. All look into the morning sun; Eleanor averts her eyes; Sara rests her hand on her daughter-in-law's knee; Franklin, a cigarette smoker, casually cradles a pipe.

26. *Sportingly clad in knickers: from the left, Marion Dickerman, Eleanor, Nancy Cook, and Marion's sister-in-law, Peggy Levenson, in 1925. That summer, Eleanor, Nancy, and Marion and three children made a camping journey to Campobello. While they were gone, Franklin supervised the construction of Val-Kill, a stone cottage and furniture factory for the three women in Hyde Park.*

27. *Eleanor with her ubiquitous knitting on the beach at Campobello, 1925.*

28. *Crew and guests on the Amberjack II off Southwest Harbor, Maine, 1933. FDR was en route to Campobello for his first visit after being struck down by polio. From the left in front: Eleanor, Franklin, and Jimmy. Behind his father is Franklin Junior. Next row: Nancy Cook, Mary Dreier, John Roosevelt, and, in the rear, Frances Kellor, Nancy Dickerman, and Antonia Hatvary.*

29. Franklin greets his neighbors during welcoming ceremonies at Welshpool, Campobello in 1933. Eleanor is in the white hat.

30. Eleanor and Sara await the arrival of the Sewanna in front of Sara's cottage, 1936.

31. Arriving at Campobello in 1936 on the Sewanna from Rockland, Maine: John, Franklin Junior, FDR, and Jimmy. The shipmate in front is unidentified.

32. A 1930s campaign poster.

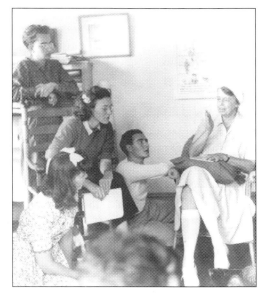

33. Eleanor meeting with students at the International Student Service Leadership Institute held at her cottage in 1941.

34. Franklin with Harry Hopkins (far left) and aides at Rockland; Maine, following the historic meeting with Winston Churchill at Argentia Bay off Newfoundland in August, 1941. At Rockland, Franklin first reported on the meeting and unveiled the principles of the Atlantic Charter.

35. *With her secretary, Maureen Coor, at Campobello in 1962, Eleanor relaxes under a tree. This was her last visit to Campobello. She died just months later.*

36. *The rear of Franklin and Eleanor's cottage in the 1960s when it became the centerpiece of the Roosevelt Campobello International Park.*

37. *The front of the cottage in the 1960s.*

38. *Linnea Calder, left, daughter of longtime Roosevelt employees and family friends, in the cottage's kitchen in the 1960s. The name on the stove, "President," is pure coincidence.*

He had his eye on a large stand of trees that the Roosevelt family had owned for fifty years. Missy LeHand replied that "The President has your letter and he wishes much that he could give you permission to cut trees on the point his Mother owns north of Herring Cove, but he has had many requests before and has had to say no because he and his Mother are very anxious to have the trees on that point left uncut and grow as much as possible. I know you will understand. . . ."[5] Both Franklin's and Sara's days on the island may have been numbered, but they fought vigorously to keep secure the ownership and protection of their Campobello homes and property.

Franklin and Eleanor were constantly concerned about the cost of operating their cottage and the only occasional use they made of the property. Their equity did not increase, although both the assessments and taxes did. They had been largely unsuccessful in renting the cottage during the summers when they were not in residence, and they worried about the maintenance costs and what they perceived to be a small but growing testiness of the islanders toward the cottagers. Several of their notes to one another reflect these concerns.

None of the Roosevelts visited Campobello in 1934, although it was on Eleanor's mind. She had been thinking ahead when she wrote to Hick, "I've been wondering the last few days what I really want for my declining years. I could completely take over the cottage at Campo & make that the place to turn to when I want to be 'at home' but it is far away not only for me but for my friends & quite out of the question for winter . . . ."[6]

By 1935, Eleanor was eager to return to Campobello. Her traveling companions for the drive through Maine to the island were Earl Miller and her longtime secretary, Malvina "Tommy" Thompson. They stopped in Portland with Eleanor's Aunt Maude and her husband David Gray, then proceeded to Campobello for several weeks of both work and play. Earl persuaded the women to try some shooting, but Eleanor had writing commitments and she and Tommy spent much of the time working. Earl rapidly became bored and was relieved that Eleanor had to shorten the visit when responsibilities required her to return to New York City and Washington. She was by now maintaining a small third floor walk-up apartment in a Greenwich Village building owned by Esther Lape and Elizabeth Read. It was another "snuggery" for Eleanor when she was not required to be in the Capitol, or didn't have the luxury of time to get to Val-Kill or Campobello.

After completing her commitments, Eleanor headed northeast once more with Tommy. This trip included a visit with friends Molly Dewson and Polly Porter in Castine, Maine. Castine was a favorite stop and an opportunity to visit good friends. This time it included a reception by the Castine Women's Club. On July 24, the Club held a special board meeting to plan a reception in her honor at what is now the Witherle Memorial Library. "How can we have a reception for a Democrat?" a Club member complained to Louise Bartlett, a Club officer. "That's not what we're doing," replied Mrs. Bartlett, "we're having a reception for the President's wife."[7]

The visit was charmingly recorded in the *Green Street News*, a mimeographed newsletter published by a fourteen-year-old Castine boy. It was headlined: "Mrs. Roosevelt Coming to Castine Friday." The *News* continued, "Mrs. Roosevelt is coming to Castine Friday. She will visit Miss Mary Dewson and have dinner with her. Miss Dewson lives of [sic] to the Porters. Then Mrs. Roosevelt the mother of the country is coming down to the Library and see everyone. Everybody can shake hands with her. She is on her way to Campello [sic]."[8]

The reception was a smashing success. Eleanor's visit was a triumph, as they so often were. Her warmth and graciousness transcended the barriers of partisan politics. An elderly member of the Club remembered fifty years later, "My father couldn't stand Eleanor Roosevelt until she came here. Then he fell in love with her."[9]

Moving on to Campobello, Eleanor settled in for a several weeks' stay. She and Emma Bugbee, a friend and a reporter for the *New York Herald Tribune*, went on a sail with Captain Calder. Eleanor took the tiller, confiding that, "I never get a chance to sail the boat myself. There are always men around . . . . One has always to let the man do the sailing."[10]

Eleanor dug into her work. She completed a children's guide to Washington and an article entitled, "Can a Woman Be Elected President?" Eleanor was aware of the probable public reaction, but believed it important to let her deeply felt feminist views be heard. "I know this is controversial and [it] will cause violent differences of opinion."[11] She sent the article to Hick to read, but not revise.

By early 1936, Franklin had suffered some deep personal losses. He had to deal with the deaths of Louis Howe and his long-time bodyguard and companion, Gus Gennerich. Louis had began to fail in the autumn of 1934, but he continued to live at the White House, still involved in the administration and beginning to plot strategy for the 1936 campaign. Eleanor finally persuaded him to move to the U.S. Naval Hospital, where he continued his steady stream of memos and telephone calls. Franklin visited often, and Eleanor went daily when in Washington. Much of his last year was spent in an oxygen tent, and on April 18, 1936, he died peacefully.

Franklin had lost his best friend. He now depended on the regular White House after-work cocktail hours for much of his amusement. Harry Hopkins, first a colleague and friend to Eleanor, transferred his allegiance to Franklin and became his closest aide, friend, and political confidant. The circle of Franklin's close friendships was small.

Franklin was winding down his first term and looking ahead toward a second. Much of the New Deal social legislation had taken root in active programs. His proactivity and the administration's public support programs were timely and widely utilized. He had used the power of the federal government to provide genuine Depression relief, and many were now convinced that government had a responsibility to provide aid, rather than depend on private volunteerism. Franklin's popularity was at a high, and the admiration was mixed with some affection, but not in all quarters.

Harvard and many of its influential alumni were loudly and pointedly critical of the New Deal in general and of Franklin in particular. Franklin loved Harvard, but his ardor was not uniformly returned. He had always been a loyal and dedicated alumnus, holding several offices in the Alumni Association and taking part in Class of '04 activities. He was elected to the Harvard Board of Overseers in 1917, and in 1929, at his twenty-fifth reunion, his classmates elected him chief marshal of the Commencement.[12]

Now, near the completion of his first term, many of Harvard's traditionally Republican alumni, some of them friends and class-mates, persistently rained criticism and insults on the President. Many of these detractors had been his personal guests at the White House in April, 1934, when he held a presidential reception for nearly a thousand classmates, their wives, and their children. The *Boston Transcript* noted that the guests "are going to get more food out of him than he got votes out of them."[13] The standard accusation many alumni hurled at him was that he was "a traitor to his class."

Harvard held its Tercentenary celebration in September, 1936. Franklin was invited to speak, but was asked to limit his remarks to ten minutes. He was furious at the wording of the invitation and its insinuation that Harvard had grudgingly invited him to speak as the Tercentenary chairman, but ignored the fact that he was the President of the United States. Franklin's acceptance letter was polite, but nec-essarily curt. His speech clearly indicated that he was speaking "in a joint and several capacity" as the President of the United States, as the Chairman of the U.S. Harvard Tercentenary Commission, and as "a son of Harvard who gladly returns to this spot where men have sought truth for three hundred years." Written in part by fellow alumnus and Supreme Court Justice Felix Frankfurter, the speech was barely ten minutes long.[14] It may have done little to silence his critics, but Franklin saw it as retribution.

The Reverend Walter Russell Bowie, a colleague from the days at the *Harvard Crimson*, wrote unhappily of "the rancorous and almost hysterical political animus which rose against him and what he stood for among the privileged groups to which many of the Harvard grad-uates happen to belong. I was amazed and disgusted to hear the way men talked of him . . . "[15]

Among the loudest alumni critics were Roosevelt family mem-bers from Theodore's Oyster Bay branch. Three of Franklin's sons were Harvard graduates and four grandsons and a great-grandson would follow. Even more of the large body of Roosevelt family Harvard alumni are from Theodore's side, including all four of his sons as well as six grandsons, seven great-grandchildren, and six great-great grandchildren. In addition, both of Theodore's daughters married Harvard men. Theodore's sons, as well as daughter Alice, were constant critics of their cousin in public and in private.

The Tercentenary year was also a national election year. That summer, Franklin once more cruised the Maine coast with his sons. They anchored one night at North Haven Island. Here, in familiar waters, Franklin was serenaded with a stirring rendition of the requisite "Hail to the Chief" by the town band. Franklin was especially pleased with the welcome of the solidly Republican townspeople who turned out to greet him. Although it was an election year, serious campaigning had yet to begin. Franklin was amused that the North Haven islanders, almost to a man, had bedecked themselves with large Alf Landon sunflower buttons.[16]

Landon, the Republican nominee, was immensely popular in Maine. He actively campaigned in the Pine Tree State, where his welcome was among the warmest he received. Maine voters still cast their ballots in September that year, and although their few electoral vote total carried little weight in the final outcome, the fact that they voted so early might prove to be some kind of an indication of the national vote. Maine had been and continued to be solidly Republican, but Franklin had been a familiar figure and a regular visitor to the state. That meant little, however, to Maine's fiercely independent voters.

Landon's campaign chose the sunflower button as an echo of his Kansas roots. The button was a popular political memento then and is extremely valuable to collectors today. Robert H. Mountain, a native Mainer, fondly remembers the Landon button. A schoolboy in Portland in 1936, Mountain remembers the excitement when Landon campaigned in Portland. He also recalled that there was a specific reason for his excitement. School ink pens of that time became easily fouled, and students required an ample supply of pen wipers. The Landon sunflower button was made of felt and served that purpose superbly. Consequently, schoolchildren vigorously collected Landon buttons for their utilitarian value.

Mountain's father took him to the local ball park to see Landon. The young man found himself standing next to a box filled with the highly prized buttons. Wasting no time, he covered himself with the sunflowers. As Landon worked his way to a dais on the pitcher's mound, a campaign worker told young Mountain, "Tonight you're going to see the next President of the United States." As fate would have it, a dense fog crept over the stadium and enveloped the pitcher's mound. Landon spoke eloquently to an audience he couldn't see and who couldn't see him. Mountain's father told him that at the least he had accumulated enough pen wipers to get him through high school. Robert lamented that he was disappointed that he had not actually seen the next President of the United States. His father quickly eased his disappointment by telling the youngster, "Mr. Roosevelt wasn't here tonight!"[17]

As Franklin sailed up the coast to Campobello, Eleanor, Nancy Cook, Marion Dickerman, and Tommy Thompson had already reached the island. Eleanor recorded somewhat tartly on Franklin's arrival, "The boys sailed in . . . today just to show off their beards. F. has side burns & looks just like his Father's portrait. Funny how men love to grow hair. I think it makes them feel virile."[18] She may well have been recollecting her many exclusions from yachting and other male-only activities.

On July 30, Franklin and Eleanor joined the Premier and Attorney General of New Brunswick for a picnic lunch. A photo in the July 31st *Portland Press Herald* shows the group seated on a rocky beach, enjoying cake after Eleanor had roasted hot dogs on an open wood fire. The group discussed the off-and-on hydro-electric power project for Passamaquoddy Bay and the recently rejected St. Lawrence Waterway Treaty. The St. Lawrence project eventually become a reality, but Passamaquoddy power, studied under federal funding during Franklin's administration, was considered too complex and too expensive, and never came into being. After a quiet overnight last stay at the cottage, Franklin left the island aboard the *USS Savannah,* headed back to Washington.

Campobello continued to cast its magic on Eleanor. She wrote to her friend Elinor, wife of the Treasury Secretary Henry Morgenthau, "It's beautiful & peaceful here. We had a good sail yesterday afternoon & this morning Marion and I walked down to the quaint little church [St. Anne's]."[19] She wrote to Hick, "How I wish you could come for even a few days." Eleanor wished that Hick were there, but knew full well that Hick "wouldn't be happy despite Campo's loveliness."[20] It was quite likely that Nan's and Marion's presence would have disappointed Hick at least as much as Campobello itself.

Eleanor was now at work on an autobiography, although she had some difficulty in acknowledging it. "I rather think I'll write up my childhood for my kids," she wrote to a friend.[21] Eleanor referred to the book as her "memoirs" when she sent it to her literary agent. The result was her popular book, published in 1937, *This Is My Story.*

To little surprise, Landon carried Maine and Vermont, but Franklin easily won the remaining forty-six states. The Roosevelt landslide was a devastating defeat for the Republican Party, whose cry had been "As goes Maine, so goes the nation." After 1936, the new maxim became, "As Maine goes, so goes Vermont." A bridge over the Salmon River dividing New Hampshire from Maine was adorned with a sign that read, "You are now leaving the U.S."[22]

Eleanor regularly made favorite stops as she drove through Maine. One was at Perry's Nut House, in Belfast, for the jars of wild strawberry and blueberry preserves that she sent to the many friends on her Christmas list. The First Lady, traveling without pomp and ceremony, provided a certain amount of pleasure to the "down home" sensibilities of Mainers. Obituaries in the *Portland Press Herald* noted the passing of former waitresses in the Maine towns of Phippsburg and Scarborough who had proudly recalled serving the First Lady. Most of these former stopping places are either gone or in new and different incarnations. The L. L. Bean store in Freeport is a notable exception. Eleanor reportedly once bought a pair of their well-known

Maine hunting shoes for Franklin. It may be difficult to picture the physically challenged President wearing "Bean boots," but the purchase was apparently made.

Eleanor traveled to Campobello in June, 1939. Franklin made a very brief and his last-ever visit to the island while cruising northeast waters on the *USS Tuscaloosa*. Franklin, Jr. and his wife Ethel, Johnnie and his wife Anne, and the Roosevelts' Hyde Park rector also made use of the cottage in this period. But, deep into the second term of Franklin's presidency, neither he nor Eleanor appeared to have either the time or occasion to visit their beloved island on a regular basis.

Franklin's second term was marked by some successes and some great disappointments. He attempted to "pack" the Supreme Court by proposing mandatory retirement from the Court when a Justice reached the age of seventy. If the Justice refused, the President would then be able to make an additional appointment. At that time, six Justices, all Republican appointees, exceeded that age. The proposal ended in a bitter legislative and public relations failure. Also, an increasingly reactionary group in Congress rebuffed many of Franklin's later New Deal programs. War in Africa and Asia, and the threat of war in Europe, dampened any enthusiasm engendered by some easing of the Depression.

The Republicans mounted an aggressive campaign for the Presidency in 1940 with an eclectically progressive candidate, Wendell Willkie. Franklin's seemingly overwhelming lead melted in October, and he had to campaign vigorously with the reluctant help of Eleanor. Franklin still enjoyed the rough-and-tumble politics of active campaigning, and his efforts brought reward.

Eleanor told friends that she did not want to spend another four years in the White House, much less campaign actively. In a rare display of humor, she described what was required of the wife of a campaigning politician: "Always be on time. Never try to make any personal engagements. Do as little talking as humanly possible. Never be disturbed by anything. Always do what you're told to do as quickly as possible. Remember to lean back in a parade, so that people can see your husband. Don't get too fat to ride three on a seat. Get out of the way as quickly as you're not needed."[23] When asked to sum up her years as the wife of an officeholder, Eleanor replied, "It's hell!"[24]

Franklin's margin of victory was not of the landslide proportions of 1936, but it was substantial. His attention stayed, necessarily, on the darkening war clouds. Japanese troops were on the march in China, the German army occupied much of Europe, and Benito Mussolini's Black Shirts had invaded North Africa. Franklin continually assessed the viability and appropriateness of active participation in support of the Allies in Europe and Chiang Kai-shek in China.

Eleanor's voice was not heard on the international crises, but she continued to badger Franklin for his attention to domestic social issues. Millions of Americans highly respected her work, including her husband, although she had occasionally opposed certain administration programs. Frances Perkins, Franklin's Secretary of Labor, confirmed that "the President was enormously proud of her ability . . . he said more than once, 'You know, Eleanor really puts it over. She's got great talent with people.' In Cabinet meetings, he would say, 'You know my Missus gets around a lot . . . my Missus says they have typhoid fever in that district . . . my Missus says that people are working for wages way below the minimum set by NRA in the town she visited last week.' "[25]

Eleanor traveled extensively and wrote prolifically. Her Secret Service protection, all but exhausted by her energetic journeys into the hinterland to meet people and understand their needs, gave her the code name "Rover." In addition to her autobiography, Eleanor wrote a syndicated daily newspaper column, "My Day," and many magazine and journal articles. She generally ended her 16- to 20-hour days, that drained most of her aides, by writing long personal letters.

She had less time to spend with many of her closest friends. By the late 1930s, her friendship with Nancy Cook and Marion Dickerman ended irrevocably following a bitter disagreement with Nan. Marion, to no surprise, sided with her partner. Nan declared that much of Eleanor's success was due to their tutelage and support.

Eleanor found the suggestion intolerable. The living arrangements had grown contentious when Eleanor's friends, family, and followers continually filled the Val-Kill home with noise and disruption, much to Nan's and Marion's distress. Eleanor offered Nan and Marion a financial arrangement, and the Val-Kill partnership and long friendship came to a disappointing end. In later years, the once-close friends maintained a cordial but distant relationship.

Eleanor's involvement with her adult children was dutiful and mostly pleasant, but fell short of great warmth. She went to their aid, when needed, but most of her time and emotional energy was committed to her work. Anna wrote, with some sadness, "Mother was always stiff, never relaxed enough to romp. Mother loved all mankind, but she didn't know how to let her children love her."[26]

Eleanor constantly sought affection and caring, but seldom received much in return for her efforts. A notable exception was her close and often choppy relationship with Lorena Hickock. The warm letters they exchanged suggest to some that a physical intimacy existed. For several years, Eleanor and Hick had written each other "romantic" letters that in today's parlance might suggest a physical relationship. But that was the thirties, and these were women who were born before the turn of the century. It was not unusual for women of that age and background to express themselves in colorful and endearing language, proclaiming their affection and regretting their separation. Eleanor and Hick certainly cared deeply for each other, but their relationship was often in turmoil. Eleanor tried, in most ways, to control Hick's life, and Hick was forced to give up her successful journalistic career because of her closeness to the First Lady.

Hick was a demanding and inflexible companion. She expressed her disapproval of many of Eleanor's friends and colleagues, and she clearly resented those who made claims on Eleanor's time and attention. Although Hick became a tireless and effective political commentator and activist, she had suffered from an abusive childhood and an adulthood of unstable relationships. Hick was constitutionally mercurial and lapsed periodically into bouts of extreme depression.

There is no question that for a time she was the most important person in Eleanor's emotional life. But as much as she cared for Hick, Eleanor grew increasingly unwilling to accede to her possessive demands and quixotic temperament. Eleanor had too much on her plate and too many friends and associates important to her who were incompatible with and unappreciative of Hick's gloom and her interference. Eleanor and Hick remained good friends, but the intensity of their relationship cooled measurably. Although Hick continued to have a room at the White House, it was often occupied by Daisy Suckley.

Despite her personal trials, Eleanor was able to throw herself into her work and meaningfully occupy the hours that were previously reserved for her private life. Her public life was challenging and satisfying. While she did not seek public approbation, she received it. But when searching for personal happiness, she most often came up empty.

11

I Have a Terrific Headache

In September 1939, the United Kingdom went to war with the Axis countries. Canada was a British Commonwealth Dominion, and Campobello families answered the call and sent their sons into battle. By 1940, the United States was anxiously trying to determine its position in the gathering storm. The isolationists in Congress were gradually losing their stranglehold on American foreign policy, and Franklin saw little chance to avoid a moral responsibility in supporting the Allied effort. Arguments persist about Franklin's motivation in moving the United States toward an active role in the war at this time. Supporters argue that he believed that American involvement was essential to the near-term survival of a free western Europe, and in the longer term to our own defense from Adolf Hitler's master plan of world dominance. Others believe that intervention was Franklin's means to rebuild his political strength and leadership after a second term whose accomplishments fell short of earlier successes. With the Depression winding down, his detractors insisted that Franklin needed a defining issue to restart the New Deal engine. International leadership, even if it meant war, could provide that momentum.

Franklin had always been a man of action, a picker of options, an experimenter, and a taker of risks. This risk was not only the greatest one of his life and generation, but perhaps the greatest in the history of the Republic. He was determined to ready the country for full-scale involvement. How well he accomplished this task is still a matter of debate.

The slumbering American industrial engine had to be energized. After the lean years of the thirties, industrial labor was plentiful, manufacturing capital was available, and entrepreneurship was encouraged. The United States would soon be ready to be an active partner in the defense of a free Europe.

Internally, military preparedness had to be developed from ground zero. Congress passed the Selective Service Act, creating a lottery system to draft able young men into the armed services. Americans prepared for war, wondering where and when it would come, but, by the summer of 1941, it seemed only a matter of time.

Eleanor had to find a role in a country preparing for war. She became active in the Red Cross, the U.S. Savings Bond drives, and organizations that provided relief to war-ravaged Europe. She also continued to remind Franklin of the important human rights and social issues to which she had dedicated herself. Eleanor realized that social and human rights issues could easily be forgotten while the country devoted itself to war preparation. She was determined and she persisted, often over the objections of Franklin's staff.

As war continued to draw closer that summer, the unused Campobello cottage offered the Roosevelts a unique opportunity. Franklin and Eleanor invited the International Student Service Leadership Institute to hold a student summer study session at the red cottage. Eleanor was a member of the Institute's executive committee, serving with educators and leading liberals. The students were nominated by the presidents of their respective colleges and were drawn from student councils, student newspaper editorships, and other campus leadership positions. Applicants to the Institute submitted essays in response to questions prepared by Margaret Mead, the noted sociologist and anthropologist.

In the first summer session, twenty-three colleges were represented by the twenty-nine participants. There was a decidedly liberal political coloration to the group, which numbered sixteen young men and thirteen young women. They reported that their religious affiliations were fourteen Protestant, ten Jewish, and five Catholic, and they ranged in age from seventeen to twenty-two. The students came from urban and rural homes, public and private colleges. Their college major concentrations included pre-medicine, ceramic engineering, and art in addition to the more likely studies of political science, history, and economics. They were to discuss the national and world issues of the day, form study groups, and prepare position papers.[1] The academic staff was headed by William A. Neilson, the retired president of Smith College, while overall direction of the Institute was in the hands of Joseph P. Lash, executive secretary of the International Student Service. Lash, Eleanor's close friend, was later her most prolific biographer.

The Institute was to be a "total experience" for the students, and Campobello's bucolic setting was a place for both serious discussion and recreation. After all, that's what the Roosevelt cottage had always been. But the cottage had been barely used for the last several years and had to be prepared for this ambitious event.

Eleanor arrived on June 18 in her usual manner, driving the ubiquitous Buick roadster. She stopped again at Perry's Nut House for a supply of jams, soaps, nuts, and wild strawberry preserves. With Tommy Thompson in tow, Eleanor knew she had much to do. Twenty additional beds were required, and Eleanor and Tommy had to sew the twenty bedcovers needed. Food and sundry supplies were fetched from Eastport and St. Andrew's. Eleanor's appearance on the streets with market basket in hand surprised and captivated the staunchly conservative Eastporters. One resident said of his wife, resignedly, "A lifelong Republican, and there she goes, chasing Mrs. Roosevelt!"[2]

After she was satisfied that the cottage was ready, but before the students arrived, Eleanor departed for commitments in New York. She left a letter for Lash: "Since I cannot be here . . . to see the young people arrive, I want to ask you to welcome them for me. I hope they will be happy in this house which has seen some tragedy but far more joy." And to the students: "These are serious times and you are all here for a serious purpose. Nevertheless I hope you will feel at home and have some pleasant vacation hours to remember. I shall look forward to meeting you . . . ."[3]

Eleanor left a list of rules, admonitions, and suggestions. Some centered on the fact that the cottage was not electrified, had a less than plentiful supply of water, and was not served by telephone. The students were not to take kerosene lamps to bedrooms and were to use no more than two inches of water for baths. Franklin had assigned the students the task of clearing brush on the slope leading to the bay, but there would be ample time for picnics, hikes, and outdoor sports.

The Institute arranged for a steady stream of distinguished visiting faculty. The nation's first family could easily accomplish that task. Among the presenters were Supreme Court Justice Felix Frankfurter; the poet Archibald MacLeish; James Wechsler, the labor editor of the left-leaning newspaper *PM*; Henry Morgenthau, Jr., the longtime Roosevelt family friend and Secretary of the Treasury; and Walter White, director of the National Association for the Advancement of Colored People.

Upon Eleanor's return, the local islanders hoped that she would participate in a dance arranged for both students and islanders at the Welshpool Community Hall. Eleanor urged all the participants at the Institute to take care not to treat the islanders as just "hired help," but accept them as equals in every way. Quite likely, the students were far less apt to look down on Campobello's residents than most of the historically typical guests at the Roosevelts' and other cottages in the island's summer community.

Eleanor arrived to join the students at the cottage and, to the islanders' delight, at their dance, serving as the event's grand marshal. She also addressed the Institute, met with students in smaller groups, and generously engaged individuals in informal conversation. They admired her dedicated grasp of major issues and her graciousness, and they enjoyed her cookies and cake as well as her poetry readings. Eleanor wanted the young people to experience Campobello in the many ways that she knew and loved.

The students published a daily newspaper, the *Camp-ISS-Bellow*, which had a rotating editorship. Split into five groups, the students cycled the responsibilities of maintaining the house and grounds, organizing recreation, and tending to the library in addition to producing the newspaper. Original editorials, reports of lectures with guest biographies, and national and incidental news filled the pages of the paper. Features covered individual students and their backgrounds, and they injected a good deal of fun and humor, albeit often sophomoric. As Eleanor suggested, they accomplished serious work and discussion, but they also had opportunities for good times.

After a few false starts, the students found that they had to lobby for a relaxation of certain curfews and time constraints. When their complaints had been successfully acknowledged, they were eagerly willing to live within rules and procedures that they helped to create or modify. Dissent was always encouraged and respected in discussions and interactions with guests as well as in procedural activities. Speakers, including Eleanor, challenged the students to make their views known clearly but always with respect.[4] In those days rife with bloody labor disputes and threats of approaching war, the students and their teachers all took a dim view of violent displays of political and social dissent.

At the closing of the Institute, the students unanimously adopted a statement of their dedication to the advancement and strengthening of the "democratic cause in this country and the world." They affirmed their opposition to all forms of Communism, Nazism, and Fascism, and ended their alliances with the American Youth Congress and the American Student Union, organizations that had decidedly moved to the left or right. Their statement closed with: "Among young people, the way to meet the appeal that Communism makes is to demonstrate that democracy has a program to establish equality of opportunity and security in the social and economic fields, and peace internationally." And typical of college students, they also prepared a mostly facetious last will and testament. Participants left Campobello with an enhanced sense of purpose and some lifelong memories.

Eleanor returned to Campobello in July to join the students and to accompany Sara on what was to be her mother-in-law's last island holiday. Eleanor drove Sara in the Buick, while the chauffeur followed in Sara's car with the luggage. They stopped for a night at a "summer place on the outskirts of Bath, Maine and enjoyed lobster."[6] Their visit was to Sebasco Lodge, a traditional summer inn in a setting of great beauty in the town of Phippsburg.

Reaching Campobello, Sara remained at her cottage until late August, hoping for a visit from her beloved Franklin. He was in North Atlantic waters, not far from Campobello, steaming toward a secret meeting with the British Prime Minister, Winston Churchill. Sara knew nothing of the meeting, nor did Eleanor. In fact, virtually everyone in his administration was in the dark about the existence of the meeting, including Franklin's Secretary of State, Cordell Hull. The complex arrangements were made in virtually total secrecy in London as well as in Washington. Apparently the only person in the presidential circle of family and friends who did know was Daisy Suckley. Her pre-knowledge of this momentous event was revealed only when her papers were examined following her death fifty years later.

In that summer of 1941, war was going badly for the Allies. The United States was morally committed to the Allied effort and materially supportive, but sensed little hope for an Allied victory without full U.S. involvement. By August, America's entry into the war seemed close to reality, but sympathetic neutrality was still the official course. Franklin had little doubt that the country would take part in the European war, but he did not know when, nor how he would persuade Congress and much of the American public that it was essential.

Franklin had kept up a steady correspondence with Winston Churchill. The Prime Minister urged closer American cooperation, and Franklin was eager to discuss war conditions directly. So, too, was Churchill. Under a veil of secrecy, the two world leaders met at sea on the North Atlantic. It was this meeting that prevented Franklin from seeing Sara that summer at Campobello.

They had met once before. Franklin remembered the event vividly; Churchill did not. Franklin had been a member of an American delegation to Britain in 1918 to help coordinate the military effort of the Allies during World War I. Churchill was a Liberal Member of Parliament, the Minister of Munitions, and a senior member of the coalition government under Prime Minister David Lloyd George. Franklin, the Under Secretary of the Navy, was a relatively junior member of the delegation, and he recalled being virtually snubbed by an impatient Churchill. Franklin was well-born and had an important family name; he was a man of some promise; and he was irritated by Churchill's barely concealed indifference. Franklin never forgot the incident. Churchill did, but, more than twenty years later, he felt compelled to say that he had then been impressed by the Assistant Secretary of the Navy.[7]

Much of the groundwork for the meeting was accomplished by Harry Hopkins, who, as Franklin's personal emissary, had flown to both London and Moscow to establish important relationships with Churchill and Soviet Premier Josef Stalin. Hopkins grew to be a great favorite of Churchill, and he was an immensely important link in the Roosevelt-Churchill alliance and friendship.

The designated place for the historic meeting was Argentia Bay, off the coast of Newfoundland. Canadian armed forces provided security, and the world knew nothing of any meeting, much less its location, until it was over. Churchill arrived first after a rough North Atlantic crossing aboard *HMS Prince of Wales*. On August 9, the heavy cruiser *USS Augusta* anchored close by, bearing the President of the United States. Both Elliott and Franklin, Jr., junior naval officers, had been summoned to the meeting, although neither of them knew what the purpose was or who would be there. They were surprised and pleased to discover their mission and to find their father in good spirits.

Elliott recalled Franklin's exuberance. "He was as delighted as a kid, boasting of how he had thrown the newspapermen off the scent by going as far as Augusta, Maine, on the presidential yacht *Potomac*."[8] Franklin was transferred from the *Potomac* to the *Augusta* in the Gulf of Maine, well off the coast. Maine's capital city of Augusta is nearly forty miles from the sea on the Kennebec River. Although the river is deep enough for naval shipbuilding at Bath, nearer its mouth, the Kennebec is too shallow for deep-draft ships at Augusta. Elliott's recollection may well have been confused by the similar names of the heavy cruiser and the city.

Churchill was also in excellent spirits, Elliott reported. "He was not only sprightly but, there is no other word for it, boyish . . . ."[9] Elliott and Franklin, Jr., were officially made aides-de-camp for reasons known only to Franklin. Eleanor, not surprisingly, would have understood. She once remarked, "Perhaps anyone who has not experienced the loneliness of being President can not appreciate what having a member of the family near one might mean."[10] Franklin wanted his sons with him at this historic event, but neglected to take either his wife or his mother into his confidence about the fact of the meeting itself.

The following morning, the *Prince of Wales* moved closer and a tender carried Churchill to their historic first meeting aboard the *Augusta*. After Franklin got over his irritation that Churchill had brought two journalists and newsreel cameramen, the meeting progressed. The newspapermen were not to publish a detailed description of the meeting for a year, and the silent newsreel was to be nothing more than documentary evidence of the event. The President saw the meeting as an opportunity to discuss American aid without entry into the war and an opportunity to receive a first-hand update on Allied military actions and plans. Churchill saw an occasion to make a direct plea for an increase in active American support and for a photo opportunity that demonstrated to the world the close cooperation and friendship between the two nations.

The remainder of that first day was devoted to social interchange. The two leaders enjoyed their meals and exchanged gifts. Churchill made a lengthy presentation after dinner in a highly emotional appeal for direct American entry into the war. Franklin listened carefully, but without comment.

The next morning, it was the President's turn to make a call. He was carefully transported and lifted to the deck of the *Prince of Wales*, where all participated in a Sunday morning religious service that was so charged with emotion that it profoundly influenced the personal bonding between the two leaders.

A series of meetings with aides followed Sunday afternoon and then again at night on the *Augusta*. The President and the Prime Minister had their differences, and there were brief flashes of anger, but they served only to strengthen the growing relationship. Later that night, Franklin revealed to his sons that "I'll be able to work with him. Don't worry about that. We'll get along famously."[11]

Monday's sessions were again held with aides present, then a long meeting with just Churchill, the Roosevelts, and Hopkins. They agreed upon the eight propositions that made up the final draft of the Atlantic Charter. The Charter was important in dramatically reinforcing the joint determination of the European Allies and the United States. Ultimately, there were to be new and specific lend-lease agreements to provide vast supplies of war materials, one of the meeting's touchstones. Another was the everlasting, undying, and absolute commitment of purpose the two men made to each other. It was wrapped in a package of friendship and respect previously unknown between twentieth-century world leaders. The course of the war, in many ways, had been determined.

After good-byes, the *Prince of Wales* departed Argentia Bay to return Churchill and his staff to England. Sadly, while on active duty only three months later, the British battleship fell victim to German torpedoes and went to the bottom of the ocean. All hands were lost.

The *Augusta* steamed south to Blue Hill Bay in Maine, where the President was again transferred to the *Potomac*. The presidential party had an unsuccessful day of fishing at Eggemoggin Reach. A Deer Isle fisherman sent a bucket of lobsters aboard for the presidential party, which had made no secret of its presence. Local fishermen complained that the naval vessels tore holes in their nets, and the Navy promised restitution. The party then proceeded to Pulpit Harbor, where, on Saturday morning, Franklin received a number of friends, some of them old neighbors from Campobello. After crossing the ten miles to Rockland, the *Potomac* docked at Tillson's Wharf.

"Rockland's Red Letter Day," headlined the local *Courier-Gazette*.[12] That red letter day was Saturday, August 16, when the President of the United States came to town. Franklin's visit was clearly a big deal for coastal Mainers. He had been in Rockland five years earlier to board the *Amberjack II* as he joined his sons for a cruise to Campobello. But now, he was coming to Rockland after his history-making meeting with Churchill off the Newfoundland coast. The *Courier-Gazette*'s editor-in-chief, F. A. Winslow, was virtually beside himself with pride and excitement about the presidential visit. He wrote that "an event of such historic interest—an event which gave Rockland, Maine, a new place in the sun throughout the civilized world—needs to be recorded at some length that future generations may hark back to it as the most momentous day in the city's history."[13] Winslow allowed as how "the tremendous importance of the occasion was due to the fact that [the President] was again setting foot on land after 14 days at sea, in the course of which occurred his conference with Prime Minister Winston Churchill."[14] The news that the meeting had occurred and that an Atlantic Charter had been agreed upon was released to the press after the *Augusta* had raised its anchor at Argentia Bay.

The highly detailed description of the afternoon's events covered the city's preparations, the displays of flags and bunting, the care taken by the Secret Service, arrangements at the wharf, the parade route, and arrangements at the railroad station. After all, this was not an extended visit. It was designed as a convenience for the President's party to disembark from the *Potomac* and a chance for him to meet with the press, to be cheered by the excited local citizenry, and to board a train for the journey back to Washington. The city of Rockland treated it as a state visit with all the pride and enthusiasm it could muster. Franklin was a "neighbor," and his arrival in Rockland was one of triumph. It was to be his last visit to a favorite area whose waters he had known intimately for a half-century.

Editor Winslow proudly displayed his White House press card, "which, I do not need to explain, will be among my valued souvenirs for the rest of my days."[15] He joined other members of the working press for an interview with the President aboard the *Potomac* shortly after it docked at Tillson's Wharf. Winslow was struck by the informality of the interview and by the President's ease and affability. Franklin took the lead in the session, telling the press precisely what he wanted to relate without releasing any meaningful information that had not already become known.

He told them that the Argentia meeting had been a joint idea, that it had been a useful exchange of views, that there were many points of agreement, and that a new lend-lease agreement was near. The Administration would ask Congress to provide aid to the European democracies, but not, at that time, to Russia. Franklin allowed that the United States was not any closer to entering the war and that further meetings and study on assistance to the Allies would be required. He also described in detail the Sunday service held on the quarter-deck of the *Prince of Wales*, calling it both historic and memorable. After posing for photographs, Franklin ended the interview on a high note of warmth and good feeling.

Franklin was assisted from the wharf to a waiting car, which drove slowly and ceremoniously past cheering crowds lined eight to ten deep. At the railroad station, large numbers of children and young adults cheered the President. Franklin was assisted aboard the train, but made his way again to the rear platform and waved to the crowd for several minutes. Always accommodating and considerate of his carefully nurtured good relationship with the press, Franklin held the train for thirty minutes so that the reporters would be able to file their stories by wire. Then, with cheers and train whistles splitting the air, the Boston & Maine *Special* puffed its way southward.

At 7:30 that evening, the *Special* pulled into Portland, Maine's largest city. The stop was merely functional, with time to check the running equipment thoroughly and to load several tons of ice for the train's air-conditioning system. The *Portland Sunday Telegram* reported that six thousand people crowded Union Station, hoping to get a glimpse of the President. They were disappointed that he did not make an appearance. Franklin was at dinner, perhaps eating the lobsters that accompanied him from Rockland. The crowd did get to cheer as a Secret Service man gave Fala, the president's dog, his daily "constitutional." A number of leaders made brief courtesy visits to Franklin, including Senator Claude Pepper of Florida, former Governor Louis Brann of Maine, and Fred Lancaster, Chairman of the Maine Democratic Party. The last leg of the trip to and from the North Atlantic Conference took Franklin from Maine for the last time.

The press assumed that the meeting with Churchill had been held off the coast of Maine. In fact, the official British newsreel, released on August 17, showed background shots of a "barren, rocky coast about a half mile away, indicating the meetings probably were held somewhere off the coast of Maine."[16] The newsreel showed Churchill handing the President a letter from King George VI. It gave the impression that the two leaders met alone. The film also showed the memorable Sunday service and American and British staff members and military personnel arriving, conferring, and departing. It offered a lighter touch by showing Franklin with his hat brim upturned and Churchill with his cap rakishly angled over his right ear. The Prime Minister was shown with his omnipresent cigar, and the narration noted the "happy coincidence" that Captain Elliott Roosevelt and Ensign Franklin Roosevelt, Jr., had been remarkably assigned to regular naval duty in the immediate area of Argentia Bay.[17]

Meanwhile, Sara waited in vain for a visit from her famous son. She was eighty-six years of age, her heart was failing, and her memory was fading. She steadfastly refused to admit that she was ill, declining to eat properly or take needed rest. Only at Franklin's insistence could she be persuaded to retain a trained nurse. True to her iron will, Sara pulled herself together for her departure from Campobello. She strode purposefully down the front stairs of her cottage and said good-bye to each member of her staff, much as she had done most summers since 1885.

Sara made the long journey back to Hyde Park and died peacefully in her sleep on September 7, 1941, in her beloved Hudson Valley home. The residents of Campobello were saddened to learn of her death only a week after her last visit. Canadian and American flags were lowered to half-staff on the island. In one of history's oddities, the largest tree on the Hyde Park estate toppled to the ground less than five minutes after her death. There was no storm, no lightning, no wind.[18] Mysteriously, but inexorably, the mighty had fallen.

Franklin, to no surprise, took Sara's death hard. He wept when he looked at a box of memorabilia that included his infant clothes and locks of his hair. Eleanor, however, took Sara's death with characteristic impassiveness. She later wrote to Anna: "I couldn't feel any emotion or any real sense of loss, and that seemed terrible after 36 years of fairly close association."[19]

It is not clear how much comfort Eleanor gave to Franklin after Sara's death. He had been extremely supportive when Eleanor's beloved brother Hall died earlier that year. But then, Franklin was far fonder of Hall than Eleanor had been of her mother-in-law.

That summer of 1941 marked the end of service for Sara's venerable cottage, and it signaled a transitional phase for Franklin and Eleanor's big red cottage. With Sara's death, the business of maintaining her cottage and its staff fast became a burden. Medley Wilson, an islander, had been caretaker for "Mrs. James" for twenty-nine years. He appealed to "Mrs. Franklin" on October 28:

> I wrote to you . . . to find out if we would still work on the place. I have been with you all for 29 years. Mrs. James always paid me—until the end of October. And I have done all the work she wanted me to do this Fall. I cut the alder all down in the bottom of your field and I shook all the carpets and rugs at your place and put them back in the rooms and put all the wood under cover and helped with all the shutters . . . . The last money Mrs. James gave me was for August, $60.00 . . . . Mrs. James always gave me $100.00 for the winter months . . . . I don't know what I would do if I was not up at the Houses, as I have never gone away from hard work. Mrs. James always told me how nice everything looked when she arrived.[20]

Looking after houses on Campobello was for many islanders the principal if not sole means of livelihood, in effect a "cottage" industry. It is not known how or whether Franklin or Eleanor handled Medley Wilson's touching appeal. Sara always paid her staff fairly and promptly. Right up until her death, Sara continued to pay many of the bills for the President's cottage. We can only hope that Franklin and Eleanor were able to maintain her considerate regularity of payment.

After the Japanese attacked Pearl Harbor on December 7, 1941, Franklin went before Congress with a declaration of war against the Axis powers. It is not possible to determine precisely when war would have begun had the Japanese not attacked. Few doubt the war's inevitability, but the timing might have been different. If the American military were not fully prepared for combat, the nation was surely in a war production mode. Lend-lease had spearheaded the development of high-speed military weapons production, and now, with full mobilization, the powerful American industrial engine was at full throttle.

Franklin felt betrayed by the sneak attack on the Pacific fleet, but he was ready for war. Churchill was relieved to have the United States finally engaged as a full comrade-in-arms, but he feared that American resources would be directed first to the Pacific rather than to the European theater of operations.

With America at war, neither Franklin nor Eleanor had the opportunity or the time to visit Campobello. If the subject even arose, it was generally because the Roosevelt island properties needed maintenance. Sara's house quickly fell into disrepair. On October 18, 1943, the President received a letter from a Campobello contractor. It contained an estimate for a new drain for the cellar, because the old drain could not be found. Franklin authorized the work and passed the letter on to Eleanor. She replied to him, "Is this our house or Mama's?"[21] It was Sara's cottage, and the work was apparently done, although the cottage was never used much again.

Eleanor's schedule and her responsibilities may have kept her from visiting Campobello during the war years, but it did not prevent her from being named "Princess Many Trails (Ow-Du-See-U)" by Bruce Poolaw, Chief of the Penobscots.[22] Honoring the First Lady, the chief was likely making reference to the many trips she took on behalf of her personal causes and those of the President.

There were occasions for Eleanor to remember happier days at Campobello and the friends she had made those many summers. One friend was the subject of her "My Day" newspaper column in 1944:

> I missed the newspaper notices, on September 1, telling the death of Dr. E. H. Bennet at the age of 96. Dr. Bennet lived in Lubec, Maine, a small town separated from the island of Campobello by a very short distance of swiftly running water. The "Narrows," as it is called, can be crossed in a rowboat, but you must know how to cross it or you will not find yourself landing where you expected to land. Dr. Bennet knew how to cross it in all weathers. He knew the people who lived on Lonely Island, on the poor farms, and in the little villages all around him, for he practiced medicine in that area for 66 years . . . he looked after me in August, 1914, when Franklin Jr. was born in Campobello. He had come over many times before that, however, to help me with some of the children's minor ailments, and once when my brother and his friends tried to climb a rock named "The Friar" and fell some distance to the stony beach below, Dr. Bennet cared for them and housed them overnight.
>
> We had few serious illnesses until my husband was stricken with poliomyelitis. Dr. Bennet traveled back with us to New York, and I have never gone to Campobello since, even for a few days, without stopping to see him. I looked upon him as a friend as well as a doctor, and I had the greatest admiration for him.[23]

By 1944, the Allies were clearly on the offensive in both Europe and the Pacific. Wartime leadership suited Franklin and enhanced his political skills. He concentrated entirely on domestic policy during his first two terms and devoted his last years to foreign affairs and the conduct of the war. But his astute political acumen was the source of his eminence.

William Leuchtenberg extols this eminence by comparing Franklin with other presidential leaders. Roosevelt, "unlike George Washington, was no heroic military leader or 'Father of his country'; unlike Abraham Lincoln he was not the deification of the common man nor did he free the slaves; unlike Thomas Jefferson he was no towering intellect or theorist of democracy; unlike Andrew Jackson he was no self-made man or military hero. In many respects he displayed opposite traits. He was a child of wealth and privilege . . . . Stricken with polio, he was able to demonstrate a 'splendid' though artfully masked, example of personal courage. . . . FDR was 'superior in the political arts of balance, circumspection, patience and cunning.' . . . All successors have operated in the shadow of FDR . . . ."[24]

Time and the war had taken their toll on the President. His work schedule had to be shortened and he took more time to rest in Hyde Park or in Warm Springs. Deep dark circles colored the skin around his eyes, he lost a significant amount of weight, and a graying pallor marked his gaunt appearance. His attention span and his generally sunny disposition suffered. Although he was easily nominated for a fourth term, he seemed to have little interest in the process. His fourth campaign began almost as one of indifference. As he grew increasingly unwell, his doctors warned him to slow down. Although it was not popularly known, Franklin was suffering from congestive heart failure. He looked aged and drawn and probably felt little would be gained by making many public appearances. His old enthusiasm for campaigning appeared to be long gone.

"I don't think Pa would really mind defeat," Eleanor wrote to Jimmy. "If elected he'll do his job well. I feel sure and I think he can be kept well to do it but he does get tired so I think if defeated he'll be content . . . ."[25] Pa Watson, the president's aide, remarked that Franklin "didn't seem to give a damn."[26] Typically, as when other approaches failed, the staff turned to Eleanor to persuade her husband to get out into the active campaign.

Franklin joined the fray, regaining sufficient strength to stand and speak from the rear of his campaign train. Although much of the vaunted Roosevelt vigor was gone, Franklin somehow found the resolve to urge his body to respond. The success of his late campaign efforts was due largely to the same kind of grit and determination he had shown in 1921 when stricken with polio. He had one more great challenge to face, and it took all his strength to face it. It was Franklin's last race, and he was determined to win by a comfortable margin.

Franklin and Eleanor waited for the final election returns at Hyde Park, as they always had. There was the usual buzz of excitement as the returns started to come in, but they did not have the same drama as in years past. Louis Howe was long dead, Missy LeHand had died of a stroke a year earlier, Sara was gone, the four Roosevelt sons were overseas at war—only Anna and her son were present. When the traditional torchlight parade of villagers arrived just before midnight, Franklin permitted himself to be wheeled out to the porch. He addressed the gathering from his wheelchair, an event unique in itself. He thanked his loyal neighbors for their support and expressed confidence in his election to a fourth term. A little after three in the morning, the Republican candidate, New York Governor Thomas E. Dewey, conceded defeat. Franklin was sound asleep.

Two days after his fourth inauguration, Franklin left for Yalta and his last summit meeting with Churchill and Stalin. Eleanor, concerned about his worsening health and his growing irritability and impatience, asked to accompany him. He turned down her request and invited Anna instead. Churchill was bringing his daughter Sarah, and Franklin thought Anna would be a more appropriate companion. It had become his custom to exclude Eleanor from participating in international diplomacy, and she had no choice but to accept his decision.

It was popularly thought at that time that the Yalta Conference went quite well. Franklin tried hard to negotiate effectively, but his failing health and flagging vigor made the task all the more difficult. Upon his return, he dutifully addressed Congress to report on the results of the conference. This time, unlike all others, he remained seated throughout his speech.

Friends reported that he looked thin, worn, and gray. His hands shook, and he suffered a noticeable loss of muscular control. He no longer drove his own car or mixed his own cocktails. Franklin was wearing out quickly, and he knew it. All he wanted to do was to get to Warm Springs and relax. In early April, he returned to "the Little White House," hoping that the warm Georgia sun would recharge his faltering batteries.

The day he died, Franklin was smartly dressed in a dark blue double-breasted suit and his favorite Harvard crimson tie. He seemed to be in good spirits. While posing for a portrait and scanning some papers, Franklin complained of "a terrific headache." He slumped forward in his chair and was quickly carried to his bedroom. His cardiologist, in residence, was summoned to his bedside, but could do nothing. Franklin Delano Roosevelt died of a cerebral hemorrhage at Warm Springs, Georgia, on April 12, 1945. He had outlived Louis Howe and Missy LeHand, and he had outlived his mother by fewer than four years. But he had not outlived the war. The conflict in Europe ended just weeks afterward. Franklin's death in Georgia took place many miles from his beloved homes in Hyde Park and Campobello, homes that had given him life and sustained him. At the end, neither his wife nor his children were with him. The only family members present were cousins Laura Delano and Daisy Suckley. Also present, unknown to Eleanor, was Lucy Mercer Rutherfurd.

In Washington, Eleanor took the news of his death calmly and without any display of emotion. She expressed her sadness for the country and her support for the new president, Harry S Truman. A funeral train carried the only president ever to be elected to four terms back to his Hudson Valley home and eternal rest at Hyde Park. Members of the public, shocked and largely unaware of the president's physical deterioration, wept at every rail crossing.

Most Americans who remember Franklin Roosevelt's death can recall precisely where they were and what they were doing when they learned that he had died. They recall this event as one of the most upsetting of their lives. Before the days of television, which provided most people with news of the assassination death of John F. Kennedy, radio newscasts, newspapers, and delayed newsreels brought them the news of Franklin's unexpected passing. The emotional effect of the loss was incalculable.

The government was prepared to send an official burial crew to Hyde Park. The long-time gardener at Springwood, William Plog, would have none of it. Plog had served the Roosevelts since Franklin was a boy. "I think the President would want his own men to do that," he said. The burial plan called for Franklin's head to rest toward the east. "That isn't right," Plog said. "We will put his head to the west. Then he will be looking always east to the rising sun and the coming of another day."[27]

At the interment service, Daisy Suckley held Fala, the president's Scotty, on a leash in the garden at Hyde Park. The guns firing military salutes frightened the dog, but Daisy held him firm. This last act of personal kindness was tendered by a distant cousin, not one of the immediate family.[28]

Eleanor had once said that if polio couldn't kill Franklin, the presidency wouldn't. If he had served one or two peacetime terms, that might well have been true. But the presidency was what he wanted, sought, and expected more than anything else in the world.

———

As peace came to Europe just weeks later, the fact that Franklin did not live to see it reinforced the nation's grief. Eleanor found it particularly difficult to rejoice in the war's end without Franklin. Japan's surrender came almost four months later, after the deployment of atomic bombs at Hiroshima and Nagasaki. President Truman had to make the excruciating decision to order the use of these weapons of mass destruction.

Harvard held an appropriate memorial service for its fallen son. Dean Willard Sperry spoke of the tragic timing of the President's death: "He died too soon. He had earned the right to see victory on land and sea and in the air. He should have seen it for himself; his eyes should have beheld it . . . ."[29]

When he heard of his friend's death, Churchill "felt as if I had been struck a physical blow. My relations with this shining personality had played so large a part in the long, terrible years we worked together. Now they had come to an end, and I was overpowered by a sense of deep and irreparable loss."[30] A "deeply distressed" Stalin heard of Franklin's death from Ambassador W. Averill Harriman, who held the Marshal's hand for a full thirty seconds. The untrusting Soviet dictator sent a message to the U.S. State Department asking that an autopsy be performed to determine whether the American President had been poisoned.[31]

In one of the more insightful statements made about the fallen President, the British philosopher Isaiah Berlin wrote, "He was one of the few statesmen in the twentieth century, or any century, who seemed to have no fear of the future."[32] Franklin was decidedly of his time. Circumstances provide the opportunity for greatness. His sense of timing in understanding the requirements of leadership was masterly and his courage unimpeachable. He could not have hoped for more success in his presidency or asked more of his destiny. His hope for personal happiness was not as high on his agenda.

Although Franklin Roosevelt's accomplishments were many, there were also extreme political and personal failures. The relocation and internment of Japanese-Americans was an unforgivable act, although born of the fear and bigotry of advisors. His inability to provide moral leadership, if action were not possible, in the slaughter of millions of European Jews in the Holocaust was enormously disappointing. He pleaded political expediency and security considerations, or fell silent to protests.

Franklin eagerly and purposefully employed any and all the resources available to him in achieving his goals. He could be manipulative, duplicitous, and opportunistic in both act and deed, although he believed that his actions were always to good purpose. Franklin listened to many and agreed with few. He used whatever information and ideas were useful and dismissed those that were not. He easily accepted the devotion, even the affection, of many, but returned it to few. Except for his family, only a select group could claim any substantive closeness with Franklin. Certainly Howe and later Hopkins could, and Churchill had a special place in Franklin's affection. Unique roles were cast for Lucy Mercer, Missy LeHand, and, perhaps, Daisy Suckley. Quite probably only Sara Delano Roosevelt received Franklin's full, everlasting, and unquestioned love.

12

The Air Has the Tang of the Sea

Dealing with Franklin's death was difficult for Eleanor, as it was for the rest of the nation. Franklin had been President through the two most momentous events of the first half of the twentieth century, the Great Depression and World War II. His sudden death came as a shattering loss just when the war was about to end. Eleanor had lost her ally and husband of forty years. The fact that their marriage had been rocky did not negate the affection and respect they held for each other.

No longer was Eleanor the wife of the sitting President. She still held the same beliefs, the same hopes, and the same needs. Would she continue to have an important public role, and what might her private life be like? How could her senior years be useful and fulfilling?

First, Eleanor had to deal with the circumstance of Franklin's death. She was well aware of his deteriorating health, his angina attacks, and his treatment for congestive heart disease. But, like others around him, she was caught up in an expectation of Franklin's vaunted recuperative powers and his demonstrated ability to overcome great physical hardship.

Eleanor had to accept the fact that Lucy Mercer Rutherfurd was with Franklin at the end. Eleanor was staggered when she learned not only that Lucy had been with Franklin in Warm Springs, but that she had also been with him at her good friend Bernard Baruch's estate in South Carolina, and had visited Franklin at the White House and in their home in Hyde Park. Finally, Eleanor had to work through with Anna the knowledge that her only daughter had been a partner to these arrangements.

Immediately after Franklin's funeral, Eleanor made herself available to President Truman to aid in the transition and to help in any way. Truman was appreciative of her graciousness, and an admirer of her skills. He believed Eleanor to be the ideal delegate to the newly formed United Nations Organization and gave her the opportunity to lead in the UN's adoption of a Declaration of Human Rights. In the span of a quarter of a century, Eleanor had grown from a limited social activism to worldwide leadership in the cause of human rights. Louis Howe would have been proud, and so, too, would Franklin Roosevelt.

When Truman asked Eleanor to be a delegate to the opening session of the UN General Assembly in London in January, 1946, she considered for a time before accepting the position. She was hesitant to take on a responsibility for what she believed to be the most important of Franklin's legacies. Eleanor was at first unsure of her own strength in filling what proved to be her most enduring appointive role.

There were also family matters that required Eleanor's attention. Among them were Franklin's estate; the fates of Springwood and Campobello; and the interests of her children and an increasing number of grandchildren. She had a lot of sorting out to do. Eleanor was sixty years old and, for the first time in her life, she was solely and completely in charge of her own future.

In the summer of 1946, Eleanor was anxious to return to Campobello. A memorial to Franklin was to be unveiled in Welshpool, and Eleanor and Fala, along with a chauffeur, headed northeast through Maine. En route, she filed a column for "My Day," dated July 31:

> After stopping overnight in Portland, Maine, I have
> driven up the coast, looking for familiar landmarks as I

went. Where was that nut shop or that place where, in the past, I stopped to buy jellies or jams? On the way up to Campobello Island, I used to make acquisitions which my family enjoyed, since it is not very easy on the island to get a variety of food. Gardens are late, but fish is always plentiful there.

I may be in time for late strawberries, because they ripen slowly. They have a wonderful flavor, somewhat like the ones grown on Ile d'Orleans, in the St. Lawrence River, near Quebec. These are famous for their delicious flavor. It used to be easy, when we had a boat, to go and come to the mainland, but a storm destroyed our boathouse and our boat last winter.

On August 1, a monument will be unveiled in the little village of Welchpool [sic], Campobello Island, N.B., in memory of my husband, who went there so often in his boyhood and early manhood and loved not only the island itself but the waters all around it. He knew the coast of New Brunswick and of Nova Scotia and was as good a sailorman thereabouts as many of the natives. They asked me particularly to try to be in Campobello on August 1, so I am glad that, with my son Elliott and his family, I will be there.[1]

Fala was a newsworthy dog often present at public and private events. No presidential pet has approached Fala's notoriety or public affection. Following is a description of one of Fala's more embarrassing experiences, from the *Portland Press Herald* in July, 1946:

> Fala Snubbed Here, Mrs. Roosevelt Departs,
> Hotel Won't Let Dog Above Lobby, Proffers Kennel
>
> Fala, most socially acceptable dog in the United States if not the World, has been snubbed. It happened in the Eastland Hotel Sunday night and as a result his famous mistress, Mrs. Franklin D. Roosevelt, passed the night in an overnight camp instead of the hotel. The proud prince

of dogdom who had the run of the White House as the constant companion of his late master, President Roosevelt, ran into a house rule and came off second best.

The house rule, invoked about a year ago at the hotel, bans dogs above the lobby. And no matter to what dizzy heights Fala had risen while attending the councils of the great with his master, he stayed at lobby level in Portland. Tongues buzzed with the gossip in the hotel lobby Monday afternoon. 'Have you heard that they wouldn't let Fala in,' was a whisper. It sounded just like gossip but Leo G. Gain, assistant manager of the hotel, confirmed it.

He said that Mrs. Roosevelt called at the Eastland desk Sunday evening to claim a reservation and ask for accommodations for her chauffeur and "my dog." She did not identify the dog as Fala. The desk clerk cited the house rule. He added that the hotel had kennels at a local garage where the dog might stay.

According to Gain, Mrs. Roosevelt was 'perfectly gracious' and left the hotel to look at the kennels. But, apparently reconsidering—or possibly she asked Fala about it— she almost immediately sent back word that she would cancel her reservations and drive on. (Mrs. Roosevelt, Fala, and the chauffeur continued on to the Royal River Cabins in Yarmouth, passed the night there, and resumed their journey to the Roosevelt summer home at Campobello, N.B. The former First Lady and Fala will be guests of honor when a memorial is dedicated there Thursday to the late President.) The report from Yarmouth Monday was that Fala passed a comfortable night undisturbed by the slight to his dignity.[2]

Eleanor responded in a "My Day" column dated August 5:

Some of the papers in the Maine area made a good deal of the fact that, on my trip up to Campobello Island,

I could not stay overnight at a hotel in Portland because I had Fala with me. Since it was a hotel rule, the clerk was quite right to stick to it and I had no complaint. . . .

The fault was mine, since I had not mentioned that I would have a dog with me. And it made no difference because, when I stopped for supper in Yarmouth, I asked if there were any cabins nearby that would take me in with a dog, and I found a place at once and had a comfortable night.[3]

It was typical of Eleanor to accept responsibility and to excuse bureaucracy and overreaction. Eleanor dined that evening at Yarmouth's Westcustogo Inn. Fala was not allowed in but was "entertained" on the restaurant's porch by the owner's daughter, who was paid one dollar for her services.

On August 1, barely sixteen months after Franklin's death, the Historic Sites and Monuments Board of Canada erected a red granite cairn and bronze tablet at Welshpool. The plaque reads: "In happy memory of Franklin Delano Roosevelt, 1882 1945, statesman and humanitarian who, during many years of his eventful life, found in this tranquil island, rest, refreshment and freedom from care. To him it was always the 'beloved island.' "[4]

Two weeks later, Eleanor was back at her New York apartment, where she met with an attorney from the firm of O'Connor & Farber. Basil O'Connor had been Franklin's law partner, a valued advisor, and a long-time friend. The subject was the disposition of the Roosevelt estate at Campobello. From an inter-office memorandum dated August 13, 1946:

When Mrs. Roosevelt was at Campobello . . . she had a careful inspection made of the property. Her report confirms the personal inspection made by . . . me . . . on July 19, 1946. The original Sara Delano Roosevelt cottage is in poor condition due to neglect over a period of many years. . . . The cottage known as the President's cottage is in fair condition. The underpinning of this cottage will have to be replaced at a number of points and some of the exterior beams, gutters and wood trim are rotted and will have to be replaced. The interior of this cottage appears to be in sound condition. The pump to the well is gone and the well should be thoroughly cleaned and a new pump installed. The boathouse at the beach is completely dilapidated and instructions were given to Medley Wilson . . . to tear it down completely.

Mrs. Roosevelt stated that upon inquiry that no property has been sold on the Island for many years and that there are a number of vacant cottages which the owners would like to get rid of, if possible, she therefor feels that the Executors will be unable to sell the property. If this is true, she and Elliott are willing to offer the Executors $1,000 in cash for all the property at Campobello, including the unimproved property at Echo Point. If her offer is accepted by the Executors, Mrs. Roosevelt intends to employ a contractor to tear down the Sara Delano Roosevelt cottage, take whatever timber, etc., that is needed to repair the President's cottage, and sell the rest of the material on a 50/50 basis with the contractor. She would then turn the President's cottage into a sort of family community house to be shared by the Grays (Eleanor's Aunt Maude and her husband David) and with the various members of the family, dividing the cost of maintenance and upkeep among them. I advised Mrs. Roosevelt that it would be necessary for the Executors to first endeavor to sell the property at the best price obtainable, but if such efforts were unsuccessful, the Executors would certainly entertain her offer. She seemed to be entirely satisfied with this arrangement. . . .[5]

It must have seemed peculiar to Eleanor to dicker over the purchase of her "own" home. The Campobello properties and the Hyde

Park holdings had passed to Franklin less than five years earlier with the death of Sara. Purchasing the cottage from the Executors was the only way for Eleanor to gain title, and the real estate values at Campobello were at rock bottom. Acquiring all the Campobello property for a mere $1,000 seems amazing, even by 1946 standards, but Campobello had long passed as a summer vacation place for the wealthy. The purchase was made and title passed to Elliott. It is more than likely that Eleanor put up the money.

It was somewhat odd that Elliott gained title to the cottage. As a child and as a young man, he showed little interest in Campobello and spent the least time on the island of all the Roosevelt children. When Franklin twice cruised to Campobello aboard the *Amberjack II* with his sons as crew, Elliott was not among them. But now, in the post-war 1940s, he was the only Roosevelt child to show some interest in Campobello, and that seemed to suit Eleanor.

By the terms of Franklin's will, the Hyde Park properties were given to the government as a national historic site to become the Franklin D. Roosevelt Library and Museum. Until that took place, Eleanor informed the Executors that Elliott intended to buy a "carload of young Texas steers to be turned loose on the property during the winter."[6] Elliott believed that the steers did not require shelter and would acclimate themselves. There was enough hay on the estate to satisfy their needs, Eleanor thought, and if the estate's income provided sufficient funds, she would ask the Executors to pay for the cattle. This was a remarkable idea and another of Elliott's schemes to make money, and another attempt by Eleanor to help him out. The very idea of Texas cattle at Hyde Park boggles the mind. If Franklin wasn't spinning in his grave, then Sara certainly was in hers.

As to the Campobello cottage and lands, it was unclear how much repair was required, who would pay for it, how it would be paid, and what future use the Roosevelts would make of the properties. It was clear, however, that Eleanor still wished to have the occasional use of the cottage. By summer, that wish was satisfied, and she wrote of her visit in "My Day" dated July 16, 1947:

This morning we are off to Maine—eight adults, four children, one puppy only a few months old, two cars, and a truck loaded with bicycles, bags, typewriters, and books. This evening we are going to descend, we hope, on Ogunquit, Maine, to see my daughter-in-law, Faye Emerson Roosevelt, act in "State of the Union." Then we will proceed to Campobello Island, New Brunswick, to spend a month there in strict retirement—devoting half of each day to work on a book and the other half to all the things that our youngsters love to do in a place where life is lived largely upon the water.

One thing that draws me back to this remote island is the sunsets as I look from my porch across the water to the mainland, where two rivers flow in on either side of Eastport, Maine. The sun sets behind the little town.

Eastport and Lubec are the two nearest mainland towns. They are not so very picturesque when you are in the streets, but from across the water they have great charm. I have sometimes thought that Lubec might almost be Mont St. Michel on the coast of France. That is just a little stretch of the imagination, however, and I like both these little towns for what they are. I get a lift of the spirit as soon as I begin to breathe the sea air of the Maine coast. . . .[7]

Eleanor wrote to a friend: "Here we are after a very long trip up. It was a caravan, truck, station wagon and my car. The children moved from car to car. Fala stayed with me . . . . The house is not in good order but it can be made very comfortable and sound in construction with comparatively little expense . . . . We've had a fog every night since we came and gray days but I hope it will clear tomorrow . . . ."[8]

The summer was productive. Eleanor was able to revise the first nine chapters of the second volume of her autobiography, *This I Remember*. The first volume, *This Is My Story*, had been written mostly in the peace and quiet of Campobello. The new book was to include a reflective portrait of Franklin, and up until then, Eleanor found it difficult to settle down and write. But once again Campobello provided a conducive setting, and she happily reported that she had begun dictating new material to Tommy Thompson. However, the process continued to be halting and she did not finish the book until 1949.

Work aside, Eleanor was happy to have an extended stay on the island. On July 26, in another "My Day" column, Eleanor described her joy at being on Campobello:

Fog which lifts every day for only a short time, but always hangs just over the edge of the island, becomes pretty monotonous—and, until yesterday, that is the kind of weather we have had since we arrived here. Someone told me that the people out on Grand Manan Island have been enveloped in fog for 47 days, and I doubt if it has even lifted in the daytime. But a good many of the island's summer visitors are artists and some of the fog effects in this region can be very beautiful. Nevertheless, every one of us greeted with joy the sunshine and the clearing west wind yesterday.

We packed our lunch baskets and in my son's little power boat we started up the St. Croix River for St. Andrew's. Some of our guests had an orgy of shopping at the craft shop there, since wool is again available and the handwoven materials, blankets, and so on, are very well made and very attractive.

Finally, we went to the little island just across the harbor from the town of St. Andrew's. We built a fire between two rocks, scrambled our eggs, cooked our bacon, and fed a hungry crowd.

It seemed the right spot to read Longfellow's *Evangeline* to the children, and so I told them the story of Nova Scotia and the Acadian peasants, and then read from a book that had belonged to their grandfather . . ."[9]

The future of the Campobello house troubled Eleanor. Elliott later wrote that "Mother was undecided about what to do with a house where wraiths seemed to hover."[10] But, on their return from another stay in Campobello in 1950, she urged him to restore the house and make it available to the whole family. "The expense . . . will be great, however, and I may not feel it worthwhile unless all of you children think you will enjoy coming here when you come east in the summer . . .," she wrote to Anna, then living in Seattle.[11]

Eleanor had also hoped that her doctor and new friend, David Gurewitsch, might spend his holiday there. David was years younger than Eleanor, but she attached great significance to this new relationship. She was eager to share with him a favorite place but, although Eleanor tried hard to have David join her in Campobello, he showed little inclination to make the effort.

Eleanor was resigned to the fact that David would not satisfy her hopes. She wrote to him, "We drove in yesterday and the air had the tang of the sea, and it was cool . . . . Elliott and I have gone all over the house and the point we own on the other side of the island on the Bay of Fundy. If we put it in order he will try to use it for six weeks in summer, and I should do the same but I will not unless it can be really useful and give pleasure to some of those I love, so I don't live only on old memories here but build some new ones."[12]

Still on the island, Eleanor wrote in "My Day" on August 25:

I have not driven a great deal since I arrived on the island. In the years when I spent long summers here we always walked or went by boat so I find it hard to remember to use the car; besides, when one has driven across the island to Herring Cove and up to the head harbor end of the island, one has been about everywhere that one can go by car, whereas by boat there are endless trips to take. One can go up the St. Croix River to Calais, or stop at St. Andrew's and see the fashionable world in the big hotel, and buy handwoven rugs and tweeds in the cottage industries shop which has flourished for many years. By now one can probably get some English china and pottery, which was not available during the war and is still not too plentiful in England itself. One can travel in a little boat among endless islands up the coast of New Brunswick, and even out to Grand Manan, and all the way around Campobello itself, joining the fishing fleet if one wants to fish.

The seining of a weir here is one of the sights no stranger should miss, for it takes one back to the days of the Bible as one watches the fisherman pulling up the seine and filling their dories with fish. One can stay in American waters and find endless picnic spots up the Denny River which flows down to the west of Eastport, as the St. Croix does on the east.

There is a little Indian village north of Eastport where the Indians still sell some of their baskets and other wares in the town. . . .

I am no happier about the way Indians have been treated in this part of our country than I am anywhere else in the United States. Had we done a really good job it seems to me that our Indians today would be educated; there would be no need of reservations; they would be fully capable of taking their places . . . .[13]

As much as Eleanor enjoyed her vacations and travels, she remained continually vigilant to social custom and the inequities that existed in American life. She had often lobbied Franklin and government officials about her concern for the treatment of Native Americans, emphasizing a need for better education and training. The Roosevelts had long had friendly contacts with Native Americans on Campobello and in Maine, and Eleanor had visited several government reservations on her trips in the West.

She wrote again to David Gurewitsch just before leaving the island. Still with some resignation, she had some hope that restoration of the house might yet happen. She allowed, however, that

Those I love have little interest in Campobello. I . . . love Campobello . . . it would have been fun to show it to you and hope that it would give you some of the lift it used to give me. Tommy will enjoy it and I will try to give her a good time but our contacts are best in the field of work and not much good otherwise tho' we love each other dearly . . . . I'll decide with Elliott what needs to be done and get contracts . . . nowadays unless I have someone I really want to be up there with, it is not a good place to be. There are good and bad memories there but the bad get the better of me when I'm there alone. I'll read a lot and practice typing and the lamps aren't too good for night reading and there the night has a thousand eyes.[14]

Not surprisingly, the cost of rehabilitation seemed prohibitive, and in 1952 Elliott sold the cottage to the industrialist Armand Hammer and his brothers, Harry and Victor. The reported sales price, $12,000, included virtually all the furnishings and effects. To the Hammers, buying a piece of history was exciting; to Eleanor, it was a bittersweet end to a much-loved family home; to Elliott it was the relief from the burden of upkeep and an opportunity to realize some money. The other Roosevelt children did not seem to have cared very much at all about the sale of their childhood cottage. But Eleanor did, although she was yet to say good-bye to Campobello.

The Hammers were in earnest about their historic purchase and what they considered to be a responsibility. They offered Eleanor a lifetime invitation to use the cottage, and they were determined to restore it accurately, completely, and functionally. In short time, they made the needed physical repairs and added appropriate period furnishings. The large floral wallpapers, although no longer stylish, were carefully restored. At long last, the cottage was electrified and a telephone was installed. The Hammers gave considerable thought and effort to carefully retaining the cottage's turn-of-the century character and charm.

Eleanor's work in the 1950s continued to be satisfying, but her personal life was less so. She continued her close friendship with David, despite his marriage to a younger woman. In 1957, Eleanor and David and Edna Gurewitsch moved into a small house on East 74th Street in New York, keeping separate apartments. In addition, the Gurewitsches had their own guest room at Val-Kill. At Val-Kill, Eleanor enjoyed the outdoor living, especially the pool that Franklin had insisted they build. She learned to be an adequate swimmer, but her diving left much to be desired. Characteristically, she persevered. David recalled that each time she dove, Eleanor held her nose and had a funny look on her face. David asked her why she continued to dive if it made her so uncomfortable. Her reply was vintage Eleanor: "It is good for my character."[15]

She wrote, ostensibly with David in mind, "The nicest men in the world are those who always keep something of the boy in them."[16] She may also have been thinking of other men in her life whom she had cared for and who had "something of the boy in them": her father, Franklin, her brother Hall, Uncle Theodore, and Earl Miller.

Eleanor continued to suffer bouts of depression that were something more than her more youthful "Griselda" moods. She had many friends, but lacked the closeness she sought. She traveled less often to Campobello because she did not have that special someone to share it with. Her work continued to be the core of her existence.

Contacts with interesting people energized her, but Eleanor maintained a cautious wariness about those she did not know well. Late in her life, a telephone caller asked to speak with her. Eleanor told her secretary, Maureen Coor, that she was too busy to take the call. "She wants something," Eleanor said after Maureen hung up. "But, Mrs. Roosevelt," her secretary asked, "don't you think people ever love you for yourself?" "No, dear," she answered, "I don't."[17]

In 1958, *Sunrise at Campobello*, a play by Dore Schary, opened on Broadway. It was a highly dramatized version of the Roosevelts' life during the critical years of 1921 to 1924. Eleanor thought the dramatization was generally well done and well acted. Ralph Bellamy played Franklin, Mary Fickett was Eleanor, Henry Jones portrayed

Louis Howe, and a young James Earl Jones played the Roosevelt butler, Edward. In a "My Day" column, Eleanor wrote that she was "happy that actors recognized it as a play and did not try to make it too real. As a result . . . I was able to see it as a drama and not think of it as depicting each individual as he or she really was." Eleanor went on to describe Mary Fickett as being "a very sweet character" in the play. Eleanor, however, most certainly did not see herself as Schary saw her.[18]

Franklin Jr., negotiated with Schary for consultation fees for the Roosevelt family. In a letter written to Jimmy on July 12, 1957, he indicated that the family would receive a minimum of five percent of the play's gross profits. They would share equally with Schary in other media interests such as film or television, with many tax implications. Everything was based on how effective Schary would be in negotiating any broadcast or movie rights.[19]

None of the agreements with and among the Roosevelt children went smoothly. Jimmy was unhappy with the way Franklin Jr., handled the negotiations and felt bedeviled by the complexities of the tax implications. Elliott, as usual, was in a financial bind and assigned his shares to others in lieu of debt. Anna and Jimmy squabbled constantly, and none of them believed that they were retaining their full shares. Meanwhile, Schary and the play's producers became increasingly annoyed with the Roosevelts, who constantly hounded the box office for free house seats.

Sunrise at Campobello was filmed on the island in 1960. The islanders were amused at the liberties that were taken with scenes and landscapes. Dissatisfied with the arrangement of the staircase in the Roosevelt cottage, the film makers moved their cameras into a neighboring house. Unhappy with the Roosevelts' dock, the production company built a new one in an even more picturesque setting. But the clincher was the director's dismissal of the island's natural geography. He had the sun rise at the cottage's back—which, of course, looks west.[20]

The actors occupied the choice hotel rooms on the island and made regular trips to Eastport to shop and dine. A native Eastporter remembers the excitement caused by the young actors who played the Roosevelt children. They brought a touch of Hollywood to a small Maine town by just "hanging around" the local drug store. The commercial business that the film brought to Eastport and Campobello is still longingly remembered.

When the film was released, Eleanor still thought it considerably more drama than reality. She enjoyed Greer Garson's portrayal of an Eleanor who was made of much sterner stuff than in the stage version. A reproduction of the ring that Franklin always wore was made for Ralph Bellamy, who repeated his stage role. The original ring had been a wedding gift to Franklin's father from his first wife in 1853. It remained on the finger of father or son for nearly a hundred years.

Eleanor noted in a 1959 "My Day" column that Campobello had been suggested as an international shrine. "Until his illness I think that [Franklin] enjoyed his holidays on the island itself as much as any other relaxation of his busy life . . . of course, polio . . . he only returned twice [three times] for brief periods, but he always remembered it with affection."[21]

In 1961 Eleanor, seventy-six and failing physically, still pressed on with her work and her regular activities. At a conference in Mystic, Connecticut, she saw the *Vireo*, then housed at the local marine museum. She recalled when it had been brought to Campobello on the deck of a U.S. Navy destroyer for the children to learn to sail. Franklin, Eleanor, and the children had sailed on Cobscook Bay on the *Vireo* the day before he lost the use of his legs.

David diagnosed Eleanor's condition as aplastic anemia, a disease of the bone marrow that inhibits the manufacture of red blood cells. She may have believed the end to be near. Only two years earlier she had written, "When you cease to make a contribution, you begin to die. Therefore I think it is a necessity to be doing something which you feel is helpful in order to grow old gracefully and contentedly."[22]

At age seventy-seven, she began a new career as a lecturer at Brandeis University. She wrote, "I suppose I should slow down, but I could not, at any age, be content to take my place in a corner by the fireside and simply look on. One must never, for whatever reason, turn his back on life."[23]

But life was turning its back on Eleanor. She refused examination or treatment by any doctor other than David, although some of her children believed that she might not be receiving the best treatment she could. By the summer of 1962, she had raging fevers and received several blood transfusions. She was so depressed that she confided that "I wish I was dead. It's my time."[24] Eleanor was now so sure that it was her time that she sent out her Christmas cards and gifts in July.

To everyone's surprise, Eleanor recovered from the fevers and insisted that she make one more trip to Campobello. The long-awaited bridge spanning the Lubec Narrows had been built, linking Campobello with the U.S. mainland. Eleanor wanted very much to be in Campobello for the dedication.

She prevailed upon the Gurewitsches to fly with her to Campobello. Trude Lash, Joseph's wife, planned to drive Eleanor back to New York after the ceremonies. Eleanor arrived on the island, but was too ill to attend the dedication. On August 9, 1962, the *New York Times* reported:

> Mrs. Franklin D. Roosevelt, weakened by a virus attack, will not attend the dedication of the Franklin D. Roosevelt Memorial Bridge between Lubec, Maine, and Campobello Island next Monday. "She will not be there as planned," her secretary said yesterday. "We . . . go to Campobello . . . but Mrs. Roosevelt is going there for a complete rest." Mrs. Roosevelt is 77 years old. She fell ill last week-end and was forced to cancel several political appearances scheduled by the New York Democratic Committee. Her fever lasted five days.

Trude Lash reported that after resting for several days, Eleanor, with Rooseveltian pluck, practiced walking up and down in front of the Campobello house so that she would be able to manage the stairs at her old friend Bishop Scarlett's house in Castine that she planned to visit. She seemed terribly frail and complained that she had forgotten how to take a deep breath and had to learn again.

Before she left Campobello for the last time, Eleanor wrote to Victor Hammer on August 19:

> On this my last day at Campobello, I want to thank you again for your great kindness in letting me stay in the cottage and for arranging everything for my comfort. I have had a most delightful time topped off today with one of the most beautiful days the Island could produce and ending in a glorious sunset.
>
> I am leaving much stronger than I came and I attribute the renewal of my strength to the peace and quiet I found here. Words cannot express my gratitude to you and Irene but I do hope you realize that it is deep and warm . . . .
>
> P.S. Your couple are wonderful. They could not have been more kind, and of course Linnea [Calder, the long-time Roosevelt housekeeper] was as good as gold.[25]

Trude Lash wrote, "We drove down the Maine coast to do once more the things she always loved to do. We visited Bishop Scarlett and his wife, Leah. We met an old friend, Molly Dewson . . . . Then we went to a place . . . where Mrs. R. . . used to stop to buy wild-strawberry preserves. She was too weak to get out of the car, and when we came back, having purchased what she wanted us to get, was only vaguely aware of what was going on . . . ."[26]

By this time, the Hammers had decided to try to sell the Campobello property. They advertised the cottage for $50,000, including all the furnishings, or for $75,000 with the inclusion of Roosevelt items they had purchased at public sales at Hyde Park. Unsuccessful in their efforts, the Hammers offered the property to the U.S. government for a memorial to Franklin Roosevelt. At the time, the governments of both the United States and Canada were discussing a joint international park as a symbol of the friendship of the two nations.

A year earlier, Eleanor had written to President John F. Kennedy encouraging the government to acquire the cottage from the Hammers in connection with any plan for an international memorial. She wrote, "It would be nice to feel that the house might be a Franklin D. Roosevelt Memorial Conference site because he was so interested in friendship between Canada and the United States and made considerable efforts to promote it."[27]

In September, following her trip to Campobello, Eleanor courageously tried to continue her work. Her feistiness and her candor were undiminished by her rapidly failing health. Emmanuel Celler, the seventy-four-year-old Congressman from New York, had offered to nominate Eleanor for the U.S. Senate. "Of course not," she replied, "I don't believe in old people running."[28]

Eleanor had planned to speak at an upcoming convention of the International Brotherhood of Electrical Workers, but she did not have the strength to appear. She had also arranged for an important television appearance on civil rights. She invited Dr. Martin Luther King, Jr., to join her in discussing the way white officials had blocked James Meridith's admission to the University of Mississippi. Dr. King agreed to participate, but Eleanor collapsed at home, ending her last attempt to contribute to the solution of America's thorniest domestic problem.

By late September, she was again hospitalized. The family had her examined by a team of physicians who concluded that she suffered from bone marrow tuberculosis. Eleanor was exhausted and constantly in extreme discomfort. She pleaded with David to let her die. Whether it was tuberculosis or aplastic anemia, the end seemed imminent to her.

Eleanor hated being hospitalized and begged her doctors to allow her to go home. In October, she was taken by stretcher to the house on East 74th Street. Convinced that she was about to die, Eleanor wrote checks in her unsteady hand to make sure everyone got their due. She refused all visitors, even favorites like former presidential candidate Adlai Stevenson and labor leader Walter Reuther. Joseph Lash tried to read newspapers to her, but she refused to listen. The Cuban missile crisis was erupting, but Eleanor had absolutely no interest in it or anything else. "Nobody makes sense," she moaned. And, in a final appeal to Lash, "All I want," she pleaded "is to be turned over!"[29]

On November 7, she peacefully slipped away. Eleanor Roosevelt was quietly buried next to Franklin in Hyde Park—in Sara Delano Roosevelt's rose garden.

13

Playing the Cards They Were Dealt

Born to nineteenth century wealth and privilege, Franklin and Eleanor Roosevelt shared the manners, mores, and expectations of the late Victorian American landed gentry. With so much similarity in their breeding and history, it was likely that they would share many personal traits and characteristics. Despite common experience and predilection, they were very different people, and Franklin and Eleanor displayed far more differences in character and personality than similarities. Some of these differences were innate and some learned, but most were significant. While some of these traits were hallmarks of greatness, others were burdens to be endured.

Franklin was athletic and daring, Eleanor awkward and cautious; he was outgoing and flirtatious, she was reserved and correct; he could be duplicitous, she was mostly loyal to a fault; he was ambitious and optimistic, she hoped for the best but had low expectations; he enjoyed pomp and ceremony, she abhorred most social convention; he loved the game of politics, she learned to use it respectfully; he was instinctive and impulsive, she was systematic and compulsive; he was warm and openly charming, she was cool and polite; and finally he was the pragmatist and experimenter while she the idealist and instigator.

But were the Roosevelts everything they seemed to be? Was

Franklin always self-assured and confident; always in control or seeking to control the events and the people around him? And when he had overcome adversity and achieved the presidency, was he happy and fully satisfied? Was it all he wanted from life?

His marriage, at least at first, was a modest success. His affair with Lucy Mercer ended, supposedly, in 1918 although they reconnected and met on occasion after his election. Missy LeHand and Daisy Suckley were faithful and devoted attendants, but their relations with Franklin were mostly personal accommodations of service and companionship. What did Franklin get from any of these relationships?

Two summers with Lucy may have been exciting, but Franklin must have realized from the start that a lasting relationship was only remotely possible. The affair was common knowledge to many in Washington, and it was inevitable that Eleanor would eventually find out. And then what would happen? Divorce from Eleanor would mean the loss of family, home, inheritance, and his all-important career. A marriage with Lucy would leave them penniless, rudderless, and with few prospects.

Missy and Daisy were "safe" relationships. Missy was an employee from a different social class, and that was of significance to any Roosevelt. Cousin Daisy was considered plain and offered unquestioning companionship. Franklin followed a safe route in each instance. Missy and Daisy attended him in much the same way as his stamp collecting, sailing, and the presence of aides served him. They helped, amused, challenged, or relaxed him. These arrangements satisfied most of Franklin's needs and served his bent for self-protection: he never had to reveal himself or his emotions to anyone. In the sum total of his personal relationships, Franklin was very much a universal receiver.

Interestingly, Lucy, Missy, and Daisy overlapped one another in service and adoration of the President. Daisy wrote often and with affection to Lucy in the last years of Franklin's life. Missy had to know of the meetings with Lucy, and she always maintained a cordial relationship with Daisy, who, in turn, expressed admiration for the secretary's long and devoted service. They were all partners in a long-suffering emotional dance with a physically challenged man who had a very prominent wife, and just happened to hold the most powerful office in the world.

Although she was fond of her, Eleanor believed that Missy overstepped her position from time to time, standing in for the First Lady at official functions. But Missy's omnipresence allowed Eleanor some slack and more time to follow her busy agenda. Eleanor likely dismissed any notion of physical relations between Franklin and Missy partly because of the difference in social class, and partly because Eleanor may well have believed that Franklin had been unable to retain sexual function.

Eleanor could not have perceived the spinsterish Daisy as any kind of threat to her marriage. Daisy, too, filled a void by her constant availability in companionship for Franklin. Her presence was much like that of an old family retainer. Daisy was barely noticed and seldom acknowledged. Other White House visitors, such as Princess Martha, were merely harmless diversions. Eleanor recognized Franklin's need to be flattered and amused by the company of women, but, in all instances, she had every expectation of propriety from her husband.

Daisy admired Eleanor's skills and her "sweetness," but she lamented that it was an "awful pity [Franklin] has not someone of his family here with him. Someone with whom to do nothing."[1] It was never Eleanor's style to "do nothing." Daisy thought that Eleanor could have made herself more available at the White House to perform certain ceremonial duties that protocol demanded. But when Eleanor did appear at events, Daisy was sometimes miffed that her favored position at Franklin's elbow was displaced, or that she was bumped from a more desirable stateroom on the presidential train.

Franklin's most enduring and most satisfying friendship was his twenty-five year partnership with Louis Howe. After Louis died in 1936, Franklin was starved for a meaningful friendship and for a reliable critic. Eleanor believed that Louis's death left "an irreparable gap" in Franklin's life. Only Louis could follow through an argument with Franklin and force him to see the other side of an issue. "After Louis's death," she wrote, "Franklin frequently made his decisions without canvassing all sides of a question."[2] Harold Ickes, Franklin's Secretary of the Interior and himself an outspoken administration voice, observed that "Howe was the only man who dared to talk to him frankly and fearlessly. He not only could tell him what he believed to be the truth, but he could hang on like a pup to the root until he got results."[3] Howe knew little of economics or policy development, but he was Franklin's political expert and his most reliable friend. With his death, Franklin lost his most honest, most faithful, and most critical insider. That responsibility fell to Eleanor, and she did her best to fill the void.

It was a difficult void for Eleanor to fill because Louis had also been an important mentor and a very good friend to her. She admired his skills and devotion to Franklin, and she was touched by his care for her. She recalled wistfully, " . . . he was interested in his power to create personages more than in a person, tho' I think he probably cared more for me as a person as much as he cared for anyone & more than anyone else ever has!"[4]

Eleanor seemed always resigned to an expectation that her closest relationships would end or fade away. She was never an equal member in the Nan Cook-Marion Dickerman connection, remaining always just a bit outside their intensely committed partnership. Earl Miller was "forbidden fruit," but he was handsome and virile, and the attention he paid to his "lady" made Eleanor feel attractive and confident. And an intense and lasting relationship with Lorena Hickock presented daunting obstacles.

Any physical liaison with another woman for the very proper First Lady appears not only quite unlikely, but also wholly counterproductive to everything that Eleanor aspired to and believed in. There are some who believe a very intimate relationship may well have existed between Eleanor and Hick. That may have been so, but evidence other than their very affectionate correspondence has not surfaced. Whatever their relationship had been, Eleanor eventually recognized its futility. Hick required Eleanor's undivided attention, and was intolerant and dismissive of many of the people and things Eleanor cared most about. One of the things Hick dismissed was Campobello, and she had scant appreciation for Eleanor's love for her island home.

After her relationships with Hick, Nan, and Marion cooled, Eleanor formed warm friendships with two younger men. Joseph P. Lash, Eleanor's Liberal Youth Movement colleague who became her prolific biographer, was a remarkably reliable friend and confidant. David Gurewitsch was also a loyal and attentive friend. Both had young wives, and they all were likely honored to be close to the world's most respected woman. David was fourteen years her junior, and he saw his role as Eleanor's healer and protector. In respect to both men, Eleanor looked for more affection than she received.

The one truly everlasting love of her life was her father and his memory. She read and reread his letters as if, by magic, to invoke his presence. In an unpublished article in 1927, Eleanor wrote:

> I knew a child once who adored her father. She was an ugly little thing, keenly conscious of her deficiencies, and her father, the only person who really cared for her, was away much of the time; but he never criticized her or blamed her, instead he wrote letters and stories, telling her how he dreamed of her growing up and what they would do together in the future, but she must be truthful, loyal, brave, well-educated, or the woman he dreamed of would not be there when the wonderful day came for them to fare forth together. The child was full of fears and because of them lying was easy; she had no intellectual stimulus at that time and yet she made herself as the years went on into a fairly good copy of the picture he had painted.[5]

If both Franklin and Eleanor often found themselves in relationships that had little chance to be fulfilling, they must have had some expectation of what was likely to happen. Were these self-fulfilling prophecies and did the Roosevelts set themselves up for failure?

Or were they just unlucky in love and content with public success? Their lifetimes of failed or disappointing relationships must have given them some clue to the reasons that intimacies foundered.

Eleanor was convinced she was unlovable, and Franklin was unable or unwilling to return affection. Only the reliable Louis Howe had a meaningful and lasting relationship with both of them.

Disappointment in human love did not diminish the fact that both Roosevelts had love of place. Franklin loved the peace and security of his boyhood home in Hyde Park, but it was not fully his until Sara's death in 1941. Eleanor observed that "his mother never allowed him to interfere with the running of the place . . . ."[6] Eleanor had Val-Kill, but for many years it was shared with Nan and Marion and not quite securely hers until the breakup of their friendship. But they both had the big red cottage on Campobello. It was, like Louis Howe, always a common denominator in their relationship.

Far from the cloistered gentility of Hyde Park, at Campobello Franklin developed and was first exposed to a broader life. On the challenging waters of Passamaquoddy Bay, he learned to sail and handle boats and crews. The pride and self-esteem developed in these early successes helped Franklin find an individuality and an independence he had not known. Trained to follow order and convention, Franklin learned at Campobello to take command, to be in control, to plot his own course. He tested his body and stamina by climbing the island's rugged cliffs and exploring its shrouded forests.

Campobello was also Franklin's social laboratory where he interacted with and even befriended people of another social class, different temperament, and contrasting lifestyle. His experience with the general population at Hyde Park, at school, and in travel was limited to servants and service people. On Campobello, he came to know islanders as friends and companions, if not equals. They taught him to sail, they showed him their work and their homes, and they shared their stories. Islanders were deferential to the cottagers, to be sure, but they demonstrated an independence of character that Franklin found both refreshing and instructive. Franklin met the islanders on their own terms, enjoyed the relationships, and learned from them.

Campobello was much unlike his prescribed life, with its privileges and its remoteness from the working classes. Here Franklin could enjoy easy friendships, because Campobello was geographically and functionally a world apart from his usual protective societal cocoon. Perhaps he realized an incipient desire to experience a kind of life that he had not previously known. On Campobello he discovered that all lives were not as secure and orderly as his own. He learned that there were people in the world engaged in pursuits that did not have the sole mission of gratifying the needs of the Roosevelts or their friends.

Franklin never forgot what Campobello had been for him and why he loved the spruce-covered island, its waters, and its people. Had it not been for the eternal damnation of polio, Campobello would have continued to play an important role in his life. He savored the memories and often rhapsodized and embellished the stories he told about his Campobello adventures to the end of his life.

Eleanor, too, matured on Campobello, as she made it her first home. Franklin made only relatively short visits from 1910 on, and she was fully in charge of her home and her activities for the first time in her life. Campobello became her security blanket and she wrapped herself in its simple pleasures. She continued to return to the island throughout her life, but it was often with mixed emotions. In time, it became more difficult for Eleanor to travel to Campobello when her friends and her children begged off and she found it too full of ghosts. On her later trips, she used the cottage as a venue for writing, or for sentimental visits, occasionally with Elliott's family. But for the forty years after polio had crippled Franklin, Eleanor always found comfort and peace on the island when she managed to get there. It was a source of respite as well as one of creativity and reflection. Campobello never disappointed her, only friends did. That didn't stop Eleanor from returning to the island even if it proved to her that in many ways she was quite alone in the world.

How did Franklin and Eleanor really feel about each other from the 1920s on? They may have made a formal pact or declaration after the Lucy Mercer affair and its disclosure. They shared some affection over the years, but they never displayed it in public and expressed it only modestly in their letters. Franklin and Eleanor certainly had mutual respect for each other's skills, and they developed a working rapport in their unique fashion.

Franklin encouraged and supported Eleanor's social activism. He admired her single-minded liberalism and her intensity. As he did with other aides and colleagues, Franklin listened to her ideas on issues that interested him, acting with his usual mixture of pragmatism and balance. He considered whether an idea or proposal was appropriate or timely and whether it was likely to work. Franklin had an extraordinary sense of what people wanted, what he believed they needed, and what government action they would accept that would make them feel better about themselves and about the nation.

Eleanor largely ignored or was intolerant of many of the political or bureaucratic machinations that Franklin saw as necessary. He was often willing to settle for half a loaf in the short term, while working longer term toward a desired goal. Eleanor wanted it all at once. She looked on most issues as right or wrong, black or white, honest or dishonest. Franklin operated in shades of gray, relying on his ability to negotiate with ease back and forth across battle lines and between camps.

Franklin trusted most of the people around him; Eleanor questioned the motives of many. When a member of his administration showed disloyalty, ambivalence, or ineptitude, he was slow to face the issue and take decisive action. Franklin disliked confrontation and happily directed others to lower a boom or settle a dispute. Eleanor abhorred disloyalty and anything less than the highest quality of performance, and she often challenged Franklin to take firm action and make what she believed to be necessary changes. While he could easily be circumspect in such matters, Eleanor was always direct and emphatic, leaving others quite certain of where she stood.

Eleanor never considered giving up the compelling life she had made for herself to provide full-time aid and comfort to a husband who neither expected nor wanted it from her. No matter what established convention required or what others expected, Eleanor was firmly committed to the fulfilling role that Franklin and Louis had helped her create. Louis, ever proud of what he had accomplished in service to Franklin, saw in Eleanor a similar greatness and, perhaps, destiny. He believed that the country might accept a woman as president and said to her shortly after Franklin's election to his second term, "Eleanor, if you want to be President in 1940, tell me now so I can start getting things ready."[7] She recalled, with more than a little satisfaction, "He always wanted to make me President when FDR was thro'"[8]

She understood that Franklin needed her help but became less than confident that he would continue on an unalterably progressive path. Eleanor realized that his quest for personal approval and political accommodation would at times divert his attention from the need to improve the conditions in the coal mines, the garment factories, and the black ghettoes. As time went on, she became impatient with his inattention, and even with his failing health.

Eleanor implored Franklin not to seek a fourth term. She was unhappy enough abiding the third. She understood that his health was failing in his last years, but, along with others, she also recognized that his leadership was supremely necessary in the last months of the war. Eleanor was eager to have Franklin live to see the end of war and to lead the international peace effort.

Eleanor represented Franklin at sorrowful events that were difficult for him to attend physically and to participate in emotionally. She went to Missy LeHand's funeral, Al Smith's memorial Mass, and the memorial service for Wendell Willkie. She was solicitous of the load that he carried, but she was unwilling to treat him as an invalid. Joseph Lash thought that Eleanor honestly believed that his sheer force of will would transcend any physical infirmity. She remembered when Woodrow Wilson's wife stood intractably between her stroke-crippled husband and the nation's desperate need for presidential leadership. Eleanor was not going to let that happen to Franklin or the nation if she had anything to say about it.

By 1945, Eleanor must have known that the end of Franklin's life was near. He was able to rise to his responsibilities only with great effort in the last year of his life. At Yalta, he was but a shadow of himself, buoyed only by one last burst of energy and by Churchill's unshakable will. In his last months, Franklin was often ill, slept a great deal, grew short of attention, and was sometimes uncharacteristically irritable. In the middle of a conversation, his memory would often wander and he would tell stories of his youth at Hyde Park or Campobello, occasionally embellishing the tale or offering one of pure invention. His mental focus was becoming fuzzy, and his joy for living and human interaction diminished. Small wonder that the undemanding Daisy Suckley became his companion of choice toward the end.

When Eleanor learned that Lucy was present in Warm Springs, that she had been with Franklin at other times, that Anna had participated in arranging meetings, and that others had conspired to keep her from knowing, she was crushed. She remained dry-eyed in public following Franklin's death and on the journey north to the funeral. When she later wrote of the events, it was with little emotion, almost detachment. She spoke of Franklin as a great leader and democrat, and although she always referred to him as "my husband," she did so with little apparent personal emotion. Eleanor never forgot Franklin's infidelity, and she was clearly unwilling to forgive any later transgressions, even in death.

When Franklin achieved what he most wanted, the presidency, his only reservation was that he might not have the strength to do the job. He proved that he did, at least for the first three terms. Eleanor's support never wavered, because she believed in him and his leadership, and she realized that she was able to draw much of her own strength from him.

It is difficult to imagine Franklin rising from the debilitation of polio without the help of a wife of such loyalty, inner strength, and purpose. But Eleanor's initial influence on Franklin and the formation of his ideals started well before polio. During their engagement, Eleanor tried to avoid the tedium of her debutante commitments by doing social work. She volunteered considerable time at the Rivington Street Settlement on New York's Lower East Side and often asked Franklin to pick her up there at day's end. It was his introduction to the lives of immigrant children and their hardscrabble tenement existence. Eleanor recalled those days with great satisfaction. In 1961 she told a friend, "I wanted him to see *how people lived* . . . and it worked. He saw how people lived and he *never* forgot."[9]

The Roosevelt partnership had been forged in family tradition and love. Challenged by shattering disloyalty, it was able to survive and flourish by a determined courage that followed a crippling illness. Franklin and Eleanor Roosevelt endured and succeeded by learning to play the cards they were dealt, and playing them well.

Epilogue

Franklin drafted a Jefferson Day address that he did not live to deliver. The last words he wrote were, "The only limit to our realization of tomorrow will be our doubts of today. Let us move forward with strong and active faith."[1] This exhortation was typical of Franklin, and it seems most appropriate for his last written remarks. He always moved forward with faith and fully expected a better tomorrow. His faith and his ability to instill hope were, perhaps, his most lasting gift to the people of the free world.

Eleanor called Franklin's a "simple faith" that was rooted in the Episcopal parish of St. James at Hyde Park and in the little St. Anne's church on Campobello.[2] Franklin was a Senior Warden at St. James, a role he was reluctant to relinquish. A simple engraved marker at St. Anne's remembers him as a faithful vestryman. His attendance at church was irregular, but, when he did participate, he did so with the usual Roosevelt gusto and intensity. Franklin held his religion and faith dear throughout his life.

In 1954, on the occasion of their fiftieth class reunion, his Harvard classmate and friend, Lathrop Brown, wrote of the qualities that sustained Franklin during the years of his presidency:

In a few weeks the nation was lifted from the pit of despair to the high ground of confidence. It was no small thing that within one man could be contained enough of faith to restore the lost morale of a great nation. All over the world were the stirrings of the lesser people of the world. England, France, Italy, Germany, and Spain fell prey to totalitarianism, socialism, fascism, or chaos. Under Franklin there was no revolution. The value of the dollar fell, but the value of the "forgotten man" rose to its full measure of dignity and decency . . . Franklin's ethics learned at home, at school, at college, and in his church . . . . gave him a sure sense of direction; and it gave him enough of faith to lead the nation.[3]

If faith fueled Franklin's leadership, that leadership was the core of his greatness. Franklin was an enigma to those who knew him best. His Dutchess County neighbor, friend, and Treasury Secretary, Henry Morgenthau, called him the most complex person he had ever known. But behind this seeming complexity, Franklin had a clear philosophy of executive process if not of leadership itself. Franklin guaranteed himself an effective flow of information and ideas. He was most comfortable, and most effective, when he balanced that flow from his official channels with that of his network of private and informal sources.

Franklin was an accessible president who welcomed ideas and opinions from a wide variety of sources. Ideas were grist for the Roosevelt mill: he encouraged, listened, sifted, balanced, and then reached his own conclusion. Franklin read the morning newspapers and an enormous quantity of official memoranda. He also gleaned considerable information through conversation. If it appeared promising, he listened. If the conversation was self-serving or otherwise off the mark, Franklin would take control until a natural conclusion was reached, or until the other participants were exhausted.

Franklin was sensitive to public criticism, but encouraged the expression of ideas with candor. Franklin knew he needed to hear both passion and conviction from trusted aides in order to reach the most appropriate conclusion. This process required a significant measure of confidence in the people he chose to have around him. More important, he had enormous self-confidence that he would ultimately make the right decision based on the information that flowed to him in torrents. He was a master of controlling that flow and selecting its product.

Franklin loved to get out among the people to the extent that he was able. However, he had little trust in opinions that were widely held in the nation's capital. He told Molly Dewson, "Pay no attention to what people are saying in Washington. They are the last persons in the country to listen to."[4] Franklin realized that his limited mobility would keep him from much of that personal contact, so he constantly encouraged his aides to get out of Washington. "Go and see what's happening," he told Rexford Tugwell. "See the end product of what we are doing. Talk to the people; get the wind in your nose."[5]

Supreme Court Justice Oliver Wendell Holmes concluded that Franklin had ". . . a second-class intellect, but a first-class temperament!"[6] There is no question that his brain was orderly and receptive. "Facts," said Rexford Tugwell, "stuck to his mind like flies to old-fashioned fly paper."[7] He had an excellent memory and was a good judge of people. He could be fooled once, but seldom twice. The flamboyant and mercurial Senator Huey Long was once a guest at the Roosevelt dinner table at Hyde Park. Sara is reported to have asked, "Who is that horrid little man sitting next to my son?"[8] Franklin recognized that Long could be valuable to him, but he was well aware of what the canny and quixotic man from Louisiana was capable of doing. Later, in a conversation with Tugwell, Roosevelt referred to Long as the second most dangerous man in America. When asked who was the first, he replied, "Douglas MacArthur."[9] Franklin did not suffer demagogues.

––––––––––

The Roosevelts were not plain folks. Linnea Calder, the daughter of their housekeeper on Campobello, reported that tourists could look into the kitchen of the red cottage with its large pine table and chairs arranged by a window and say they could imagine ". . . the Roosevelts eating their breakfast. I don't say anything, but the Roosevelts were not ones to eat in the kitchen."[10] But millions of Americans believed that this president would eat in their kitchens. And they welcomed him into their living rooms through radio, they hung his picture on their walls and they invited his protection.

For nearly a generation, Franklin Roosevelt was the only president many Americans had ever known. He had led them together through their darkest days: the Great Depression and the greatest of wars. When all seemed darkness, Franklin Roosevelt brought light. When he took office, nine out of ten families in rural America had no electricity, few had pensions, and millions were without work. The Tennessee Valley Authority and other projects electrified the powerless, Social Security provided old-age insurance, and public works projects and conservation programs provided jobs and, more important, the dignity of work. Franklin Roosevelt was a man of cheer and vitality, a benevolent and favorite uncle. He was not the champion of Wall Street and of corporate executives, but he was the people's champion. They loved his smile and his good humor, his sunny optimism and his promise. They believed that he made their lives far better. The American Dream may have been tattered during the early part of the Depression, but it was still alive and its reaffirmation occurred on Franklin Roosevelt's watch.

Journalist Daniel Schorr recalls that Franklin Roosevelt saw to it that the government regulated the securities business, insured bank deposits, provided his mother with a Depression-era relief check, and helped him attend college through the aid of the National Youth Administration. He wonders what his life might have been like without these sustaining programs.[11]

Meeting Franklin Roosevelt, Winston Churchill said, was like uncorking your first bottle of champagne. Churchill had the habit of uncorking bottles on a regular basis, so his first had to be memorable. The Prime Minister also had an eye for natural beauty and its sustaining powers. He insisted that Franklin share with him the sunset over the Atlas Mountains in Marrakech as the Casablanca

Conference was ending. Churchill then painted the scene and presented it to him. The sheer peace and beauty reminded Franklin of the vistas from his Campobello home, and how sunsets touched his soul.

The country was heartbroken at Franklin's unexpected death. He was the one man the free world needed most, they believed, and he was gone. How could it have happened? What were they to do? The people mourned for him, but they mourned mostly for themselves. There was an overwhelming feeling of uncertainty, a fear of being rudderless. In Franklin's death, many felt the single greatest sense of loss they had ever known.

Franklin's death was felt very deeply on Campobello. In 1946, the cairn unveiled in Welshpool was the first memorial to the fallen president erected on foreign soil. And on a summer morning in 1955, parishioners and guests gathered in the wood-paneled St. Anne's Church for the dedication of a bronze plaque that read: "To the Glory of God. In Memory of Franklin Delano Roosevelt, 1882–1945. Honorary Vestryman of St. Anne's Church." Eleanor was in Europe on a mission for the United Nations and Jimmy, then a Congressman from California, was in the air over the tiny island, unable to land because, not surprisingly, of a persistent fog.

In 1956, a simple shaft was erected to Franklin's memory in front of the little Campobello library that he had long supported. It was clear that the islanders were honoring not a world leader, but the memory of a neighbor who had spent so many happy years among them.

More than sixty years have passed since Franklin last visited Campobello. It has been even longer since he last hiked its cliffs, jogged its paths, and frolicked with his children in its waters. The Roosevelt Campobello International Park draws visitors and latter-day pilgrims across the bridge that bears his name. Franklin Roosevelt and Campobello Island are infinitely and inexorably intertwined. It is remarkable that Campobello and its people have changed little since that day in 1883 when a teething baby was first brought to visit its shores.

That Eleanor kept going back to Campobello to the very end is testament to how she felt about her island. The rugged physical activities of Campobello were not the special appeal. She sought the quiet, calming life where she could shut out the noise, the frustrations, the disappointments, and the demands of an outside world that constantly challenged and often frustrated her.

Eleanor's life had been a litany of obligations and obstacles, but also one of challenges and triumphs. The once shy and retiring person who early showed few signs of greatness was a liberated woman. But, according to Arthur Schlesinger, Jr.:

> Her liberation was not an uncovenanted gift. She attained it only through a terrifying exertion of self-discipline. It was terrifying because the conviction of her own inadequacy was so effectively instilled in Eleanor Roosevelt as a child, and because her adult life had so much disappointment and shock, that it required incomparable and incessant self-control to win maturity and serenity. If her mastery of herself was never complete, if to the end of her life she could still succumb to private melancholy while calmly meeting public obligation, this makes her achievement and character all the more formidable. Her life was both ordeal and fulfillment. It combined vulnerability and stoicism, pathos and pride, frustration and accomplishment, sadness and happiness.[12]

It is small wonder that the end of her life was as painful as the start. Only with the sheer force of will was she able to make that last, sentimental journey to her island in 1962. She was resigned to impending death, but she was determined to say good-bye to Campobello, to her friends in Maine, and to a way of life that had passed not only for her, but also for all North Americans.

Lois Lowry's 1975 description of Campobello remains as apt today as it was then, and as it was in the nineteenth century:

It hasn't changed much since the summers of the Roosevelts. The charm . . . relies on the natural phenomena that need neither maintenance, updating nor embellishment: the caves are still there, and the rugged pinnacles, and the peat bogs, and the wind-torn hilltop trees . . . you can stand on the craggy peak at Friar's Head and look out through the fog to Thrumbcap Island, and if you're barefoot your feet will be stained blue from berries, and there won't be a plastic souvenir stand in sight.[13]

When Eleanor made that last trip to Campobello, her frustration was apparent to all around her. But her mind was still agile, and she was intent on completing her last book, *Tomorrow Is Now*. It is only appropriate that she filed one of her last "My Day" columns from her island:

Next Monday they will be dedicating the Franklin D. Roosevelt Memorial Bridge between Lubec, Maine, and Campobello Island.

The "beloved island" was what Mr. and Mrs. James Roosevelt called Campobello after they first discovered it in the summer of 1883, when they were looking for a good climate for their young son Franklin to spend his second summer. From that time on, part of every summer was spent on the island itself and sailing the waters nearby. James Roosevelt loved to sail and bought a two-masted schooner called the "Half Moon" in which he explored the coast and neighboring waters, and by the time little Franklin was seven he was presented with a small sailboat of his own.

One of the best sailors on the island, Captain Eddie Lank, taught the youngster the mysteries of the Bay of Fundy tides, and how to be a really good sailorman. In fact, Franklin Roosevelt was one day to be probably as good a navigator of the coast as could be found, with a very intimate knowledge of all the inlets and rivers and harbors, so that even in a fog he could usually get into port . . . . When my husband was a boy there was fine timber on the island, but forest fires and speculators have taken much of that away. You can still walk on mossy paths through dark mysterious woods and come out at a number of points on the other side of the island. If you face the rivers, you can have the most beautiful sunsets laid before you in an unbelievable panorama. If you stay a little distance from Lubec, you can almost think you are looking on Mont Saint-Michel on the coast of France. There are an endless number of islands to visit, an endless number of waterways and constantly changing scenery, but everywhere the rocks come down to the pebbly beaches, with the pine trees clinging precariously as far as they can cling and the water lapping the beaches and the rocks below.

If you cross the island and look out toward the Bay of Fundy and Grand Manan Island in the far distance where the gulls have their nesting place, you find yourself on the most beautiful crescent beach called Herring Cove. Here the fishermen put out their lobster pots. Inside the beach, which is more or less sandy, there used to be a lake called Glen Severn in which it was warm enough to swim. There are also ponds on the island which, when the sun reaches them, warm up and make pleasant swimming pools. But unless you are a hardy native, you had better stay out of the waters of the bay on either side or you will turn blue after a very few seconds . . . .

When we lived there the one telephone, which could hardly be called a good connection, was at the postmistress' office in the village. There was no electric light, and the water supply for use in the house was somewhat sketchy and always restricted. Lamps had a horrible way of smoking, and going to bed by candlelight was no great joy to those who wished to read at night in bed. But you never had hay fever or any of the other allergies which beset people in summer climates. The sun was warm and delightful in the daytime, and at night your pine logs took the chill off the evening air. So it was always the "beloved island" and it remained so in memory when my husband was no longer able, because of the attack of polio, to go there and live the life he enjoyed.

Now there will be a bridge from Lubec to the island instead of the little ferry which always took our cars across in the later years. People will cross with ease, and there will be less and less division between the U.S. and Canada. Still, those of us who remember the past will have a nostalgic feeling for the days when you could spend a month or six weeks, virtually cut off from the world and all its troubles, enjoying to the full the "beloved island."[14]

The Roosevelt Campobello International Park was officially dedicated on August 24, 1964. The First Ladies of the United States and Canada, Mrs. Lyndon B. Johnson and Mrs. Lester B. Pearson, cut the ribbon. Looking on was Franklin D. Roosevelt, Jr., who was born in the family cottage fifty years earlier. The proposal for a memorial to Franklin was made by President John F. Kennedy during a visit to Brunswick, Maine, in 1962. Eleanor had suggested it to him, and the Hammers had offered the cottage to the U.S. government for that purpose. The U.S. Congress and the Canadian Parliament passed enabling legislation in June 1964, and President Johnson signed it into law in the United States. Queen Elizabeth II's proclamation establishing the Park under Canadian law closely followed.

Franklin and Eleanor's cottage is the centerpiece of the Park, and the Franklin D. Roosevelt Memorial Bridge carries thousands of visitors each year to its welcoming door. One can only expect that the Roosevelts would find that most fitting.

Appendix A

Chronology

1882 Franklin Roosevelt born January 31 in Hyde Park, New York.

1883 James, Sara, and one-year-old Franklin Roosevelt visited Campobello for the first time. They stayed at the just-completed Tyn-y-coed Hotel. Friends who were associated with the Campobello Company, the developers of the island's summer colony and facilities, suggested it to James as an appropriate resort.

1884 The Roosevelts had a cottage built. They did not visit the island, traveling much of the summer in England. Anna Eleanor Roosevelt born October 11.

1885 The cottage was completed; the Roosevelts arrived in July to spend the summer.

1886 The family spent eight weeks on Campobello.

1887 The family occupied the cottage from mid-July to early September.

1888 The Roosevelts were again on the island from mid-July to mid-September.

1889 The Roosevelts spent the entire summer in Europe.

1890 After an early summer trip to Europe, the Roosevelts were on Campobello from mid-July to mid-September.

1891 The Roosevelts spent the entire summer in Europe.

1892 The Roosevelts were in Europe for several months, then on Campobello from late July to mid-September.

1893 Breaking the pattern, the Roosevelts were on Campobello from late June to early August, then sailed for Europe.

1894 The Roosevelts stayed on Campobello from mid-July to mid-September.

1895 First in Europe again, the Roosevelts were on Campobello from early August until mid-September.

1896 The Roosevelts spent the entire summer in Europe. They rented the cottage to the Hartman Kuhn family, whose cottage was under construction.

1897 The Roosevelts took an early trip to Europe, then summered on Campobello from mid-July to mid-September.

1898 The family made a longer summer visit, from early July to mid-September.

1899 The family made a shorter summer visit, from early August to mid-September.

1900 Franklin, now eighteen years old, served as secretary-treasurer of the fledgling Campobello Golf Club. The family stayed from early July to mid-September, when Franklin entered Harvard. James died in December.

1901 Sara and Franklin spent the summer traveling in Europe.

1902 Sara and Franklin were on Campobello from mid-July until mid-September. By this time, Franklin's Harvard friends were regular visitors and companions.

1903 Franklin spent the early part of the summer in Europe. He returned in late July to Campobello. Eleanor, who was summering in Isleboro, Maine, made her first visit, suitably chaperoned, for five days in late summer.

1904 Sara and Franklin were on Campobello for the entire summer. Franklin, now a Harvard graduate, was secretly engaged to be married to Eleanor, who visited for the month of August.

1905 Franklin and Eleanor were married in New York in March. The young couple honeymooned in Europe while Sara spent part of August on Campobello.

1906 Daughter Anna was born in May, and, shortly after her christening, the young family headed to Campobello in early July.

1907 Franklin, Eleanor, and Anna spent the entire summer in Sara's cottage while she summered in Europe. This lengthy period on the island was their first without Sara. Son James was born in December.

1908   The fragile physical condition of young James prompted Franklin and Eleanor to rent a cottage in Seabright, New Jersey, for the summer, in order to have doctors and medical facilities nearby. Sara remained in Hyde Park so she could visit the young Roosevelts.

1909   Son Franklin, Jr., was born in March and died in November. Sara purchased the cottage next door for Franklin and Eleanor. Eleanor arrived first, and they were there until mid-September. Eleanor was thrilled at having a home of her own.

1910   Eleanor and the two children spent the summer on Campobello while Franklin campaigned for the New York State Senate. Elliott was born shortly after their return in September.

1911   Eleanor and the three children were on Campobello for the summer; Franklin was in Albany until August. They all departed in early September.

1912   Eleanor and the three children spent the summer on Campobello while Franklin took part in the Democratic convention that nominated Woodrow Wilson for president. Franklin managed only a short visit to the island.

1913   Eleanor, Franklin, and the children traveled to Campobello in June. Franklin returned to Washington to his duties as Assistant Secretary of the Navy. He brought a battleship to Eastport for the Fourth of July celebration and returned to Campobello for about a week at the end of August.

1914   Eleanor and the children were on Campobello for the summer. Franklin was in Washington until August. Franklin, Jr. (the second), was born on Campobello in August, the only Roosevelt to be born on foreign soil. Franklin returned to Washington, then returned again to Campobello on a destroyer in September.

1915   Eleanor and the four children were on Campobello and Franklin was in Washington until mid-July, when he returned to the island to recuperate from an emergency appendectomy.

1916   Son John was born in March, and Eleanor and the family summered on Campobello. Franklin was in Washington most of the summer, visiting Campobello for about two weeks. He campaigned in Maine in support of Democratic congressional candidates. Eleanor and the children remained on Campobello until early October, at Franklin's insistence, because of the extensive polio epidemic in the eastern United States.

1917   The United States entered World War I. Eleanor and the children arrived on Campobello in mid-July after the younger boys had recovered from whooping cough. Franklin stayed in Washington except for a two-week trip to Campobello.

1918   None of the Roosevelts was on Campobello. Eleanor performed Red Cross support activities in Washington for much of the summer, and then she and the children went to Hyde Park. Franklin was in Europe during this last summer of the war. On his return, Eleanor discovered his romance with Lucy Mercer, her former personal secretary.

1919   Eleanor took the children to the Delano family summer home in Fairhaven, Massachusetts.

1920   Eleanor and the children returned to Campobello for the summer. Franklin visited for a week in August on the destroyer *Hatfield*, returning to Washington to campaign unsuccessfully as the Democratic vice-presidential candidate.

1921   The fateful summer. Eleanor and the children were on Campobello from July on. Franklin arrived in August and soon became ill. After several weeks, he was diagnosed with polio. Franklin would never again walk unaided on his beloved island, or anywhere else.

1922   Sara took Anna and James to Europe, resuming the Roosevelt family tradition. Eleanor remained with the other children in New York City and Hyde Park. Franklin spent part of the summer at the Marion, Massachusetts, vacation home of Louis Howe.

1923   Eleanor and the children remained in New York City; Franklin was in Marion.

1924   Eleanor devoted herself to politics and social service activities in New York City; Franklin was again in Marion.

1925   Eleanor, with friends Nancy Cook and Marion Dickerman, took Franklin, Jr., John, and their friends on a motor tour through the Adirondacks and Quebec before reaching Maine and Campobello. It was a remarkable camping trip for unescorted women and children to undertake.

1926   Eleanor occupied her own stone cottage, Val-Kill, in Hyde Park with Cook and Dickerman, and began teaching in New York City. Franklin was now involved with Warm Springs, Georgia, at a facility that offered him some hope for relief from polio.

1927   Franklin was in Warm Springs for the summer. Eleanor was at Val-Kill except for a brief trip to Campobello with Cook, Dickerman, and the younger boys.

1928   Eleanor remained in Hyde Park and New York City. Franklin took part in the Democratic National Convention. He was elected Governor of New York, succeeding Al Smith, the Democratic candidate for President. The cottage was rented for the summer.

1929   Eleanor went to Europe with Cook and Dickerman, Franklin, Jr., and John. Franklin summered in Warm Springs. The cottage was rented out for the summer.

1930   Franklin, with Eleanor's assistance, campaigned successfully for his second term as governor.

1931   Eleanor worked actively to promote Franklin as a presidential candidate while he remained at work in Albany.

1932   Franklin was nominated and elected the 32nd president of the United States.

1933   Franklin made a triumphant and symbolic return to Campobello as president, his first visit in twelve years. He arrived on the *Amberjack II* with three of his sons. Eleanor and an entourage met him there, with celebrations in Lubec, Eastport, and Campobello. He departed on the *USS Indianapolis*. Eleanor and a friend, Lorena Hickock, toured

Quebec and Maine, visiting Campobello for two weeks later that summer.

1934 Eleanor visited the western United States; Franklin vacationed in the Caribbean.

1935 Eleanor stayed on Campobello for several weeks after visiting friends in Maine.

1936 Eleanor and friends were on Campobello; Franklin and three sons sailed in for a brief stay.

1937–1938 Two of the children made brief visits to the cottage. Franklin was a trustee of an association of summer residents.

1939 Eleanor was on Campobello in late June. Franklin made a brief visit, his last, while cruising aboard the *USS Tuscaloosa*.

1941 The Campobello Leadership Institute of college students met at the Roosevelt cottage from late June to early August. Eleanor preceded the group in June, preparing the cottage for them, and visited again with Sara in late August. Sara died shortly after her return to Hyde Park. No members of the family visited Campobello during World War II. All of the sons were in military service.

1945 Franklin died at Warm Springs, Georgia. The war ended in Europe in May and in the Pacific in September.

1946 Eleanor visited Campobello in late July. Elliott, the new owner, was in residence.

1947 Eleanor returned in mid-July to write and to spend time with Elliott's children.

1950 Eleanor made her last extended visit, staying several weeks. Elliott put the cottage up for sale.

1952 Elliott sold the cottage to Armand, Harry, and Victor Hammer, who made extensive repairs and installed electricity and a telephone. They invited Eleanor to visit at any time.

1962 President John F. Kennedy proposed a Campobello Park as a memorial to Franklin Roosevelt. Eleanor made her final visit to Campobello. She was ill and unable to participate in the dedication of the Franklin D. Roosevelt Memorial Bridge, connecting Campobello and Lubec. She made one last sentimental journey homeward by auto through Maine, visiting old friends, and died in New York shortly after the trip.

1963   Armand Hammer offered to give the cottage and lands to the U.S. government for a Roosevelt memorial. Officials from the Departments of State and Interior entered into negotiations with their counterparts in the Canadian government.

1964   Congress passed and President Lyndon B. Johnson signed an act establishing Roosevelt Campobello International Park. The Canadian Parliament approved similar legislation. Queen Elizabeth II issued a formal proclamation. On August 20, the First Ladies of the United States and Canada, Mrs. Lyndon B. Johnson and Mrs. Lester B. Pearson, officially opened the Park. Franklin D. Roosevelt, Jr., was the only family member present.

Appendix B

Cottage for Sale, 1957

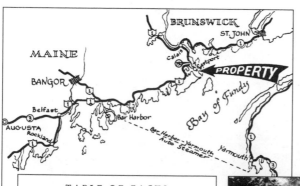

OFFERED AT:
$50,000 with
complete Campobello
furnishings and
equipment. $75,000
with additional
furnishings brought
from Hyde Park.

TABLE OF FACTS

LOCATION: Easterly shore of Friars Bay, Campobello Island, New Brunswick, Canada, facing Eastport, Maine, across the bay. Free ferry landing, about 1 mile; 5-minute run across short channel to Lubec. Good shopping at either point. New York City, about 530 miles from Lubec over Route 1, turnpike and parkways; Boston, approx. 320 miles. RR and airport at Eastport.

PROPERTY: Approx. 15 acres. Lawn around residence, facing highway; balance in natural spruce woods extending to clean, rocky shore and beach. Magnificent views across water.

RESIDENCE: 23 Rooms (11 master bedrooms; 4 baths). 2½-story Dutch Colonial house with ell at either end. Exterior of painted red shingles. Cedar shingle roof. Foundation, concrete piers. Mostly hardwood floors. UTILITIES: Abundant water from artesian well, electric pump and pressure tank. Canadian Public Service electricity. Telephone.

FIRST FLOOR: Entrance Porch. Large Entrance Hall with wide staircase to second and third floors. Coat closet and Powder Room in rear hall. Drawing Room (about 34'x24'), large brick fireplace, doors to Porch overlooking water. Dining-Room with fireplace. Library with fireplace. Down three steps to private wing of the late President: Hall; 2 single Bedrooms; Bathroom; Roosevelt's Office with fireplace, overlooking ocean. Kitchen Wing; Large Kitchen; butler's pantry, cabinets, laundry. 2 large pantries. Back Hall, back stairs, back door to drying yard. Ample closets. Maid's Lavatory and Shower Room.

SECOND FLOOR: South wing over Presidential office: Suite of very large Bedroom with fireplace; covered Porch with view of ocean; single Bedroom; large Bathroom. 4 double Bedrooms; Sewing Room or small Sitting Room. Bathroom. Each room has at least one large, deep closet. Ample broom and linen closets. 6 additional single rooms.

THIRD FLOOR: 3 double Bedrooms; Bathroom. Ample closets and storage space, small unfinished attic.

241

Notes

CHAPTER 1

1. Geoffrey C. Ward, *Before the Trumpet: Young Franklin Roosevelt*. New York: Harper, 1985, p. 66.

2. Ibid., p. 112.

3. This was an 1880s English novel by Frances Hodgson Burnett. Its aristocratic protagonist was a girlishly handsome small boy.

4. Mrs. James (Sara) Roosevelt, *My Boy Franklin,* New York: Ray Lang and Richard Smith, 1933, p. 13.

5. Ward, *Before the Trumpet*, p. 163.

6. "Muscular Christianity" was a 19th century English movement of strongly encouraging schoolboys to play games hard and well, and play them for God's sake.

7. Geoffrey C. Ward, *A First Class Temperament: The Emergence of Franklin Roosevelt,* New York: Harper, 1989, p. 18.

8. David McCullough, "Mama's Boys," *Psychology Today*, 17/3, March 1983, p. 38. Of course, Freud could have been describing any number of prominent people who might fall into the same category; General Douglas MacArthur for one.

9. Ward, *A First Class Temperament,* p. 18.

10. Ward, *Before the Trumpet*, p. 189. Franklin never wavered in his esteem for Peabody. The Reverend was included in many Roosevelt family events and was a lifelong guest and friend. Many other "Grotties" shared Franklin's affection for their mentor.

11. Ibid, p. 260. Eleanor probably did realize how "ghastly" her childhood was, but, for the most part, was unable or unwilling to articulate it.

12. Ibid, p. 266.

13. Ibid.

14. Ibid, p. 269. Eleanor's choice of words is interesting. "Fear," of course, was a touchstone word in Franklin's first inaugural address. The use of "crippling" may have been an unconscious reference to Franklin's polio.

15. H. D. Graham, "The Paradox of Eleanor Roosevelt: Alcoholism's Child," *Virginia Quarterly Review*, 63/2, Spring 1987, p. 219. Eleanor was plagued by the alcoholism of those close to her. Her father and brother, two uncles, and several of Franklin's friends including Livy Davis succumbed to its ravages. Franklin enjoyed his cocktails, and it was not unusual for Sara to cut him off gently some evenings at Hyde Park. Eleanor took a very occasional glass of wine only, and she was angered by alcoholic excess in her home. She was seldom a participant in Franklin's White House after-hours martini parties. Missy LeHand, and later Anna, generally acted as hostess at these events.

16. Ward, *Before the Trumpet*, p. 286. Eleanor's deeply held and often professed affection for her father all through her adult life probably surpassed what actually took place in the precious few years they actually spent together.

17. Griselda was a figure in *The Canterbury Tales* by Geoffrey Chaucer. Her husband subjects her to a long string of humiliations in order to test her character.

18. Ward, *Before the Trumpet*, p. 298. It was Eleanor's first and most important exposure to leftist ideas.

19. Ibid, p. 301.

20. Ibid, p. 303. Eleanor's esteem and affection for Mlle. Souvestre was no less avid than Franklin's for Peabody. The teacher's advanced age and her death abbreviated their span of companionable time. Eleanor kept a photograph of her mentor prominently displayed throughout her life.

21. Ibid, p. 303. Victorian letters from women to women often expressed feelings and emotions vividly. Unlike the letters between Eleanor and Lorena Hickock, this one has not has raised any suggestion of an intimate relationship.

22. Arthur M. Schlesinger, Jr., *The Age of Roosevelt: The Crisis of the Old Order, 1919-1933*, Boston: Houghton Mifflin, 1957, pp. 326–7.

23. Ibid.

CHAPTER 2

1. Elizabeth B. Goodman, "A Home of Her Own," *National Parks*, 56/7–8, July/August 1982, p. 7.

2. Alden Nowlan, *Campobello, the Outer Island*, Toronto: Clarke, Irwin & Co., 1975, p. 2. "Old man's beard" is a grey-green lichen that clings to evergreen trees in the Northeast. It takes on a particularly droopy look and feel in fog-shrouded forests.

3. Stephen O. Muskie, *Campobello: Roosevelt's "Beloved Island,"* Lubec, ME: Roosevelt International Park Commission, 1982, p. 4. Muskie is a son of Senator and Secretary of State Edmund S. Muskie of Maine. Senator Muskie was appointed to the Roosevelt Campobello International Park Commission at its creation, along with FDR, Jr., former Maine Governor Sumner T. Pike, and three Canadian dignitaries.

4. Ibid, p. 3.

5. Nowlan, *Campobello, the Outer Island*, p. 15.

6. "Spell of Campobello, Maine's Neighbor Isle, Summer Home of President Roosevelt," *Lewiston Journal*, July 8, 1933.

7. Nowlan, *Campobello, the Outer Island*, pp. 64–5.

8. Andrew Sackett, *The Views in Every Direction Are Enticing: Campobello Island as a Summer Resort, 1880-1910*, 1995, p. 3. This booklet was prepared for Design Research, St Andrew's, New Brunswick, in August, 1995, in conjunction with the design and production of a display at the Roosevelt Campobello International Park Reception Center.

9. Ibid. p. 4.

10. Ibid.

11. Kenneth S. Davis, *FDR: The Beckoning of Destiny, 1882–1928*, New York: Putnam: 1971, p. 56.

12. Sackett, *The Views in Every Direction Are Enticing*, p. 5.

13. Nowlan, *Campobello: The Outer Island*, p. 90.

14. Sackett, *The Views in Every Direction Are Enticing*, p. 10.

15. Goodman, "A Home of Her Own," p. 5. Kate Gannet Wells was the unofficial historian of Campobello in the late 19th Century. Her writing, while rich in hyperbole, is fairly typical late Victorian "elitist" prose.

16. Sackett, *The Views in Every Direction are Enticing*, pp. 12-13

17. "Roosevelt's 'Beloved Island'—Campobello," *Down East*, August 1958, p. 29.

18. Cecilia Rasmussen, "A Party Ship's Last Voyage," *Los Angeles Times*, February 15, 1998, p. 28. *Harvard* and *Yale* were plying coastal Pacific routes by 1910. Both served as troop transports in the English Channel during World War I, and then as cruise ships on the Pacific Coast. *Harvard* struck a reef and sank in 1931, and *Yale* was scrapped in 1949 following its service in World War II.

19. "Roosevelt's 'Beloved Island,'—Campobello," August 1958, p. 28.

CHAPTER 3

1. Nowlan, *Campobello: The Outer Island*, pp. 91-2.

2. Ibid, p. 93.

3. Interview July 29, 1996, with Anne Newman, Roosevelt Campobello International Park.

4. Goodman, "A Home of Her Own," p. 5. And many others.

5. Hugh Gregory Gallagher, *FDR's Splendid Deception*, New York: Dodd, Mead, 1985, pp. 4-5. This excellent volume is a treatise on Franklin's polio and the obstacles that were overcome. Here Gallagher notes the root of Franklin's resolve to handle pain. It stood him in good stead during his "trial of fire."

6. Harold F. Gosnell, *Champion Campaigner, Franklin D. Roosevelt*, New York: Macmillan, 1952, p. 9.

7. Rexford G. Tugwell, *FDR: Architect of an Era*, New York: Macmillan, 1967, p. 10.

8. R. H. Kiernan, *President Roosevelt*, London: George C. Harrap and Company, Ltd., 1948, p. 16.

9. James N. Rosenau, *The Roosevelt Treasury*, Garden City, NY: Doubleday, 1951, p. 19.

10. Nathan Miller, *The Roosevelt Chronicles*, Garden City, NY: Doubleday: 1979, p. 228. Many men such as Halsey met Franklin early in his career and then played major roles in the military, the administration, or the Congress when Franklin was President.

11. Alden Hatch, *Franklin D. Roosevelt: An Informal Biography*, New York: Henry Holt & Co., 1947, p. 25.

12. Mrs. James Roosevelt, *My Boy Franklin*, pp. 49-50. This story may be a bit hard to swallow. The text also says that the captain of the nefarious vessel actually told Franklin he was running human cargo. However, Sara claimed the story was true.

13. Ward, *Before the Trumpet*, p. 203.

14. "Roosevelt's 'Beloved Island,'" August 1958, p. 28. And several others. An often repeated story.

15. Ibid.

16. Confidential source, Campobello, FDR Papers, Franklin D. Roosevelt Library. Also, Ward, *A First Class Temperament*, p. 578f.

17. Ibid.

18. Ward, *A First Class Temperament*, p. 578f.

19. Ward, *Before the Trumpet*, p. 254. Alice Sohier was Franklin's first "romance." She was quite young at the time, and there is little indication of her feelings. Franklin was short on courting experience but long on vitality and Alice deflected his ardor. Members of her family were something less than impressed with the situation, and they spirited Alice off to Europe for an extended tour. Eleanor claimed knowledge of the relationship, but it's not known if she heard of it from Franklin.

20. Ibid, p. 308.

21. Ibid, p. 313. The author has no knowledge how the code was "broken" or when. Apparently it served Franklin's purposes.

22. Joseph P. Lash, *Eleanor and Franklin: The Story of Their Relationship*, New York: W.W. Norton, 1971, p. 107.

23. Ward, *Before the Trumpet*, jacket flap.

24. Doris Kearns Goodwin, *No Ordinary Time: Franklin and Eleanor Roosevelt: The Home Front in World War II*, New York: Simon & Schuster, 1994, p. 79.

25. Kenneth S. Davis, "Miss Eleanor Roosevelt," *American Heritage*, 22/6, October 1971, p. 50. It is doubtful that Franklin ever did or would have talked about girls with his mother. In the unlikely event that he did, his words would have fallen on deaf or disbelieving ears.

26. John T. Bethell, "Frank Roosevelt at Harvard, and What Became of Him Later," *Harvard Magazine*, 99/2, November-December 1996, p. 6.

27. Ward, *Before the Trumpet*, p. 236.

28. Ibid, p. 334.

29. Lash, *Eleanor and Franklin*, p. 134.

30. Ward, *Before the Trumpet*, p. 334. Maids, chaperones, and others made it extremely difficult for proper young ladies and gentlemen to spend much time alone.

31. Ward, *A First Class Temperament*, p. 32. For Eleanor to use the pet name "Nell" for Franklin is indicative of her love for him. It's not clear how long this continued in their relationship.

32. Ward, *Before the Trumpet*, p. 335. The interest Mrs. Kuhn took at first in Franklin and then in Eleanor is important. She allowed her house to pass through Sara to Franklin and Eleanor as a token of her affection for the young couple.

CHAPTER 4

1. Goodwin, *No Ordinary Time*, p. 79.

2. Ibid. At this time, Eleanor sensed Sara's discomfort, but probably misunderstood its basis. She thought Sara believed she was losing Franklin when, it seems, Sara was sending the message that she was not about to be excluded from anything. She wasn't.

3. Davis, "Miss Eleanor Roosevelt," p. 51.

4. Ward, *Before the Trumpet*, p. 340. Franklin copied much from his cousin. He, too, would insist on taking center stage.

5. Geoffrey C. Ward, "The Wonderful Husband," *American Heritage*, September–October 1989, p. 58.

6. Ward, *Before the Trumpet*, p. 342.

7. Sackett, *The Views in Every Way Are Enticing*, p. 19. There probably were forty days of fog, but the changing times slowed Campobello's popularity, not the weather.

8. Elliott Roosevelt, editor, and James N. Rosenau, *F.D.R · His Personal Letters, 1905–1928*, New York: Duell, Sloan and Pearce, 1948, p. 90.

9. Ibid, p. 91. Apparently Eleanor took many pictures over the years at Campobello, but very few survive.

10. Ibid, p. 94. Sara was short on humor, but never on propriety.

11. Ibid.

12. Ibid, p. 100.

13. Livy Davis served as a special assistant to Franklin in the Navy Department and later in the American Relief Administration under Herbert Hoover. Until Franklin's election as governor of New York, the playful and hard-drinking Livy was a regular chum and playmate for Franklin in Washington and later during the early polio rehabilitation. Eleanor neither liked nor trusted Livy, who eventually resented Franklin's success and unavailability. Franklin declined an invitation to Livy's wedding in Maine in 1927 and Livy declined an invitation to the inauguration in 1932. Shortly thereafter, suffering from depression and acute alcoholism, Livy went to the shed behind his Massachusetts home and shot himself.

14. Roosevelt and Rosenau, *F.D.R.: His Personal Letters, 1905–1928*, p. 112.

15. Ibid, p. 113.

16. Ibid.

17. Ibid.

18. Ibid, p. 127. There is indication that this letter got Franklin's attention. There were no further written chastisements from Sara. He always took care not to displease his mother.

19. Ibid, p. 131.

20. Ibid, p. 132.

21. Ibid, p. 133

22. Ibid, p. 134.

23. Ibid, p. 136. The association of cottagers did not take over the ownership and management of the common lands until long after the growth period and well into the post-war 1920s. An elected board and a hired agent managed the properties.

24. Ibid, p. 139. Franklin held no enthusiasm for practicing law but he assumed it was the appropriate thing for him to do. Although he passed the New York State Bar exam, he never finished his studies at Columbia or received a jurisprudence degree.

CHAPTER 5

1. Ward, *A First Class Temperament*, p. 85. It may have been arrogance on Franklin's part, but he was remarkably prescient.

2. Ibid.

3. Ibid, p. 80.

4. Goodman, "A Home of Her Own," p. 5. The Kuhns were from Boston and built their cottage in 1897. There is no question that Grace was fond of the younger Roosevelts, but it's not clear that she understood the extent of Sara's domination of her son and daughter-in-law.

5. Blanche Wiesen Cook, *Eleanor Roosevelt: Volume I 1884–1933*, New York: Viking: 1992, p. 182.

6. Tugwell, *FDR: Architect of an Era*, p. 35. This was the most telling and most concise statement Eleanor made about how Sara made her feel in their Hyde Park "home."

7. Ward, *A First Class Temperament*, pp. 274-5.

8. Ibid, p. 99.

9. Ibid.

10. Ibid, p. 109. Franklin's visits were brief, and Hall was out west that summer, and Eleanor longed for adult kin.

11. Roosevelt and Rosenau, *F.D.R.: His Personal Letters, 1905–1928*, p. 170.

12. Eleanor Roosevelt, *This Is My Story*, New York: Harper, 1937, p. 178.

13. James Roosevelt, *My Parents: A Differing View*, Chicago, Playboy Press, 1976, p. 127.

14. Ward, *A First Class Temperament*, p. 580.

15. Roosevelt, *My Parents: A Differing View*, p. 52. Actually, Jimmy's word for the pool water was "stank."

16. Miller, *The Roosevelt Chronicles*, p. 278. When in ill health, the 19th century author Robert Louis Stevenson moved to the island of Samoa to a home he named "Valima." His condition soon worsened and he died. Franklin's condition, of course, was a temporary one. Had Franklin not been indisposed at this time, he might not have involved Howe in this particular campaign. It is, however, difficult to imagine that they would not have come together in their joint mission at some point.

17. Lash, *Eleanor and Franklin*, p. 186. She may not have looked forward to entertaining naval officers, but she was certainly good at doing so.

18. Ward, *A First Class Temperament*, p. 580. Isabel Ferguson was Eleanor's best friend and was married to a much older Bob Ferguson, who had once been linked romantically with Theodore's sister, Bamie. Ferguson was tubercular and they lived most of their married life in New Mexico. This was one more instance when Eleanor felt deserted (although she well understood) by someone she very much cared for.

19. Elliott Roosevelt, *Eleanor Roosevelt With Love: A Centenary Remembrance*, New York: E.P. Dutton, 1984, p. 20.

20. Alfred Steinberg, *Mrs. R.: The Life of Eleanor Roosevelt*, New York, Putnam, 1958, p. 98.

21. Frank Friedel, *Franklin D. Roosevelt: The Apprenticeship*, Boston: Little Brown, 1952, p. 253. Nomura's message was strictly a courtesy; they were only casual acquaintances.

22. Ibid, p. 276. Franklin did get involved in Haiti after his return to Washington. He later claimed to have written Haiti's constitution, but there is little substantiation. His participation was minimal.

23. Roosevelt and Rosenau, *F.D.R.: His Personal Letters, 1905–1928*, p. 135. Again, Franklin's perception proved somewhat faulty. During Franklin's active political career, Maine never elected a Democrat to a federal office. He was always warmly welcomed in Maine, but Mainers never gave him their vote.

24. J. William T. Youngs, *Eleanor Roosevelt: A Personal and Public Life*, edited by Oscar Handlin, Boston: Little Brown, 1985, p. 108. Franklin's fear of polio was real and constant. It was, essentially, a fear for the well-being of his children.

25. Lois Scharf, *Eleanor Roosevelt: First Lady of American Liberalism*, Boston: Twayn, 1987, p. 50.

26. Lash, *Eleanor and Franklin*, p. 199.

27. Ted Morgan, *FDR: A Biography*, New York: Simon & Schuster, 1985, pp. 172–4.

28. Bernard Asbell, *The F.D.R. Memoirs*, , Garden City, NY: Doubleday, 1973, p. 256. Did Franklin fear that Eleanor really knew what was going on between him and Lucy Mercer? At any rate, he tried to put any suspicions she might have to rest.

29. Lash, *Eleanor and Franklin*, p. 226. Alice didn't save all her gossip and her tartness for Franklin and Eleanor, but Eleanor was certainly a favorite target. Franklin and Alice had some friendly moments until the final break between the two family branches came in the early 1920s.

30. Ibid, p. 224.

31. William M. Rand, *Cap's Story,* West Concord, MA: Concord Press, 1968, pp. 73–5.

32. Lash, *Eleanor and Franklin,* p. 224.

33. Roosevelt and Rosenau, *F.D.R.: His Personal Letters, 1905–1928,* p. 351. "Bosch" was a pejorative term for Germans widely used in England and America before and during World War I. Rumors flew throughout the war about German submarines along the Maine coast, as they did again during World War II, when German U-boats did clandestinely put ashore two "saboteurs" in Vanceboro. They were captured later, but there were suggestions that submarines had cracked the net thrown across Casco Bay off Portland where the U.S. Navy maintained a large facility and refueling depot. One story had a German spy nabbed in Portland with a movie theatre stub in his pocket!

34. Miller, *The Roosevelt Chronicles,* p. 287.

CHAPTER 6

1. Lash, *Eleanor and Franklin,* p. 227. Although she never did forget or fully forgive, Eleanor never wavered in her esteem for Franklin or her belief in his leadership. She always referred to him in the third person, and probably never forgot the love they once had. As with her father, Eleanor held dearly onto the memory of her loves.

2. Ward, *A First Class Temperament,* p. 313. Whether she did really find sex an ordeal or not, Eleanor delivered six babies in nine years. Most of them were large infants, and the second, Franklin Jr., had a particularly long and difficult birth. She was through after John's birth, and abstention was her guarantee of no more.

3. Graham, "The Paradox of Eleanor Roosevelt: Alcoholism's Child," p. 227.

4. Cook, *Eleanor Roosevelt, Volume I,* p. 261.

5. Lash, *Eleanor and Franklin,* p. 231. Eleanor adored her Uncle Theodore when she was a child. She may have recorded his death with little noticeable emotion, but she must have felt his loss.

6. Peter Collier with David Horowitz, *The Roosevelts: An American Saga,* New York: Simon & Schuster, 1984, p. 121.

7. Cook, *Eleanor Roosevelt, Volume I,* p. 257. This may have been one of the last times Eleanor felt need to apologize to Sara for disagreeing with her. Never rude to her mother-in-law, Eleanor elected to remove herself more often from Sara's presence.

8. Ibid, p. 249.

9. Ibid. Eleanor may have feared that in some ways she was too much like her grandmother

10. Ibid, p. 262.

11. Roosevelt and Rosenau, *F.D.R.: His Personal Letters, 1905–1928,* p. 483. Maude and David Gray were great favorites of Eleanor and had a warm relationship with Franklin.

12. Cook, *Eleanor Roosevelt, Volume I,* p. 273.

13. Lash, *Eleanor and Franklin*, p. 252. This response attests to the warmth that Eleanor still felt toward Franklin. She missed him when he was absent from Campobello.

14. Ward, *A First Class Temperament*, p. 516.

15. John Gunther, *Roosevelt in Retrospect*, New York: Harper, 1950, p. 9. This comment was probably made just for its effect. Franklin took the walk often because he enjoyed it. Theodore made these kinds of activities an absolute and did them with scheduled regularity. Franklin was governed by impulse.

16. Lois Lowry, "Where F.D.R. Sunned," *New York Times*, June 1, 1975, p. 18.

17. Ward, *A First Class Temperament*, p. 540. Franklin and Theodore Junior had a strained relationship throughout their lives. Although Ted was considerably over age for combat in World War II, Franklin generously raised his rank to brigadier general and he was able to see a great deal of action. General Roosevelt participated in the invasion of Normandy, where he died of a heart attack.

18. Ibid, p. 534.

19. Ibid, p. 557.

CHAPTER 7

1. Lash, *Eleanor and Franklin*, p. 262.

2. Ibid, p. 264. It was obvious that Eleanor delighted in her newfound ability to get up in front of a group and speak her mind. It is also apparent that she was most appreciative of Franklin's coaching and his interest in helping her.

3. FDR Personal File, Box 10, Franklin D. Roosevelt Library.

4. Cook, *Eleanor Roosevelt, Volume I*, p. 306.

5. Ward, *A First Class Temperament*, p. 570. Franklin could not have been very surprised by the summons, but he was extremely disappointed.

6. Ibid, p. 573. The fact that the sub-committee's findings and the newspaper headlines had only a momentary impact on the public is surprising by today's media standards. The story was probably not covered in much depth, if at all, by other than major metropolitan newspapers. With newspapers the only public medium, the scandal was likely unknown to the vast majority of Americans.

7. Ibid, p. 574. Eleanor was continually supportive and, most often, a clear voice of reason.

8. Ibid, p. 575.

9. Ibid, p. 577. The Calders, more than any other Campobello family, provided two generations of service and friendship to the Roosevelts.

10. Ibid, p. 581. Many of the children's happiest memories of Franklin as an active father were Campobello events. His most notable parenting success was in play and sporting instruction.

11. Asbell, *The F.D.R. Memoirs*, p. 259. The waters of Passamaquoddy Bay were legendary in their coldness. It is unlikely that Franklin had often, if ever, been in the waters at this particular depth. The beach water, while still very cold, is less so as tides are warmed as they reach shoreward.

12. Ibid.

13. Miller, *The Roosevelt Chronicles*, p. 302.

14. Lela Stiles, *The Man Behind Roosevelt: The Story of Louis McHenry Howe*, Cleveland: World Publishing Co., 1954, p. 332.

15. Ward, *A First Class Temperament*, p. 587. As proud as she was of her nursing skills, Eleanor made it very clear that she was not going to serve in that capacity on a full-time basis.

16. Miller, *The Roosevelt Chronicles*, p. 303.

17. Richard Thayer Goldberg, *The Making of Franklin D. Roosevelt: Triumph Over Disability*, Cambridge: Abt Books, 1981, p. 30. Why the lumbar puncture did not take place remains a mystery. Perhaps the difficult trip to Bangor was a factor. It is now generally accepted that not performing the relatively simple procedure was a mistake.

18. Ward, *A First Class Temperament*, p. 592. Both Rosy and Sara's brother Frederick were always available for assistance to Franklin. Uncle Fred had a vast network of useful connections, and Rosy, who lived next door in Hyde Park, was always big brotherly.

19. Ibid, p. 593.

20. Asbell, *The F.D.R. Memoirs*, p. 34. It may be hard to understand that Sara and Franklin could maintain stiff upper lips for each other's benefit, as well as for others, but they did. This ability, or curse, was one of the many iron-like bonds they shared.

21. Ward, *A First Class Temperament*, p. 596. Louis could maintain a sense of humor in most situations. His comment about the watches and their vast difference in cost is an example. The Radiolite was a 1921 equivalent of today's inexpensive digital watches, costing just a few dollars.

22. Ibid, p. 599. As he was carried on the stretcher, Franklin had his fedora covering his hands clasped over his chest. The intent was to shield the paralysis that then existed from his children's eyes.

23. Lash, *Eleanor and Franklin*, p. 272.

24. Alfred B. Rollins, Jr., *Roosevelt and Howe*, New York: Alfred A. Knopf, 1962, p. 176.

CHAPTER 8

1. Gunther, *Roosevelt in Retrospect*, pp. 226–7.

2. Ibid, p. 229. Franklin's indictment of water as the cause of his polio was not rational, but an emotional observation.

3. Gallagher, *FDR's Splendid Deception*, pp. 28–33.

4. Ward, *A First Class Temperament*, p. 621.

5. Ibid, pp. 616–17. Howe had gambled his career, his family, and his soul for the opportunity to serve Franklin. If he didn't devoutly believe that Franklin would eventually become President, he could not have justified his actions, let alone his conscience.

6. Ibid, p. 628. Howe's attempt to soothe Eleanor was proof not only of his service to her, but his deepening friendship.

7. Ibid, p. 699. Had television been a reality in 1924, Franklin might have achieved instant national stardom. Still, this appearance was a public relations masterpiece.

8. Ibid, p. 700.

9. Lash, *Eleanor and Franklin*, p. 298.

10. Cook, *Eleanor Roosevelt, Volume I*, p. 328.

11. Ibid.

12. Lash, *Eleanor and Franklin*, p. 298.

13. Lash, *Love, Eleanor: Eleanor Roosevelt and Her Friends*, Garden City, NY: Doubleday, 1982, p. 93. It was quite amazing that activists such as Schneiderman, Swartz, and Simkhovitch would go to such a distance to visit Eleanor at Campobello. It speaks to both her influence and her abilities.

14. Kenneth S. Davis, *Invincible Summer: An Intimate Portrait of the Roosevelts, Based on the Recollections of Marion Dickerman*, New York: Atheneum, 1974, p. 42.

15. Frank Friedel, *Franklin D. Roosevelt: The Ordeal*, Boston: Little Brown, 1954, p. 235. Howe was livid that Franklin accepted the nomination without first telling him. He got over it quickly.

16. Cook, *Eleanor Roosevelt, Volume I*, p. 379. Eleanor had much to learn about handling the press. By the time she was First Lady, she had a much better sense of control. Lorena Hickock became her teacher as well as her close friend during Franklin's first term.

17. Richard Harrity and Ralph G. Martin, *The Human Side of FDR*, New York: Duell, Sloan and Pearce, 1960, p. 13.

18. Eleanor Roosevelt, *This I Remember*, p. 25.

19. Tugwell, *In Search of Roosevelt*, p. 53.

20. Frances Perkins, *The Roosevelt I Knew*, New York: Viking Press, 1946, p. 29. Perkins was an able labor activist and a competent Secretary of Labor. She was not, however, close to Franklin. Eleanor first brought her to his attention.

21. Christopher Clausen, "Summer Addresses," *The New Leader*, 80/14, September 8, 1997, p. 11.

22. Ibid.

23. Ibid.

24. Lash, *Eleanor and Franklin*, p. 462.

25. James A. Farley, *Behind the Ballots*, New York: Harcourt Brace, 1938, p. 189. Perhaps the proudest day of her life, but probably not the happiest.

CHAPTER 9

1. Geoffrey C. Ward, editor, *Closest Companion: The Unknown Story of the Intimate Friendship Between Franklin Roosevelt and Margaret Suckley*, New York: Houghton Mifflin, 1995, p. x. Daisy Suckley believed, or fantasized, that she and Franklin would live together after his Presidency in Top Cottage, the retreat he built in the late

1930s. She believed they had a "defining" moment and that they would, somehow, live together.

2. "Welcome to the President," *Lubec Herald,* June 29, 1933, p. 1. (Not to be confused with an article of the same headline in the June 22, 1933, issue.)

3. "Welcome to the President." *Lubec Herald,* June 22, 1933, p. 1. (Not to be confused with an article of the same headline in the June 29, 1933, issue.)

4. Ibid.

5. Ellen MacDonald Ward, "Sunset at Campobello," *Down East,* 41/9, April 1995, pp. 97–8. This was an early message to Franklin about security requirements. The Secret Service learned to adapt to his needs, particularly those that involved getting close to the people. No President had ever been as anxious to "press the flesh" as Franklin. Hoover never wandered far from the Oval Office, but Franklin, despite his limited mobility, longed to make personal contact with ordinary citizens.

6. *Lubec Herald,* June 29, 1933, p. 8.

7. Ibid.

8. Lash, *Eleanor Roosevelt on Campobello,* Campobello: Roosevelt Campobello International Park (no date), p. 9. Eleanor was, undoubtedly, happier enjoying Campobello with her good friends than she was in anticipation of all the hoopla that would surround Franklin's arrival. In fact, when he did arrive, she was annoyed by his disdain for her careful preparation. He hosted a raucous cocktail party that much delayed her planned dinner, and she had to deal with her sons who had too much to drink. Eleanor's memories of dear ones consuming too much alcohol must have been painful for her. This was, however, typical behavior for both Franklin and Eleanor. He liked gay parties at the expense of schedules and protocol, and she was bound to keeping to schedules and observing appropriate decorum. But, grudgingly, Eleanor understood that this was Franklin's party, not hers.

9. Lash, *Love, Eleanor,* p. 162.

10. Davis, *Invincible Summer,* p. 115.

11. Ibid, p. 116.

12. Ibid. Although Marion waxed poetic about the scene, there is no doubt that Franklin's arrival was dramatic, colorful, and everything that was expected of it. It is interesting that this vivid version was penned by Marion Dickerman, not Eleanor.

13. FDR Personal Files, Box 15, Franklin D. Roosevelt Library.

14. Don Wharton, *The Roosevelt Omnibus,* New York: Alfred A. Knopf, 1934, pp. 92–3. This story was published barely a year after the event took place. If anything, it provides even more credibility for its accuracy.

15. Eleanor Roosevelt, *This I Remember,* p. 124.

16. Ibid, p. 125. Hick encountered more than the ladder. Although she had Eleanor to herself at Campobello during this trip, she did not seem to take to the island. Perhaps, at this stage in their relationship, she found Campobello competing with her for Eleanor's attention. Or she was displeased that Eleanor had happy memories of times spent there with others, most particularly trips to the island with Nan and Marion.

17. Lash, in Muskie, *Campobello: Roosevelt's "Beloved Island,"* p. xx.

CHAPTER 10

1. FDR Personal Files, Box 561, Franklin D. Roosevelt Library.

2. Ibid.

3. FDR Personal Files, Box 160, Franklin D. Roosevelt Library.

4. Ward, *A First Class Temperament*, p. 577f.

5. FDR Personal Files, Box 561, Franklin D. Roosevelt Library.

6. Lash, *Love, Eleanor*, p. 191. For just a moment, Eleanor allowed herself to consider Campobello for extended living. The cottage was hardly a candidate for winterization, and Eleanor knew that precious few of her friends, or family for that matter, would make the journey northeast very often.

7. Miriam Anne Bourne, *The Ladies of Castine*, New York: Arbor House, 1986, p. 127.

8. "Mrs. Roosevelt Coming to Castine Friday," *The Green Street News*, July 26, 1935, Wetherle Memorial Library, Castine, ME. Author unknown.

9. Bourne, *The Ladies of Castine*, p. 127.

10. Lash, in Muskie, *Campobello: Roosevelt's "Beloved Island,"* p. xix. Eleanor had come a long way from her early fear of the sea. Fiercely competitive by this stage in life, she regretted not making Franklin give her the opportunity to sail the many years they spent together on the water.

11. Lash, *Love, Eleanor*, p. 162. Eleanor did not shy from controversy, and opposed Franklin occasionally in print. It may not have pleased him, but he made little effort to try to contain her free expression. Had he done so, it is unlikely that it would have had much effect.

12. Bethell, "Frank Roosevelt at Harvard, and What Became of Him Later," p. 47. Franklin was often at odds with members of the Class of '04. A vocal and numerically superior number of classmates resided in the Cambridge/Boston area and regularly opposed allowing members from outside the area to hold class offices. Franklin threw himself against these forces, often with success.

13. Ibid, p. 49.

14. Ibid. Justice Frankfurter was Franklin's candidate for Solicitor General. After discussion with his wife, he turned it down. However, he continued to be very much a Roosevelt insider.

15. Ibid.

16. Ward, "Sunset at Campobello," p. 100.

17. Robert H. Mountain, "Flower Power," *American Heritage*, 48/5, September 1997, p. 32.

18. Lash, *Love, Eleanor*, p. 233. This was the last time that Franklin sailed in his favorite waters. His brief return in 1939 was aboard a naval ship. His trip to meet Churchill in 1941 was again aboard naval vessels.

19. Ibid, p. 225. The house was full that visit. In addition to Nan, Marion, and Elinor Morgenthau, guests included Molly Dewson, Rose Schneiderman, and Helen Keller.

20. Ibid.

21. Lash, *Eleanor Roosevelt on Campobello*, p. 10.

22. William E. Leuchtenberg, *The FDR Years: On Roosevelt and His Legacy*, New York: Columbia University Press, 1995, p. 147. Since the 1950s, Maine has elected a number of Democrats to the governorship and to both the U.S. Senate and House of Representatives. So has Vermont. The old saw no longer has significance or accuracy.

23. Eleanor Roosevelt, *My Day*, Vol. 2, David Eldridge, editor, New York: Pharos Books, 1990, p. 360.

24. Ibid.

25. Goodwin, *No Ordinary Time*, p. 81.

26. James Roosevelt, *My Parents: A Differing View*, p. 59.

CHAPTER 11

1. Lash, *Eleanor Roosevelt: A Friend's Memoir*, Garden City, NY: Doubleday, 1964, p. 244.

2. Ibid, p. 243.

3. "Roosevelt Cottage on Maine's Neighboring Island, Campobello, Becomes Home of Unique Summer School, the Student Leadership Institute," *Lewiston Journal*, July 12, 1941.

4. Lash, *Eleanor Roosevelt: A Friend's Memoir*, p. 244.

5. Statement, Campobello Leadership Conference, Roosevelt Campobello International Park Library, Supplement, p. 3.

6. Harold Richard and Kenneth Cushman, "Memoirs." In Franklin P. Cole (ed.), *Nathan A. Cushman, a Rugged Individualist*, Portland, ME: Casco Printing Co., 1984. p. 117.

7. Keith Alldrit, *The Greatest of Friends, Franklin D. Roosevelt and Winston Churchill, 1941-1945*, New York: Duell, Sloan and Pearce, 1995, p. 30. Churchill understandably had no memory of their first meeting: Franklin had a relatively minor position in a large contingent. Even if he had remembered, there was nothing distinguishable about Franklin's participation to jog that memory.

8. Elliott Roosevelt, *As He Saw It*, New York: Duell, Sloan and Pearce, 1946, p. 19. All four of the Roosevelt sons served on active duty during the war and saw action. Franklin must have taken some satisfaction that, although he was denied service, his sons carried the standard.

9. Alldrit, *The Greatest of Friends*, p. 57. One of the many things that drew Franklin and Churchill to each other was their playfulness and high spirits. They had a good time together although the occasion for each meeting was extraordinarily serious in nature.

10. Elliott Roosevelt, *As He Saw It*, p. viii. Interesting comment for Eleanor to make. When she had her triumphs, no member of her family was nearby.

11. Ibid, p. 39. Franklin's judgement of who he would be comfortable working with was unerring.

12. "President Roosevelt's Rockland Visit," *Rockland Courier Gazette*, 96/99, August 19, 1941, p. 1.

13. Ibid.

14. Ibid.

15. Ibid.

16. "Roosevelt, Churchill Met Off Maine Coast, Films Indicate," *Portland Press Herald*, August 18, 1941, p. 1. There were a great many American citizens who could easily confuse Newfoundland with Maine. It is likely that many were unsure of what was American and what was Canadian in the North Atlantic.

17. Ibid.

18. Nathan Miller, *F.D.R.: An Intimate History*, Garden City, NY: Doubleday, 1983, p. 466. No one could provide a satisfactory reason for the tree to fall. The planting and maintenance of trees on the Hyde Park estate was of tremendous importance to Franklin, and Sara as well.

19. Peter Collier, with David Horowitz, *The Roosevelts: An American Saga*, New York: Simon & Schuster, p. 401. Eleanor would have liked a different relationship with her mother-in-law. She was eager to have a mother in her life, but it was clear early on that Sara would not fill that role. It took some time for Eleanor to shrug Sara off, but she eventually did. Sara admired Eleanor's abilities, but openly criticized her mothering. Sara's death removed an enormous barrier between Eleanor and Franklin. By then, however, it was too late.

20. FDR Personal Files, Box 561, Franklin D. Roosevelt Library. It's not that Franklin was irresponsible in making payments, he was just inexperienced. When Sara paid the bills, she took the responsibility. Eleanor became a proficient keeper of home books.

21. Ibid. Typically, Franklin trusted most people, Eleanor few.

22. "Princess Many Trails," Indian Clipping File, Maine State Historical Society Library.

23. Eleanor Roosevelt, "My Day," in Ryerson and Lois Johnson, *Two Hundred Years of Lubec History*, Lubec, ME: Lubec Historical Society, 1976, p. 134. Eleanor was a devoted friend to Dr. Bennet who, in time, became comfortable enough to call her his friend. He served the Lubec and Campobello area with humility and distinction.

24. John M. Cooper, Jr., "Great Expectations and Shadowlands: American Presidents and Their Reputations in the 20th Century," *Virginia Quarterly Review*, 72/3, Summer 1996, p. 381.

25. Lash, *Eleanor and Franklin*, p. 709.

26. Ibid.

27. Davis, *Invincible Summer*, p. 166. Plog served the Roosevelts for nearly 60 years. They relied heavily on his judgement and skill in maintaining the Springwood property.

28. "Bringing the President Home," *American Heritage*, 46/2, April 1995, p. 4.

29. Bethell, "Frank Roosevelt at Harvard, and What Became of Him Later," p. 87.

30. Goodwin, *No Ordinary Time*, p. 605.

31. Ibid. Was Stalin paranoid? He regularly had his food tested/tasted before he would touch it.

32. Ibid, p. 607.

CHAPTER 12

1. Eleanor Roosevelt, *My Day*, Vol. 2, p. 69.

2. "Fala Snubbed Here . . . .," *Portland Press Herald*, August 1, 1946, p. 1.

3. Eleanor Roosevelt, *My Day*, vol. 2, pp. 69–70. During the 1930s, Eleanor kept large and aggressive dogs. They were annoying to most visitors, and even nipped a congressman or two. Fala was really Franklin's dog. Eleanor kept the Scottie after Franklin's death for companionship and not for newsworthiness.

4. Nowlan, *Campobello: The Outer Island*, p. 117.

5. Basil O'Connor Files, Box 1, Franklin D. Roosevelt Library.

6. Ibid.

7. Eleanor Roosevelt, *My Day*, vol. 2, p. 104. Eleanor wrote both privately and for publication about Campobello's beauty and charm. She wanted her readers to get some sense of the strong feelings she had for her island home. Those of us who have their spirits lifted just by breathing the air of our special place will understand.

8. Lash, *Eleanor Roosevelt on Campobello*, p. 11.

9. Eleanor Roosevelt, *My Day*, vol. 2, pp. 106–7.

10. Lash, *Eleanor Roosevelt on Campobello*, p. 11.

11. Ibid.

12. Lash, *A World of Love: Eleanor Roosevelt and Friends*, Garden City, NY: Doubleday, 1984, pp. 229–30.

13. Eleanor Roosevelt, *My Day*, Vol. 2, p. 210.

14. Lash, *Eleanor Roosevelt on Campobello*, p. 11. In some ways, this is the most poignant of Eleanor's letters from the island. She does not foresee much future for her at Campobello any more. The cottage was sold to the Hammers not long after.

15. A. David Gurewitsch, *Eleanor Roosevelt: Her Day*, New York: Quadrangle, 1973, p. 37.

16. Edna P. Gurewitsch, "Remembering Mrs. Roosevelt," *American Heritage*, December 1981, p. 15.

17. Ward, "The Wonderful Husband," p. 74.

18. Eleanor Roosevelt, *My Day*, vol. 3, David Eldridge, editor. New York: Pharos Books, 1991, pp. 157-8.

19. FDR Personal Files, Box 31, Franklin D. Roosevelt Library.

20, Lowry, "Where F.D.R. Sunned," p. 18.

21. Eleanor Roosevelt, *My Day*, Vol. 3, New York: Pharos Books, p. 290.

22. James Roosevelt, *My Parents: A Differing View*, p. 296.

23. Ibid.

24. Ibid.

25. Johnson and Johnson, *Two Hundred Years of Lubec History*, unnumbered page.

26. Lash, *Eleanor Roosevelt: The Years Alone*, New York: W.W. Norton, 1972, pp. 325–6.

27. Ibid.

28. Allida M. Black, *Casting Her Own Shadow: Eleanor Roosevelt and the Shaping of Postwar Liberalism*, New York: Columbia University Press, 1996, p. 196.

29. Ibid, p. 197.

CHAPTER 13

1. Ward, *Closest Companion: The Unknown Story of the Intimate Friendship Between Franklin Roosevelt and Margaret Suckley* , p. 227.

2. Schlesinger, *The Age of Roosevelt: The Coming of the New Deal*, Boston, Houghton Mifflin, 1959, p. 515.

3. Ibid.

4. Lash, *Love, Eleanor*, p. 298.

5. Lash, *Eleanor and Franklin*, p. 46. This may have been, in some way, a kind of catharsis for Eleanor. The thought is one that is deeply personally felt, but expressed in the third person.

6. Eleanor Roosevelt, *Franklin D. Roosevelt and Hyde Park: Personal Recollections of Eleanor Roosevelt*, Washington, DC: U.S. Department of the Interior, 1980, p. 15. Eleanor clearly recognized that Springwood was Sara's home and not fully Franklin's until his mother's death. This passage suggests Eleanor's displeasure that Sara withheld passing title and responsibility too long.

7. Lash, *Eleanor and Franklin*, p. 390. This statement was clearly startling for the time, but it attests to Howe's perception of Eleanor's potential and, perhaps, to his own perceived skills in being able to elect presidents.

8. Lash, *Love, Eleanor*, p. 298.

9. Ward, *Before the Trumpet*, p. 319f.

EPILOGUE

1. Bethell, "Frank Roosevelt at Harvard, and What Became of Him Later," p.87.

2. Merlin Gustafson and Jerry Rosenberg, "The Faith of Franklin Roosevelt," *Presidential Studies Quarterly*, 19/3, Summer 1989, p. 561.

3. Bethell, *Harvard Magazine*, p. 87. Lathrop Brown was Franklin's oldest friend. While they were not especially close during Franklin's political career, they always had a cordial and reliable friendship. When Franklin's half-brother Rosy was abroad and unavailable, Brown served as Franklin's best man.

4. Schlesinger, *The Age of Roosevelt: The Coming of the New Deal*, p. 525.

5. Ibid.

6. Ward, *A First Class Temperament, p. xv.* Justice Holmes's observation is now widely held. It was made just after the newly elected President made a surprise courtesy call on the 92-year-old jurist, whose list of acquaintances spanned from John Quincy Adams to FDR.

7. S. G. F. Spackman, "Roosevelt," *History Today*, 10, June 1980, p. 39.

8. Rexford G. Tugwell, *The Brains Trust*, New York: Viking Press, 1968, p. 433. Long was at first a wary supporter of Franklin, but by the time of his assassination in 1935, he was solidly in the opposition camp.

9. Ibid. Franklin's view of MacArthur was undoubtedly influenced by the general's use of excessive force in routing the Bonus Marchers from Washington in 1932.

10. Lowry, "Where F.D.R. Sunned," p. 18.

11. Daniel Schorr, "The Real Roosevelt," *The New Leader*, LXXIX/8, November 4–18, 1996, p. 211.

12. Lash, *Eleanor and Franklin*, p. xi.

13. Lowry, "Where F.D.R. Sunned," p. 18.

14. Eleanor Roosevelt, *My Day.* Vol. 3, pp. 314–16.

Bibliography

Alldritt, Keith. *The Greatest of Friends: Franklin D. Roosevelt and Winston Churchill, 1941–1945.* New York: St. Martin's Press, 1995.

Alsop, Joseph. *FDR: A Centenary Remembrance.* New York: Viking, 1982.

Asbell, Bernard. *The F.D.R. Memoirs.* Garden City, NY: Doubleday, 1973.

Bethell, John T. "Frank Roosevelt at Harvard, and What Became of Him Later." *Harvard Magazine*, 99/2, November-December 1996.

Black, Allida M. *Casting Her Own Shadow: Eleanor Roosevelt and the Shaping of Postwar Liberalism.* New York: Columbia University Press, 1996.

Black, Ruby A. *Eleanor Roosevelt: A Biography.* New York: Duell, Sloan and Pearce, 1940.

Bourne, Miriam Anne. *The Ladies of Castine.* New York: Arbor House, 1986.

Brogan, Hugh, and Mosley, Charles. *American Presidential Families.* New York: Macmillan, 1993.

Brownstein, Elizabeth Smith. *If This House Could Talk.* New York: Simon & Schuster, 1999.

Bugbee, Emma. "Happy Days at Campobello." *New York Herald Tribune*, July 7, 1963.

Burns, James MacGregor. *Roosevelt: The Lion and the Fox.* New York: Harcourt Brace, 1956.

_____. *Roosevelt: The Soldier of Freedom.* New York: Harcourt Brace, 1970.

"Cambridge 02138." *Harvard Magazine*, 99/3, January-February 1997.

Caroli, Betty Boyd. *The Roosevelt Women.* New York: Basic Books, 1998.

"Celeste M. Wallace, Obituary." *Portland Press Herald*, September 12, 1996.

Clausen, Christopher. "Summer Addresses." *New Leader*, 80/14, September 8, 1997.

Cole, Franklin P.(ed.), *Nathan A. Cushman, a Rugged Individualist.* Portland, ME: Casco Printing Co., 1984.

Collier, Peter, with David Horowitz. *The Roosevelts: An American Saga.* New York: Simon & Schuster, 1984.

Cook, Blanche Wiesen. *Eleanor Roosevelt: Volume I, 1884–1933.* New York: Viking, 1992.

_____. *Eleanor Roosevelt: Volume II, 1933–1938.* New York: Viking, 1999.

Cooper, John Milton Jr. "Great Expectations and Shadowlands: American Presidents and their Reputations in the 20th Century." *Virginia Quarterly Review,* 72/3, Summer 1996.

Davis, Kenneth S. *FDR: The Beckoning of Destiny, 1882–1928.* New York: Putnam, 1971.

_____. *FDR: The New Deal Years, 1933–1937.* New York: Random House, 1986.

_____. *FDR: Into the Storm, 1937–1940.* New York: Random House, 1993.

_____. *Invincible Summer: An Intimate Portrait of the Roosevelts, Based on the Recollections of Marion Dickerman.* New York: Atheneum, 1974.

_____. "Miss Eleanor Roosevelt." *American Heritage,* 22/6, October 1971.

Delano, Daniel W. *Franklin Roosevelt and the Delano Influence.* Pittsburgh: James S. Nudi, 1946.

Edens, John A. *Eleanor Roosevelt: A Comprehensive Bibliography.* Westport, CT: Greenwood Press, 1994.

Emery, Charles, and Marsh, S. P. *Description of the Island of Campobello.* Boston: Press of Rockwell & Churchill, 1874.

Faber, Doris. *The Life of Lorena Hickock.* New York: Morrow, 1980.

"Fala Snubbed Here . . . ." *Portland Press Herald,* August 1, 1946, p. 1.

Farley, James A. *Behind the Ballots.* New York: Harcourt Brace, 1938.

Farr, Finis. *FDR.* New Rochelle, NY: Arlington House, 1972.

Franklin D. Roosevelt Library, President's Personal File:

    Box 561, Campobello Island, Campobello Library Association.

    Box 15, Campobello Island, Extemporaneous Remarks.

    _____. President's Official File:
    Box 1, Campobello (1).
    _____. Campobello (2).
    _____. Campobello (3).
    _____. Campobello Cruise.
    _____, President's Secretary's File:

    Box 97, Campobello.

    Box 160, Roosevelt, Franklin—Finances: Campobello.

    _____, F, B, & P File:
    Box 10, Campobello.
    Box 18, Guestbooks: Campobello.

    _____. Joseph P. Lash File:
    Box 3, Campobello.
    Box 26, International Student Service: Campobello School.
    Box 39, Eleanor Roosevelt to Lash—Campobello.

    _____. Basil O'Connor File:

Box 1, Campobello: Deeds, Bill of Sale.
Box 8, Roosevelt, Franklin D.: Estate: Campobello.

_____. O'Connor/Farber File:
Box 31, Roosevelt, Franklin D.: Estate: Siblings, Roosevelt Siblings Agreement with Dore Schary. *Sunrise at Campobello*: Correspondence, Papers re Tax Court Case. Memoranda. Miscellaneous Papers. Franklin D. Roosevelt, Jr.: Tax Papers.

_____. Leila Styles File:
Box 10, *Sunrise at Campobello*: Clippings.

_____. Marion Dickerman File:
Box 2, Campobello Visit 1933.

_____. James Roosevelt (son) File:
Box 181. *Sunrise at Campobello*.

_____. Louis Howe File:
Box 84, Maine.
Box 85, Maine.

Freeman, Allen. "FDR's Place." *Preservation*, September–October 1996.

Freedman, Russell. *Franklin Delano Roosevelt*. New York: Clarion Books, 1990.

Friedel, Frank. *Franklin D. Roosevelt: The Apprenticeship*. Boston: Little Brown, 1952.

_____. *Franklin D. Roosevelt: Launching the New Deal*. Boston: Little Brown, 1973.

_____. *Franklin D. Roosevelt: The Ordeal*. Boston: Little Brown, 1954.

_____. *Franklin D. Roosevelt: A Rendezvous With Destiny*. Boston: Little Brown, 1990.

_____. "The Election of 1932." in *The Coming to Power: Critical Presidential Elections in American History*, ed. Arthur M. Schlesinger, Jr. New York: Chelsea House, 1981.

Gallagher, Hugh Gregory. *FDR's Splendid Deception*. New York: Dodd Mead, 1985.

Gies, Joseph. *Franklin D. Roosevelt: Portrait of a President*. Garden City, NY: Doubleday, 1971.

Goldberg, Richard Thayer. *The Making of Franklin D. Roosevelt: Triumph over Disability*. Cambridge: Abt Books, 1981.

Goodman, Elizabeth B. "A Home of Her Own." *National Parks*, 56/7–8, July-August 1982.

Goodwin, Doris Kearns. *No Ordinary Time: Franklin and Eleanor Roosevelt: The Home Front in World War II*. New York: Simon & Schuster, 1994.

Gosnell, Harold F. *Champion Campaigner, Franklin D. Roosevelt*. New York: Macmillan, 1952.

Graf, Robert D., & Ginna, Robert E, text by Roger Butterfield. *FDR*. Based on the American Broadcasting Company's television series "FDR." New York: Harper, 1962.

Graham, H. D. "The Paradox of Eleanor Roosevelt: Alcoholism's Child." *Virginia Quarterly Review*, 63/2, Spring 1987.

Graham, Otis L. Jr. and Wander, Meghan Robinson, (eds.). *FDR, His Life and Times: Franklin D. Roosevelt Encyclopedia*. Boston: G. K. Hall, 1985.

"Greetings to President Franklin D. Roosevelt, the Cruise of the Amberjack II." *Eastport Sentinel*, June 28, 1933.

Gunther, John. *Roosevelt in Retrospect.* New York: Harper, 1950.

Gurewitsch, A. David. *Eleanor Roosevelt: Her Day.* New York: Quadrangle, 1973.

Gurewitsch, Edna P. "Remembering Mrs. Roosevelt." *American Heritage,* 33/1, December 1981.

Gustafson, Merlin, and Rosenberg, Jerry. "The Faith of Franklin Roosevelt." *Presidential Studies Quarterly,* 19/3, Summer 1989.

Hammer, Armand. *Hammer.* New York: Putnam, 1987.

Harrity, Richard, and Martin, Ralph G. *The Human Side of FDR.* New York: Duell, Sloan and Pearce, 1960.

Harvard Magazine, "Cambridge 02138." 99/3, January-February 1997.

Hassett, William D. *Off the Record with F.D.R., 1942–1945.* Westport, CT: Greenwood Press, 1958.

Hatch, Alden. *Franklin D. Roosevelt: An Informal Biography.* New York: Henry Holt & Co., 1947.

Hersham, Stella K. *The Candles She Lit: The Legacy of Eleanor Roosevelt.* Westport, CT: Praeger, 1993.

Hoff-Wilson, Joan, and Lightman, Marjorie (eds.). *Without Precedent: The Life and Career of Eleanor Roosevelt.* Bloomington: Indiana University Press, 1984.

Holmes, Theodore C. "A History of the Passamaquoddy Tidal Project." University of Maine, M.A. Thesis, 1955.

"How to Get the Most Out of Life." *Toronto Star,* August 30, 1958.

An Informal History of Rockland, Maine. Rockland Bicentennial Commission, 1976.

Johnson, Gerald W. *Roosevelt: Dictator or Democrat?* New York: Harper, 1941.

Johnson, Ryerson, and Johnson, Lois. *Two Hundred Years of Lubec History.* Lubec, ME: Lubec Historical Society, 1976.

Judd, Richard W., Churchill, Edwin A., and Eastman, Joel W. (eds.). *Maine: The Pine Tree State from Prehistory to the Present.* Orono: University of Maine Press, 1995.

Kiernan, R. H. *President Roosevelt.* London: George C. Harrap and Company, Ltd., 1948.

Kleeman, Ruta Halle. *Gracious Lady: The Life of Sara Delano Roosevelt.* New York: Appleton-Century, 1935.

Klein, Jonas. "The Making of a President: Franklin Delano Roosevelt, the First Fifty Years." Syracuse University, MSSc. Thesis, 1985.

Lash, Joseph P. *Eleanor and Franklin: The Story of their Relationship.* New York: W. W. Norton, 1971.

_____. *Eleanor Roosevelt: A Friend's Memoir.* Garden City, NY: Doubleday, 1964.

_____. *Eleanor Roosevelt on Campobello.* Campobello: Roosevelt Campobello International Park, n.d.

_____. *Eleanor: The Years Alone.* New York: W. W. Norton, 1972.

_____. *Love, Eleanor: Eleanor Roosevelt and her Friends.* Garden City, NY: Doubleday, 1982.

_____. *A World of Love: Eleanor Roosevelt and Friends, 1943-1962.* Garden City, NY: Doubleday, 1984.

Leuchtenburg, William E. *The FDR Years: On Roosevelt and His Legacy.* New York: Columbia University Press, 1995.

_____. *Franklin D. Roosevelt: A Profile.* New York: Hill & Wang, 1967.

_____. "Why the Candidates Still Use FDR as their Measure." *American Heritage,* 39/1, February 1988.

Lourie, Walter. "Roosevelt and the Passamaquoddy Bay Tidal Project." *History,* 30, 1968–69.

Lowry, Lois. "Where F.D.R. Sunned." *New York Times,* June 1, 1975.

Mackenzie, Compton. *Mr. Roosevelt.* New York: E. P. Dutton, 1944.

Maney, Patrick J. *The Roosevelt Presence: A Biography of Franklin Delano Roosevelt.* New York: Twayne Publishers, 1992.

McCarthy, A. "Message at Campobello: Eleanor Roosevelt and Human Rights." *Commonweal,* 111/4589, September 7, 1984.

McCullough, David, "Mama's Boys." *Psychology Today,* 17/3, March 1983.

McElvaine, Robert S. *The Great Depression: America, 1929-1941.* New York: Times Books, 1983.

McGehee, A. J. "Bringing the President Home." *American Heritage,* 46/2, April 1995.

Miller, Nathan. *FDR: An Intimate History.* Garden City, NY: Doubleday, 1983.

_____. *The Roosevelt Chronicles.* Garden City, NY: Doubleday, 1979.

Morgan, Ted. *FDR: A Biography.* New York: Simon & Schuster, 1985.

Mountain, Robert H. "Flower Power." *American Heritage,* 48/5, September 1997.

Muskie, Stephen O. *Campobello: Roosevelt's "Beloved Island."* Lubec, ME: Roosevelt Campobello International Park Commission, 1982.

Nowlan, Alden. *Campobello: The Outer Island.* Toronto: Clarke, Irwin & Co., 1975.

Perkins, Frances. *The Roosevelt I Knew.* New York: Viking Press, 1946.

"Portlanders Unable to Glimpse President." *Portland Sunday Telegram,* August 17, 1941.

"President Picnics with Canadian Guests." *Portland Press Herald,* July 31, 1936.

"President Roosevelt's Rockland Visit." *Rockland Courier Gazette,* August 16, 1941.

"President's Yacht Ideal for Cruise." *Eastport Sentinel,* June 28, 1933.

Rand, William M. *Cap's Story.* West Concord, MA: Concord Press, 1968.

Rasmussen, Cecilia. "A Party Ship's Last Voyage." *Los Angeles Times,* February 15, 1998.

Rollins, Alfred B., Jr. *Roosevelt and Howe.* New York: Alfred A. Knopf, 1962.

"Roosevelt, Churchill Met Off Maine Coast, Films Indicate." *Portland Press Herald,* August 18, 1941.

Roosevelt, Eleanor. *Franklin D. Roosevelt and Hyde Park: Personal Recollections of Eleanor Roosevelt.* Washington, D.C.: U.S. Department of the Interior, National Park Service, 1980.

_____. *It Seems To Me.* New York: W. W. Norton, 1954.

_____. *My Day.* Vol. 1. Rochelle Chadakoff (ed.). New York: Pharos Books, 1989.

_____. *My Day.* Vol. 2. David Eldridge (ed.). New York: Pharos Books, 1990.

_____. *My Day.* Vol. 3. David Eldridge (ed.). New York: Pharos Books, 1991.

_____. *The Autobiography of Eleanor Roosevelt,* New York: DaCapo, 1992.

_____. *This Is My Story.* New York: Harper, 1937.

_____. *This I Remember.* New York: Harper, 1949.

Roosevelt, Elliott. *As He Saw It.* New York: Duell, Sloan & Pearce, 1946.

_____. *A Rendezvous with Destiny: The Roosevelts of the White House.* New York: Putnam, 1975.

_____. *Eleanor Roosevelt with Love: A Centenary Remembrance.* New York: E. P. Dutton, 1984.

Roosevelt, Elliott, and Brough, James. *The Roosevelts of Hyde Park: An Untold Story.* New York: Putnam, 1973.

Roosevelt, Elliott (ed.), assisted by James N. Rosenau. *F.D.R.: His Personal Letters, Early Years.* New York: Duell, Sloan and Pearce, 1947.

_____. *F.D.R.: His Personal Letters, 1905-1928.* New York: Duell, Sloan and Pearce, 1948.

Roosevelt, James. *My Parents: A Differing View.* Chicago: Playboy Press, 1976.

Roosevelt, James, and Shalett, Sidney. *Affectionately, FDR.* New York: Harcourt Brace, 1959.

Roosevelt, Mrs. James, as told to Isobel Leighton and Gabrielle Forbush. *My Boy Franklin.* New York: Ray Lang and Richard R. Smith, Inc., 1933.

"Roosevelt's 'Beloved Island'—Campobello." *Down East,* August 1958.

"Roosevelt's Cottage on Maine's Neighboring Island, Campobello, Becomes Home of Unique Summer School, the Student Leadership Institute." *Lewiston Journal,* July 12, 1941.

Rosenau, James N. *The Roosevelt Treasury.* Garden City, NY: Doubleday, 1951.

Rosenman, Samuel I. *Working With Roosevelt.* New York: Harper, 1952.

"Ruth H.M. Ahlquist, Obituary." *Portland Press Herald,* October 1, 1999.

Sackett, Andrew. *The Views in Every Direction Are Enticing: Campobello Island as a Summer Resort, 1880-1910.* St. Andrew's, New Brunswick: Design Research, 1995.

Scharf, Lois. *Eleanor Roosevelt: First Lady of American Liberalism.* Boston: Twayne, 1987.

Scheer, R. "Eleanor to H.R.C." *The Nation,* 264/8, March 3, 1997.

Schlesinger, Arthur M. Jr. *The Age of Roosevelt: The Crisis of the Old Order, 1919-1933.* Boston: Houghton Mifflin, 1957.

_____. *The Age of Roosevelt: The Coming of the New Deal.* Boston: Houghton Mifflin, 1959.

_____. "Historic Houses: Campobello." *Architectural Digest,* 42, March 1985.

_____. "The Man of the Century." *American Heritage,* 45/3, May/June 1994.

Schorr, Daniel. "The Real Roosevelt." *New Leader,* LXXIX/8, November 4–18, 1996.

Spackman, S. G. F. "Roosevelt." *History Today,* 30, June 1980.

"Spell of Campobello, Maine's Neighbor Isle, Summer Home of President Franklin D. Roosevelt." *Lewiston Journal,* July 8, 1933.

Steinberg, Alfred. *Mrs. R.: The Life of Eleanor Roosevelt.* New York: Putnam, 1958.

Steitmatter, Roger (ed.). *Empty Without You: The Intimate Letters of Eleanor Roosevelt and Lorena Hickock.* New York: The Free Press, 1998.

Stiles, Lela. *The Man Behind Roosevelt: The Story of Louis McHenry Howe.* Cleveland: World Publishing Co., 1954.

Tugwell, Rexford G. *The Brains Trust.* New York: Viking Press, 1968.

_____. *The Democratic Roosevelt.* Garden City, NY: Doubleday, 1957.

_____. *FDR: Architect of an Era.* New York: Macmillan, 1967.

_____. *In Search of Roosevelt.* Cambridge, MA: Harvard University Press, 1972.

"A Visit to Campobello." *Ford Times,* April 1963.

Ward, Ellen MacDonald. "Sunset at Campobello." *Down East,* 41/9, April 1995.

Ward, Geoffrey C. *Before the Trumpet: Young Franklin Roosevelt, 1882-1905.* New York: Harper, 1985.

_____. *A First Class Temperament: The Emergence of Franklin Roosevelt.* New York: Harper, 1989.

_____, editor and annotator. *Closest Companion: The Unknown Story of the Intimate Friendship Between Franklin Roosevelt and Margaret Suckley.* New York: Houghton Mifflin, 1995.

_____. "Reexamining Roosevelt." *American Heritage,* 46/2. April 1995.

_____. "The Wonderful Husband." *American Heritage,* 40/6, September-October 1989.

Watkins, T. H. *The Great Depression: America in the 1930s.* Boston: Little Brown, 1993.

Weinberg, Steve. *Armand Hammer: The Untold Story.* New York: Little Brown, 1989.

Weiss, Stephanie. "Remembering the Roosevelts." *NEA Today,* 15/3, October 1996.

"Welcome to President Franklin D. Roosevelt." *Lubec Herald,* June 22, 1933.

"Welcome to President Franklin D. Roosevelt." *Lubec Herald,* June 29, 1933.

Wharton, Don. *The Roosevelt Omnibus.* New York: Alfred A. Knopf, 1934.

Wilson, Theodore A. *Roosevelt and Churchill at Placentia Bay, 1941.* Lawrence: University Press of Kansas, 1991.

Winfield, Betty Hanchin. "The Legacy of Eleanor Roosevelt." *Presidential Studies Quarterly,* 20/4, Fall 1990.

Youngs, J. William T. *Eleanor Roosevelt: A Personal and Public Life,* edited by Oscar Handlin. Boston: Little Brown, 1985.

Index

Acadia, 19, 203
Adams, Clover, 89
Adams, Henry, 89, 135
Albany, N.Y., 71, 72, 74, 129, 130, 131, 137, 138
Algonac, 10, 152
Allenswood School, 14, 90
Alsop, Corinne Robinson, 10
Amberjack II, 140-3, 148, 201
American Student Union, 178
American Youth Congress, 178
Annapolis, Md., 33
Annapolis Royal, N.S. 19
Argentia Bay, Newfoundland, 180-2, 185
Armistice, 89
Arnold, Benedict, 20
Aroostook County, Me., 149-50
Assistant Secretary of the Navy, 74, 82, 83, 84, 180
Astor, Vincent, 118
Atlantic Charter, 182-5
Atlas Mountains, 228
Atomic Bomb, 192
Augusta, Me., 180
Ayers Junction, Me., 68

Baker, Ray Stannard, 127
Barbados, 37
Bar Harbor, Me., 3, 17, 24, 40, 46, 61, 71, 77, 82, 109, 140
Baruch, Bernard, 88, 196
Bath, Me., 179, 181
Batson, Price, 153
Bay of Fundy, 2, 18, 19, 36, 84, 108, 118, 204, 231, 232

Beacon, N.Y., 10
Beal, Thomas B., 59
Bear Mountain, N.Y., 104
Bellamy, Ralph, 207, 209
Bennet, Eban, 72, 76, 77, 109, 110, 111, 112, 114, 115, 117, 188, 256*n*
Beverly, Mass., 36
Black, Van Lear, 100, 107, 108
Blackley, Charles Harrison, 25
Blue Hill Bay, Me., 182
Boothbay Harbor, Me., 142
Boston, Mass., 17, 25, 36, 37, 68, 79, 107, 111
Boston & Maine *Special*, 184
Boston Transcript, 166
Bowdoin College, 92, 104
Boy Scouts (Council), 100
Brain(s) Trust, 31, 134
Brandeis University, 209
Brann, Louis, 143, 145, 185
British Royal Navy, 77
Brittanic (ship), 11
Brown, Lathrop, 36, 43, 225, 258*n*
Browning, Robert, 40
Bugbee, Emma, 156

Calder, Aubrey 154
Calder, Franklin, 30, 69, 102, 105, 114, 115, 116, 150, 154, 156
Calder, John, 30, 143, 146, 154
Calder, Linnea, 106, 211, 227
California, 133, 229
Cambridge, Mass., 36, 66
Campbell, Lord William, 19
Camp-ISS-Bellow, 178

Campobello Company, 17, 21, 22, 63, 65
Campobello Debating Society, 30
Campobello Dramatic Club, 29
Campobello Golf Club, 34, 51
Campobello Island, 2, 3, 4, 16-26, 27-41,
    45-50, 59-66, 74, 76-81, 82, 84-5, 93-6,
    102-3, 105-16, 140-7, 150, 152-4, 163,
    164, 168-9, 170, 175-8, 179, 185-6,
    187, 188, 196-9, 201-6, 210-1, 212,
    223, 225, 229, 230, 234-40, 241, 246n
Campobello Island Club, 152, 153, 247n
Canada, 3, 17, 72, 85, 141, 146, 152, 174,
    180, 186, 199, 212, 228
Carter, Evelyn, 37, 41
Carter Ledyard and Milburn, 58-9
Casablanca Conference, 228
Casco Bay, 142
Castine, Me., 126, 154, 164, 211
Castine Women's Club, 164
Cherokee (ship), 82-4
Celler, Emmanuel, 212
Chebeague Island, 142
Chiang Kai-shek, 171
China, 6, 171
Churchill, Sarah, 190
Churchill, Winston, 179-83, 185, 187,
    190, 193, 222, 228, 229, 254n, 255n
Clausen, Christopher, 131-2
Cleveland, Grover, 109
Cobscook Bay, 108, 209
Columbia Law School, 44, 67, 247n
Congress, 79, 140, 170, 175, 232
Cook, Blanche Wiesen, 69
Cook, Nancy ("Nan"), 122, 123, 125, 127,
    138-41, 144, 145, 148, 152, 168, 169,
    171, 172, 217, 218
Coor, Maureen, 207
Court of Saint James, 39
Cow Bell, 29
Cox, James, 94
Cranberry Point, 24
Cuba, 78, 213
Cumberland (ship), 26
Cutler, Me., 71

Daniels, Josephus, 87, 79, 86, 90, 102,
    103, 104
Dark Harbor, Me., 32, 40
Davis, Livingston ("Livy"), 51, 59, 123,
    243n, 246n

Davis, Norman H., 145, 146
Dean, F. W., 22
Declaration of Human Rights, 196
Deer Isle, Me., 182
Delano, Deborah ("Dora" or "Aunt Doe"),
    6, 62, 90, 113
Delano, Frederick ("Uncle Fred"), 111,
    113, 115, 251n
Delano, "Kassie" (Aunt), 113
Delano, Laura, 137-8, 191
Delano, Warren Delano, 5
De La Noye, Phillipe, 5
Democrats, Democratic Party, 39, 71, 78,
    94, 96, 97, 101, 114, 125, 129, 132,
    149, 248n
Democratic National Committee, 78
Democratic National Convention, 93, 124,
    133
Derby, George, 92
Dewey, Thomas E., 190
Dewson, Molly, 122, 123, 126, 138, 164,
    211, 227
Dickerman, Marion, 122, 123, 125, 127,
    138-41, 144, 145, 148, 152, 168, 169,
    171, 172, 217, 218, 253n
Disarmament Conference, 146
Dolphin (ship), 79, 80
Draper, George, 117, 123, 125
Dreier, Mary, 140, 142
Dreyfus, Alfred, 14
Duffy (Roosevelt family dog), 48
Dutchess County, N.Y., 37, 226

Eastland Hotel, 197
Eastport, Me., 23, 25, 37, 41, 49, 58, 60,
    61, 64, 69, 75, 80, 95, 105, 106, 107,
    113, 115, 141, 145, 146, 148, 152, 176,
    202, 205, 209
Eastport Sentinel, 141
Eggemoggin Reach, Me., 32, 182
Elizabeth II, Queen, 233
Emmett, Marvin and Roosevelt, 99

Fairhaven, Mass., 91
Fala (Roosevelt family dog), 185, 192, 196-
    99, 257n
Farley, James A., 132, 134
Ferguson, Bob, 248n
Ferguson, Isabella, 75, 92, 248n
Ferguson, Martha, 76

Fickett, Mary, 207
Fidelity and Deposit Company, 100
Fourteen Points, 90
Frankfurter, Felix, 166, 177, 254*n*
Franklin D. Roosevelt International Bridge, 2, 210, 231, 233
Franklin D. Roosevelt Library, 59, 201
Freeport, Me., 140, 169
Friar's Bay, 4, 20, 69
Friar's Head (Rock), 20, 72, 180, 231

Garrison, William Lloyd, 20
Garson, Greer, 209
Gaspé Peninsula, 148
Gennerich, Gus, 147, 165
George VI, King, 146, 185
German submarines, 48, 79, 85, 182, 249*n*
Gibbs, Captain 140, 142
Gloucester, Mass., 20
Goldberg, Richard Thayer, 130
Goodwin, Doris Kearns, 38
Grand Manan Island, 23, 32, 33, 84, 203, 205, 232
Gray, David, 92, 163, 249*n*
Gray, Maude Hall (Eleanor's aunt) 92, 163, 195, 249*n*
Great Depression, 1, 130, 133, 135, 140, 153, 165, 170, 174, 228
Green Street News, 164
Grey, Sir Edward, 90
Groton School, 8-10, 33, 35, 37, 59, 97, 122, 130
Gurewitsch, David, 204-5, 207, 209, 210, 212, 218
Gurewitsch, Edna, 207, 210

Haiti, 77, 248*n*
Half Moon (boat), 31, 35-7, 40, 41, 46, 48-9, 60, 61, 62, 65, 72, 104, 231
Halifax, N.S., 19
Hall, Anna (*see* Roosevelt, Anna (Hall))
Hall, Edith ("Aunt Pussie"), 13, 92
Hall, Mary Livingston Ludlow, (Grandmother Hall), 10, 13, 14, 91
Hall, Maude Livingston (*see* Gray, Maude Hall)
Hall, "Tissie," (Aunt), 92
Hall, Jr., Valentine G., 10
Halsey, William F. ("Bull"), 32, 245*n*

Hammer, Armand, Harry, and Victor, 206, 211-2, 223, 257*n*
"Happy Warrior" speech, 124
Harbour de L'Outre, 18
Harding, Warren G., 104
Harriman, W. Averill, 193
Harvard (ship), 26
Harvard Board of Overseers, 166
Harvard College (University), 9, 22, 33, 36, 39, 59, 63, 130, 165-7, 191, 192, 225, 254*n*
Harvard Crimson, 39, 166
Harvard Fly Club, 105
Harvard Infantile Paralysis Commission, 111
Harvard Tercentenary Commission, 166-7
Head Harbor, 73
Hearst, William Randolph, 95, 133
Herring Cove, 24, 60, 163, 204, 232
Hickock, Lorena ("Hick"), 144, 148-50, 163, 165, 169, 172-3, 217-8, 243*n*, 252*n*, 253*n*
Hiroshima, 192
Hitler, Adolf, 174
HMS *Prince of Wales*, 180-2, 184
Holmes, Oliver Wendell, 227, 259*n*
Holocaust, 193
Hong Kong, 8
Hoover, Herbert, 133-4
"Hoovervilles," 134
Hopkins, Harry, 136, 165, 180, 182, 184
Hotel Owen, 21, 65
Hotel Touraine, 68
Hotel Tyn-y-Coed, 22, 28, 65, 154
Hotel Tyn-y-Maes, 22, 65
Howe, Grace, 102
Howe, Hartley, 102, 105, 110
Howe, Louis
  Roosevelt, Eleanor, and, 121, 134, 143, 217, 222, 251*n*
  Roosevelt, Franklin, and, 74, 88, 91, 109-16, 128, 130, 136, 194, 217, 248*n*, 251*n*, 252*n*
  Roosevelt family and, 97, 120, 251*n*
Howe, Mary, 97, 114
Hudson River (Valley), 5, 99, 104, 128, 185, 191
Hull, Cordell, 179

Hyde Park, 2, 11, 17, 26, 37, 43, 44, 47, 59, 60, 64, 66, 68, 69, 71, 78-80, 87, 88, 90, 91, 94, 118, 120, 127, 185, 186, 247*n*, 251*n*, 256*n*

Ickes, Harold, 217
International Brotherhood of Electrical Workers, 212
International Congress of Working Women, 92
International Student Service, 176
International Student Service Leadership Institute, 72, 175-8
Isleboro, Me., 40

Japan, 77, 112, 171, 187, 192
Japanese-Americans, 193
Johnson, Lyndon B., 233
Johnson, Mrs. Lyndon B., 233
Jonesport, Me., 81, 143
Jones, Henry, 207
Jones, James Earl, 208
Joseph, Chief Tomah, 59, 72, 150

Keen, W. W., 109-11
Kennebec River, 142, 181
Kennedy, John F., 192, 212, 228
Kennedy, Joseph P., 133
Kidd, Captain, 32
King, Jr., Martin Luther, 212
Kronprinzessen Cecile, 77
Kuhn, Mrs. Hartman (Grace), 37, 41, 68, 246*n*, 247*n*

Lake (Loch) Severn, 108, 232
Landon, Alf, 167-9
Lank, Eddie, 30, 146, 152, 231
Lape, Esther, 100, 123, 138, 164
Lash, Joseph P., 38, 86, 134, 176, 210, 213, 218, 221
Lash, Trude, 210
Law, Nigel, 81
League of Nations, 90, 94
League of Women Voters, 100
Leahy, William D., 80
LeHand, Marguerite A. ("Missy") 123, 130, 137, 139, 142, 152, 163, 190-1, 194, 215, 216, 221, 243*n*
Lend Lease, 182, 184, 187
Levine, Samuel, 111
Liberty Point, 18

Little Lord Fauntleroy, 7
L. L. Bean, 140, 169-70
Lloyd, Andrew, 20
Lloyd George, David, 180
Lodge, Henry Cabot, 90
Long, Huey, 227, 259*n*
Longfellow, Henry Wadsworth, 203
Longworth, Alice Roosevelt, 43, 81, 90, 248*n*
Lovett, Robert W., 111-2, 114, 117, 123
Lower East Side, 223
Lubec, Me., 2, 17, 23, 49, 58, 72, 76, 109, 117, 126, 141, 143, 144, 150, 152, 188, 202, 231, 232
Lubec Herald, 141, 143
Lubec Narrows, 32, 76, 84, 94, 145, 146, 188, 210

MacArthur, Douglas, 134, 227, 242*n*, 259*n*
MacGillivary, Campobello Club Agent, 153
MacLeish, Archibald, 177
Mahan, Alfred T., 31
Maine, 2, 16-18, 25, 33, 56, 59, 67, 77-9, 96, 107, 193, 142-3, 148-9, 163, 167, 169, 185, 202, 205, 230, 248*n*, 255*n*
Marion, Mass., 140
Maritime Provinces, 16, 17, 48
Marrakech, 228
Martha, Princess of Norway, 138, 216
McAdoo, William, 133
McCormick, Vance, 70
McGowan, Anna, 106
Mead, Margaret, 167
Mercer, Lucy (*see* Rutherfurd, Lucy Mercer)
Meredith, James, 212
Miller, Earl, 138-9, 152, 163, 207, 217
Mitchell, Captain, 146
Moley, Raymond, 141
Mont Saint-Michel, 202, 232
Montreal, P.Q., 17, 26
Morgenthau, Elinor, 169
Morgenthau, Jr., Henry, 145, 169, 177, 226
Moses, Robert, 129
Moskowitz, Belle, 129
Mount Desert Island, 32, 140
Mount Washington, 126
Museum of Natural History, 63
Mussolini's Black Shirts, 169
"My Day," 171, 188, 196-7, 198-9, 201-2, 203-4, 209, 231-3

Mystic, Conn. 209

Nagasaki, 192
National Association for the Advancement
   of Colored People, 177
National Youth Administration, 228
Native Americans, 16, 59, 62, 69, 150, 205
New Brunswick, 2, 16, 18, 25, 36, 49, 92,
   143, 144, 146, 149, 168, 197, 205
New Deal, 133, 140, 165, 170, 174
New England Coast, 17, 36
Newfoundland, 180
New Moon (boat), 31, 32, 35
Newport, R.I., 3, 17, 24, 46, 122
Newport Naval Base, 102-4, 250*n*
New York City (Manhattan), 12, 17, 25,
   37, 43, 44, 47, 62, 64, 65, 68, 71, 78,
   105, 108, 112, 113, 114, 115, 117, 120,
   121, 122, 127, 130
New York Democratic Party, 94, 99, 128,
   132, 202
New York Herald Tribune, 148
New York Journal, 95
New York State Assembly, 67
New York State Senate, 70, 71, 99
New York Times, 103, 116, 202
Newburgh, N.Y., 6
Nomura, Kichisaburo, 77, 248*n*
North Atlantic, 77, 179-80, 185
Northeast Harbor, Me., 32, 36, 71
North Dakota Primary, 132
North Haven Island, Me., 59
Nova Scotia, 19, 89, 203

O'Connor & Farber, 199
O'Connor, Basil, 199
Opium Wars, 6
Owen, Squire David, 20
Owen, William Fitzwilliam, 20, 154
Owen, William, 19-20
Oyster Bay, N.Y., 6, 37, 90, 101, 166

Palmer, Mitchell, 93
Parish, Henry, 50, 59
Parish, Susan Ludlow (Cousin "Susie"), 43,
   45, 50, 59, 71, 122
Passamaquoddy Bay, 16, 23, 59, 141, 145,
   168, 219, 250*n*
Peabody, Endicott, 9, 10, 43, 242*n*
Pearl Harbor, 77, 112, 187
Pearson, Mrs. Lester B., 233

Pell, Frances, 41
Penobscot Tribe, 188
Perkins, Frances, 110, 125, 131, 155, 252*n*
Perry's Nut House, 169, 176
Phippsburg, Me., 169, 179
Platt, Charles A., 62
Plog, William, 192, 256*n*
PM (newspaper), 177
Polio (Infantile Paralysis), 78, 111-16,
   130-1, 135, 136, 188
Porcellian, 39
Porter, Alexander, 28
Porter, Polly, 126, 138, 164
Portland, Me., 92, 142, 163, 167, 196, 199
Portland Press Herald, 158-9, 197
Portland Sunday Telegram, 184
Potomac (ship), 180, 182-6
Poughkeepsie, N.Y., 70, 78, 87, 120
Prendergast, Tom, 124
Presbyterian Hospital, 117
President of the United States 38, 67, 126,
   132, 135, 145, 147, 168, 193
Prohibition, 20, 120, 124
Pulpit Harbor, Me., 182

Quebec, 25, 125, 148, 149, 197
Queens County Council, 152

Rand, William M., 81-5
Read, Elizabeth, 100, 123, 138, 180
Redbook (magazine), 129
Red Cross, 175
Republicans, Republican Party, 36, 71, 90,
   96, 97, 134, 142, 162, 167, 170, 190
Reuther, Walter, 213
Rivington Street Settlement, 45, 223
Robinson-Owen, Cornelia, 21
Robinson-Owen, James, 21
Rock Creek Park, 89
Rockey, Edna, 115
Rockland, Me., 79, 183-4
Rockland Courier-Gazette, 183
Roosevelt, Alice (*see* Longworth, Alice
   Roosevelt)
Roosevelt, Alice (Theodore's first wife), 11
Roosevelt, Anna Eleanor (daughter), 45,
   46, 50, 60, 61, 64, 87, 95, 112, 120,
   130, 180, 190, 196, 208, 243*n*
Roosevelt, Anna Hall (Eleanor's mother),
   10-13
Roosevelt, Anna ("Aunt Bamie"), 12, 248*n*

Roosevelt, Betty ("Rosy's" wife), 77
Roosevelt, Eleanor
    Campobello and, 2, 4, 37, 40, 45, 46-
        48, 59-66, 68-72, 74, 75, 76, 78-81,
        85, 94-5, 97, 102, 105-16, 125-7,
        132, 139-44, 150, 163-4, 168-9, 175-
        82, 186, 188, 196-206, 210-1, 219-
        20, 227, 228, 230-2, 233, 250n,
        252n, 253n, 254n, 257n
    Children and, 45, 46, 49, 50, 60, 61, 64,
        75-7, 91, 93, 105, 121-2, 160, 172,
        202, 203, 208, 249n
    Cook, Nancy, and Dickerman, Marion,
        and, 122-3, 125, 127, 138-41, 144,
        145, 148, 152, 168, 169, 171, 172,
        217, 218
    Cottage and, 68-70, 72, 106, 199-200,
        206, 210-1, 232-3, 246n
    Friends and, 92, 122-3, 126-7, 164,
        204-5, 207, 210, 212-3, 218, 252n
    Hickock, Lorena ("Hick"), and, 144,
        148-50, 152, 169, 172-3, 217-8,
        243n, 252n, 253n
    Howe, Louis, and, 121, 134, 143, 217,
        222, 251n
    Miller, Earl, and, 138-9, 152, 163
    Moods (Griselda), 44, 89, 121
    "My Day," 196-7, 198-9, 201-2, 203-4,
        209, 231-3
    Politics and public service, 101, 124-5,
        129, 134, 151, 170, 172-3, 174, 196,
        212, 252n
    Roosevelt, Anna Hall (mother), and,
        12-3
    Roosevelt, Elliott (father), and, 10-3,
        218, 243n
    Roosevelt, Franklin, and, 4, 11, 37, 38,
        40-5, 47, 85, 86-8, 89, 90, 101, 109-
        10, 118, 142, 143, 220-1, 223-4,
        246n, 248n, 250n
    Roosevelt, Hall (brother), and, 12, 37,
        59, 72, 186
    Roosevelt, Sara Delano, and, 37, 38, 41,
        42, 44, 47, 48, 50, 64, 69, 91, 92,
        113-4, 156, 159, 186, 246n, 247n,
        249n, 256n, 258n
    Val-Kill and, 127, 138, 152, 196
    Victorianism and, 1, 90, 151, 214
Roosevelt, Elliott (Eleanor's father), 10-3,
    243n

Roosevelt, Elliott (son), 71, 76, 89, 105,
    108, 130, 139, 180, 181, 185, 197, 200,
    201, 204, 206, 208
Roosevelt, Jr., Elliott (Eleanor's baby
    brother), 12
Roosevelt, Faye Emerson (son Elliott's
    wife), 202
Roosevelt, Franklin Delano
    Assistant Secretary of Navy, 33, 67, 74,
        75, 82, 248n
    Campobello and, 2, 4, 28-36, 40-1, 45,
        46-8, 70, 73-5, 77, 80, 85, 94-5, 102-
        3, 106-116, 132, 140-48, 161-3, 168,
        219-20, 227-8, 229-32, 233, 250n
    Children and, 45, 49, 60, 67, 76, 85, 93,
        106, 108, 122, 124, 140, 142, 168,
        180-2, 250n, 255n
    Church and, 180-2, 183, 184, 193, 228-9
    Cottage and, 68, 70, 73, 106, 232, 246n
    Groton School and, 8, 9, 33, 35
    Harvard and, 9, 39, 63, 165-7, 254n
    Hobbies and activities, 8, 33, 39, 45, 60,
        63, 73, 104
    Howe, Louis, and, 74, 88, 93, 109-17,
        128, 130, 134, 136, 165, 217, 248n,
        251n, 252n
    Hyde Park and, 2, 94, 219
    LeHand, Marguerite ("Missy"), and, 123,
        130, 137, 142, 163, 215-6
    Polio and Rehabilitation, 109-19, 130-2,
        244n, 248n, 251n
    Politics, 70-1, 74, 78, 90, 93-4, 96-8, 99,
        102-3, 124-5, 128, 160, 168-9, 172-3
    President of the United States, 135-6,
        140, 170-1, 174-5, 187, 189-91, 193,
        226
    Roosevelt, Eleanor, and, 4, 11, 37, 38,
        40-5, 47, 85, 86-88, 89, 90, 101, 118-
        19, 220-1, 223-4, 246n, 250n
    Roosevelt, James (father), and, 3, 6, 35
    Roosevelt, Sara Delano, and, 3, 5-6, 7, 9,
        34, 36, 38, 39, 41-2, 44, 47-8, 51, 63-
        4, 69, 87, 113-4, 186, 194, 227,
        245n, 247n
    Rutherfurd, Lucy Mercer, and, 81, 86-9,
        122-3, 136, 191, 194-5, 215-6, 223,
        248n
    Sailing and ships, 30-2, 35-6, 48, 50, 59-
        61, 65, 71, 75-6, 80, 81-5, 94-5, 107,
        108, 140-4, 168, 171, 231

Smith, Alfred E. ("Al"), and, 124, 128-9, 133
Women and, 137-8, 191, 194, 215-6, 245*n*, 252*n*
Roosevelt, Jr., Franklin D. (1st) (son) 68, 70
Roosevelt, Jr., Franklin D. (2nd) (son), 73, 77, 125, 126, 130, 140, 142, 170, 180, 181, 185, 188, 208, 233
Roosevelt, Hall (Eleanor's brother) 12, 37, 59, 61, 71, 72, 186, 207, 247*n*
Roosevelt, James (Franklin's father), 5, 6, 11, 17, 26, 28, 30, 33, 35, 36, 43, 53, 231
Roosevelt, James ("Jimmy") (son), 67, 68, 72, 93, 95, 107, 105, 108, 120, 122, 124, 130, 140, 142, 189, 208, 229
Roosevelt James Roosevelt ("Rosy"), 43, 77, 111, 251*n*, 258*n*
Roosevelt, John (son), 80, 125, 130, 140, 142, 170
Roosevelt, Sara Delano
Campobello, and, 28, 29-30, 113, 179, 185-6
Delano family and, 5, 6, 90
Grandchildren and, 68, 97, 120
Hyde Park and, 3, 69, 185-6
Roosevelt, Eleanor, and, 37, 38, 41, 42, 44, 48, 69, 91, 113-4, 186, 246*n*, 247*n*, 249*n*, 256*n*
Roosevelt, Franklin Delano, and, 3, 5, 6, 7, 9, 34, 36, 38, 39, 41, 42, 44, 48, 63-4, 69, 87, 113-4, 142, 143, 179, 186, 194, 227, 243*n*, 245*n*, 247*n*
Roosevelt, James (husband), and, 3, 5, 6
Travel, 8, 28, 46, 112-3
Roosevelt, Theodore, 6, 10, 33, 39, 43, 77, 90, 96, 149, 166, 207, 249
Roosevelt, Jr., Theodore, 96, 125, 250*n*
Roosevelt Campobello International Park, 3, 17, 229, 232
Roosevelt International Bridge, Franklin D., 2, 210, 231, 233
Rozenvelt, Niklaus, 5
Royal River Cabins, 198
Rough Riders, 33
Rutherfurd, Lucy Mercer, 81, 86-7, 122, 138, 144, 191, 194-5, 215-6, 220, 223

Sabalo (boat), 107-8
St. Andrew's, N.B., 25, 49, 144, 176, 203, 204
St. Anne's Anglican Church, 20, 154, 169, 225, 229
St. Croix River, 19, 144, 203-5
Saint-Gaudens statue, 89
St. James Episcopal Church, 225
St. John, N.B., 36
St. John Daily Sun, 23
St. John River, 19
St. Lawrence Seaway, 168, 197
St. Patrick's Day, 43
Salmon River, 169
Sarreau, Jean, Sieur de St. Aubin, 19
Scarborough, Me., 140, 169
Scarlett, Bishop, 211
Schary, Dore, 207-8
Schneiderman, Rose, 126
Schorr, Daniel, 228
Seabright, N.J., 68
Seacoast Canning Company, 65
Sebasco Lodge, 179
Secretary of Labor, 110, 252*n*
Secret Service, 183, 185, 253*n*
Seguin Island, Me., 142
Selective Service Act, 175
Seven Years War, 19
Shaler, N. S., 23
Simkhovitch, Mary, 126
Sirocco (boat), 131
Smith, Alfred E. ("Al"), 93, 124, 128, 129, 213
Socialist Party, 134
Sohier, Alice, 36, 245*n*
South Carolina, 88, 188
Southwest Harbor, Me., 140, 142
Souvestre, Marie, 14, 90, 243*n*
Sperry, Willard, 208
Springwood (Hyde Park estate), 11, 43, 69, 91, 122, 127, 192, 256*n*, 258*n*
Stalin, Josef, 180, 193, 257*n*
State of Maine (ship), 26
Stevenson, Adlai, 213
Stevenson, Robert Louis, 37, 82, 248*n*
Sturgis, Gertrude, 34
Suckley, Margaret ("Daisy"), 137, 138, 173, 179, 191-2, 194, 215, 216, 223, 252*n*
Sunrise at Campobello, 207-9
Swartz, Maude, 126

Tammany Hall, 71, 93, 99, 128
This I Remember, 150, 202
This Is My Story, 169, 202
Thomas, Norman, 134
Thompson, Malvina ("Tommy"), 163, 164, 168, 176, 203
Tiffany & Company, 42, 114
Tilley, L. P. D., 144, 146
Tillson's Wharf (Rockland), 183-4
Time (magazine), 130-1
Tivoli, N.Y., 13
Todhunter School, 127, 139
Tomorrow Is Now, 231
Tories, 49
Treat Island, N.B., 71
Truman, Harry S, 124, 191, 196
Tugwell, Rexford, 31, 131, 227
Twain, Mark, 27

United Kingdom, 174
United Nations (UN), 196
U.S. Army, 134
U.S. Marines, 77
U.S. Naval Academy, 33
U.S. Navy, 82, 94, 182, 209
U.S. Navy Department, 33, 75, 86, 100, 136, 151
U.S. Savings Bonds, 175
U.S. State Department, 193
U.S. Supreme Court, 170
U.S. Treasury Department, 160
USS *Augusta*, 180-2
USS *Bernardon*, 143
USS *Ellis*, 143
USS *Hatfield*, 94
USS *Indianapolis*, 140, 143, 145, 148
USS *North Dakota*, 75-6, 148
USS *Tuscaloosa*, 170
University of Mississippi, 212
Urry, John, 23

Val-Kill, 127, 130, 138, 152, 164, 170
Vassar College, 97
Veblen, Thorstein, 27
Vermont, 169, 255*n*
Veterans' Bonus March, 134

Vice-President of the United States, 95, 97
Victorianism, 1, 17, 21, 28, 46, 90, 122, 151, 214
Vireo (boat), 94, 95, 102, 209
Virginia, 12-3

Wall Street, 88
Warm Springs, Ga., 88-9, 128, 132, 137, 138, 189, 191, 195
Washington, D.C., 74, 79, 80, 86, 89, 107, 151, 165, 191, 227
Waterbury Radiolite, 114
Watson, Edwin ("Pa"), 189
Webster-Ashburton Treaty, 17
Wechsler, James, 177
Wells, Kate Gannet, 24, 26, 244*n*
Welshpool (also Welchpool), 25, 32, 69, 103, 105, 107, 144, 145, 146, 154, 177, 196, 197, 229
West Quoddy Head, 84, 145
White House, 33, 38, 88, 95, 131, 137, 139, 142, 145, 153, 165
White Mountains, 125
White Rocks, 24
White, Walter, 177
Willkie, Wendell, 170, 221
Wilson, Medley, 186-7, 200
Wilson, Woodrow, 33, 74, 77, 78, 86, 90, 93, 94, 133, 221
Wilson's Beach, 49, 60, 72, 105
Winslow, F. A., 183
Winston, Owen, 63
Women's Democratic News, 129
Women's Division of the Democratic Party, 124-5
Women's Trade Union League, 126
World Monetary and Economic Conference, 141, 151
World War I, 23, 33, 86
World War II, 1, 26, 187, 195

Yale (ship), 26
Yalta Conference, 190, 222
Yarmouth, Me., 198-9
York Harbor, Me., 75-6

1/00

ML